69 @ 69

A Naive Widow Swipes Right into the World of Online Dating

JACQUELINE T. MAY

Copyright © Jacqueline T. May 2025. All rights reserved.

This book or any portion thereof may not be reproduced or used in any manner whatsoever without the express written permission of the publisher except for the use of brief quotations in a book review.

Strenuous attempts have been made to credit all copyrighted materials used in this book. All such materials and trademarks, which are referenced in this book, are the full property of their respective copyright owners. Every effort has been made to obtain copyright permission for material quoted in this book. Any omissions will be rectified in future editions.

Note that all names, identifying features, and locations have been changed to protect anonymity of those involved.

Cover image by:
Book design by: SWATT Books Ltd

Printed in the United Kingdom
First Printing, 2025

ISBN: 978-1-0683072-0-1 (Paperback)
ISBN: 978-1-0683072-1-8 (eBook)

J T May
Wetherby, West Yorkshire

www.69at69.co.uk

Dedicated to :

My daughters

My Girl Tribe

Shirley

CONTENTS

Introduction 7

CHAPTER 1	Now Alone	11
CHAPTER 2	Past, Present and What's Next?	19
CHAPTER 3	Online Dating Website Virgin	29
CHAPTER 4	Diamond Mine	33
CHAPTER 5	One Shade of Role Play	41
CHAPTER 6	Awakening	67
CHAPTER 7	Come In Vicar	81
CHAPTER 8	The Narcissist and His Shoes	95
CHAPTER 9	Armani Man	115
CHAPTER 10	Toothpaste and More Dates	121
CHAPTER 11	The Music Man	127
CHAPTER 12	Dancing Stew and Heather Paul	135
CHAPTER 13	Testicles, HIV & STIs	143
CHAPTER 14	Dating Apps and Old Rockers	149
CHAPTER 15	Norton Rob the Sex Texter	157
CHAPTER 16	The Boring Love Lost Engineer	165
CHAPTER 17	Daddy Day Care – Drinker	171
CHAPTER 18	The Uncommitted Charmer	181
CHAPTER 19	Catfish Reflection and Support	201
CHAPTER 20	Friend With Benefits – Part 1	209
CHAPTER 21	"Big Foot" - The 6'5" Man Child	241
CHAPTER 22	Friend With Benefits – Part 2	247
CHAPTER 23	Soldier and Teddy Bears	255
CHAPTER 24	A Man Who Nearly Died in My Bed	263

CHAPTER 25	The Obsessive Rock Climber	273
CHAPTER 26	The Pandemic and Unrequited Love	283
CHAPTER 27	Mr Ted	295
CHAPTER 28	The Lord of the Manor	301
CHAPTER 29	The Fishing Romantic	309
CHAPTER 30	The Competitive Cyclist	315
CHAPTER 31	The Blue Danube and the Proposal	323
CHAPTER 32	A Date with Mr Parkinson	333
	About the Author	341

INTRODUCTION

69@69

Will you swipe right on "69@69?" It's a tale of love, laughter, grit, tears and the unexpected joys of late-life romance.

Should I find a new man?

After the loss of my beloved husband, widowed and grieving for three years, I'm ready to embark on a new journey—one that involves more than volunteering and crossword puzzles. How hard can it be to find someone who will be my soul mate, best friend, travel partner, maybe life partner in their mid- 60's

Swipe Right!

You could say I am a pretty impulsive-spirited woman. It is typical of me that I jumped head-first into the world of online dating. Why? After 42 years in a cosy relationship bubble, and finding myself a widow, grieving for three years, I yearned for companionship and adventure. So, with sheer determination, a smartphone, and a dash of humour, I set sail on the digital sea of matchmaking. I had lots to learn.

I didn't expect to face scammers, charmers, catfishing, friends with benefits and obsessive suitors; many tested my resilience. Along the way, I discovered not to take everything at face value and searched for authenticity, finding the true meaning of companionship.

A Rollercoaster Ride of Laughter

I encounter so many crazy scenarios—from awkward first dates (toothpaste and fish and chips) to unexpected connections and unfathomable obsessions (Toes, a schoolgirl uniform, and motorbikes); backbreaking sex with several teddy bears staring at me; and the Lord of the Manor, who nearly made my dog sick with his home-fried liver.

Heartache and tears

There are moments of vulnerability, too. I grapple with heartache, loss and deceptions, yet I (sometimes foolishly) continue to bounce back, determined to find joy amidst the swipes and emojis. I am dealing with online stalking, sex text bombardment and catfishing. My four-year saga of chasing an uncommitted Toy Boy who struggled to leave me alone and only wanted 'Friends With Benefits'.

Wine, Laughter, and Solidarity

My loyal Girl Tribe, my precious mates, are always here to listen to my stories and woes, sip wine, laugh, and cheer me on. Even if they take the Micky out of my disastrous naïve decisions, I value their input and derision, which usually involves a few appropriate swear words.

Poetry

Some of my dates inspired me to write poetry. These short verses, range from humorous, anger and sadness.

Why 69@69?

Why did I choose the title 69@69? Well, I celebrated my 69th date in my 69th year. After reflecting on my life's wild ride with my Girl Tribe, I decided to write about my memorable encounters, throwing in some wisdom, humour, and unapologetic candour. And yes, the sexual innuendo of "69" isn't lost on them, nor the sexual experiences I encountered on my way.

Warning

Please be aware that this book contains adult content including descriptions of sex and erotic acts; and is not recommended to readers below the age of 18.

JACQUELINE T. **MAY**

CHAPTER 1
NOW ALONE

I'm sitting here in this cold mediaeval church. His oak casket adorned with lilies. This place of worship where he was a choir boy when I first met him. A skinny lad who met me at the bus station for our first date, wearing what I called his Rupert Bear trousers, supported on his hips by a huge brown leather belt. I remember noticing his eyebrows; they seemed to dance as he spoke and greeted me with a cheeky smile.

I remember, too, the attraction and excitement I felt when I first started dating my first boyfriend. I was 16, he was 18. I laugh now, as I thought he was so mature, and his scooter was a bonus, too.

I hadn't noticed the congregation standing while my mind was reminiscing. The music of "Journey to the Centre of the Earth", chosen by our daughters, has finished at the part where the sound of a heavy screw lid is being turned and then falls off. The congregation made a few suppressed giggles at the unexpected sound. I knew he would appreciate this moment, too. This and the feeling of a gentle tug on my elbow by my eldest daughter took me back to the moment as she passed me the order of service with tears in her eyes. I cannot cry; I wish I could; the mental numbness is in charge of my emotions, and I can feel over 100 pairs of eyes staring at me in pity. My sister Kitty is crying and blowing her nose in the background. It all feels surreal.

This couldn't be all there is to end a life, could it? Has the last 42 years of marriage come to this? No warning of losing the man who shared my bed and meal times, reared our children and provided for us. My rock. Yet he also caused me heartache, doubts, anger and frustration. I could not understand the mood swings, control and disrespect when he couldn't get his way. I cannot remember him telling me he loved me more than three times. However, I know he did by his actions. Was this the end of him breathing, laughing, moving and hugging me and my family on greeting us? Famous in this congregation for turning up with his battered old toolbox to fix something for them, he just knew how everything worked. But he could not fix himself.

The vicar stands before the oak casket with brass handles that we chose for the scallop shells. Tony loved walking and had always dreamt of walking the pilgrim's way in Spain. The scallop is a symbol of that walk. Maybe one day I'll do it for him. As the remorse over those scallop shells cuts into my heart, my head is flooded with his plans.

My throat feels like it's closing as everyone starts singing from the Order of Service I haven't opened. His picture there in front of me is blurred, not from tears but from an overwhelming feeling of wanting to be sick. Thankfully, my daughters see me sway and help me sit back in my seat. Still staring at Tony's photo on the Order of Service, wearing his faded blue jeans and white shirt, holding a cup of coffee in one hand, he looks so relaxed and happy. I hear my youngest daughter's beautiful voice as she stands alone on the alter steps, singing one of Tony's favourite Fleetwood Mac songs. She is a mother of three children, in her 30s and is often described as "mini-me" with her long auburn hair and freckles. Her older sister, also a mother of two, resembles her father's family with dark brown eyes, hair, and olive skin. Next, she takes her place on the alter steps and reads a poem she wrote for her dad. Both girls were so amazing. All I could think was that I wished he was here to witness this, his wonderful daughters showing how much he meant to them.

Why the fuck did you leave Tony? They don't deserve this heartbreaking day, I scream silently in my head. As the girls returned to me, they both wrapped their arms around my stationary body and sobbed. I cannot cry. I cannot wait for it all to be over. Please, God, if you exist, let me cry and squash all this hurt and fear for my future without him.

The bucket list

Travel will become my obsessive focus now. Tony and I had quite an extensive bucket list of places we wanted to visit, and somehow, I will find a way to achieve many of them.

I start our ambitious list over the next three years with Australia, New Zealand, Canada, Crete, Croatia, Madeira, Latvia, Lithuania, Estonia, Montenegro, Spain, Turkey, the Danube, Edinburgh, Cardiff, Anglesey, Alaska, and South America.

Many destinations had their highlights, but Alaska is my most memorable.

Paddling a canoe around a huge iceberg blew me away. Although I was scared, not having rowed before in open seas, my Inuit guide did most of the rowing.

I watch his broad back, wearing a fluorescent yellow Hi-Vis life jacket, mesmerised by his arms heaving the oars through the water. Once the canoe started moving, he beckoned me to start rowing, too. There was probably more splashing than rowing on my part, but I felt I was playing my part in a small way. In the distance, I can see what looks grey at first, but as we slowly approach, I am overwhelmed by a colossal ice island jewel with its various colours, pearlescent and blue, shifting to turquoise in deep creases. This beauty contrasts with the black ocean below.

We lifted our oars to stop rowing, which allowed the canoe to drift. The scale of the iceberg made me feel small. I expected silence, but the ocean's ripples and the cracking ice flow nearby made sounds I had never heard before. Gulls noisily squawk above my head, soaring in search of fish. The sounds around me mix peace with a sense of nature's vastness and my insignificance in this fantastic place. I feel like an imposter, out of place, knowing humans only destroy everything we touch. I'm sure many before me feel the same "How lucky am I to be here on this magical day."

I cannot return to my old self. There's so much more to live for and explore. So, I head back to the tourist desk to see what else I can do.

Looking at the list of activities for the next seven days, I'm thrilled to take a seaplane ride over Vancouver and drive a quad bike across the Alaskan tundra, drenched in ice melt and snow from head to toe. I know it'll be an exhilarating experience that'll make me feel younger than I have in years. Bring it on!

One of our coach trips dropped us off at the entrance to Lake Louise, where winter's thaw was underway. The mountains are still wearing their snowy and icy coats, glistening in the sunlight. The frozen lake was blanketed with snow, except for turquoise streaks of water that snaked around the edges. The mountains rose sharply from the water, surrounding the lake like a big, white embrace.

The scenery is breathtaking, and the air is so pure that I can feel my lungs expanding with pleasure. As I tread carefully along an icy pathway, I see something unexpected. It's a heartwarming sight of a little metre-high snowman against the vast scenery. A twig smile and arms stuck out at 45 degrees. I look around. Someone must have brought twigs to build this charming structure in one of Canada's most famous spectacular views. I take a photo, one of my best, which I cherish deeply today. It captures my emotions at a time of loss and isolation, yet there he is, smiling and optimistic. That snowman and that view will affect my attitude from now on. I might be alone, but life will always give me unexpected smiles. I will keep looking, enjoy, and return to my photographs and their memories.

Flying solo has become second nature, and packing a suitcase is routine. But I learned the hard way that it's smart to pack a few essentials in my carry-on. After five days in Argentina without my bags, I saw I needed so few clothes to travel. Despite the excitement, I felt something was missing. I missed the joy of sharing experiences with others. Hotel rooms, ship cabins, and my caravan felt like emotional voids. I longed for conversations, like "What did you think of that?" moments and sharing funny stories. I could write a book about those trips. But travel journals are a dime a dozen. Interestingly, none of my adventures led me to meet Mr. Right. Instead, I made great female friends on my travels. They showed me that women are more adventurous than men regarding solo travel. On a tour of Eastern Bloc countries, 13 of 18 travellers were women. Only five were men. Of those, three lived with their mothers, and two were married. That says it all.

I surprised myself with achievements I had never imagined doing years ago. After years as a navigator while my late husband towed our caravan across Europe. I finally dared to tow it alone to the Yorkshire coast, Edinburgh, and Cardiff. On my first venture out, I realised he had inflated his role as a driver and caravan tow operator. He made it seem like a huge, complex responsibility. Surprisingly, I found it easy and was in danger of forgetting I was towing a 12-foot-long caravan. The caravan swayed behind me, threatening to roll the car! It reminded me of the phrase, "the tail wagging the dog."

—

To make my point about adventurous female solo travellers, I joined a group of 25 in South America. Of the 25, 23 were female; one was a gay male, and another was a male who had previous 'goings on' with one of the women. My experience was that solo travel was about adventure and making friends. It was definitely not about finding a heterosexual relationship. If I wanted to be a lesbian, there were plenty of opportunities, and to say I didn't consider the thought would be a lie … but I don't see myself going down on another woman!!! Consequently, I knew it was time to look at other ways of meeting men. I have tried the Art Club, the Walking Club, and the Creative Writing Club. I even tried croquet, for God's sake. I am now a volunteer fundraiser for a charity. I felt like it was time to give something back and meet like-minded people. It's fun to do, but again, it's dominated, in the main, by women.

I tried to join a Canasta Cards Club with a broken shoulder. But, holding and placing cards was nearly impossible. The sour-faced woman opposite me gave me a look that said, "I'll bet she broke her shoulder when she was drunk."

"Oh, you broke it on holiday. Were you partying?"

No way was I going to tell her I fell off a riverboat, drunk on pomegranate juice and who knows how much raki in Turkey. The boat's captain was also intoxicated and hadn't secured the vessel to the moorings.

"Well, yes, you could say I was," I replied. I tried to sound mysterious. I wanted to say I was rescuing an elderly lady who fell off a boat. I wanted to say that the boat crashed against my shoulder and, in turn, I was rescued by a handsome captain. He drove me to the hospital in his Mercedes and held my hand while I was treated. The bit about him rescuing me was true. But my sister found it less than gallant as he grabbed my shorts and gave me a painful "wedgy" while lifting me onto the jetty. Luckily I was unconscious, too. My sister screamed for help. Would you believe an ambulance was just around the corner? I awoke to two gorgeous paramedics who didn't speak English, other than shouting at me, "Allergic? Allergic?"

Back to Canasta. I thought hiding my reasons for a broken shoulder from these boring, card-wielding women was wise. So, I made a quick exit.

"I'll come back when my shoulder is better," I announced hastily, then fled, never to return.

Eight weeks of healing and sleeping upright in a chair led me to seek other ways to meet men. My girlfriends, whom I have known for over twenty years, are not enough to fulfil my other needs.

First, I ask myself who I am and what I want. It's a phrase I asked myself when I began writing this story of the highlights of my life. After much searching through old, fading photos and memories, I realise my life has been shaped by those who seem to know 'who' they are. I have spent most of my life trying to emulate them. I am trying to prove that I can do most things if I put my mind to it. Today, I am less influenced by personalities I meet but fascinated by what makes them tick. After 60 years, I am finally happy with my identity. I now have the confidence to try new things and find someone to fill the void Tony left in my life. However, he was a hard act to follow, and I am trying to accept my lost lifestyle, security, and friendship; there are no guarantees I will find the same again; I have to be open-minded.

66 years old

Retired and a widow for three years. I'm staring at my computer screen with Pink Floyd's "Wish You Were Here" playing from my "favourites list", wondering what to do next. What would excite me? I had done so much but didn't feel fulfilled; that empty pit in my stomach gnawing at my loneliness in widowhood. My lovely home had never had so much attention. The garden bloomed, the lawn was manicured, and the floors and surfaces gleamed. But...it was a never-ending cycle. Menopause is over. My health is okay. My daughters and grandchildren no longer need my help. I now needed more from life.

JACQUELINE T. **MAY**

CHAPTER 2
PAST, PRESENT AND WHAT'S NEXT?

My mother was a strong woman and a great role model for her seven children, who are all achievers in different ways. I am the eldest. I still see her throwing a wet dishcloth at us, often hitting our faces, if we were disruptive at meals. It was made all the funnier by the fact these dishcloths were my father's old vests. A cricketer would be proud of her throwing accuracy. Sadly, she was a single mother for a few years when I was fifteen. This coincided with my school exams. I had no alternative but to support my mother by doing chores and helping with my little siblings. So, I left school at fifteen with no qualifications. My first weekly wages were essential to support the family. So, responsibility was instilled in me from an early age.

I am largely self-taught. My first job was in administration, and I became a personal assistant. According to my boss, due to my dyslexia, I was rubbish at it. However, according to my boss, I made a good cup of tea and sounded good on the telephone.

At the age of twenty-one, I married and had two wonderful daughters. For the next decade, I was a stay-at-home mum. I re-entered the workforce in my mid-30s.

My return to employment initially involved various temporary positions. Eventually, I found my niche in sales, mainly telesales. I then progressed to senior management in the Internet industry. It was an unusual position for a mature woman in the 1990s. As an international business development executive, I was used to travelling alone throughout Europe and America. My final management role was running a department promoting the new technology of online data storage (The Cloud).

I retired in my mid-50s, mid-menopause, and mid-Dotcom crash. It was time to leave a fast-moving industry and join my husband in retirement.

Many believe that heartaches and tragic losses have the greatest impact on us. However, I found that it was puberty and menopause that truly shaped my emotions. The profound hormonal shifts during these life stages were tumultuous. These biochemical changes and significant physical transformations can deeply affect us, influencing our personal lives, friendships, and careers.

During these times, we women may gain or lose weight. We may see changes in our appearance and libido. We have no choice but to confront these changes, the realities of ageing, and their impact on our relationships and family dynamics. Yet, internally, we remain the same, navigating emotional highs and lows driven by hormonal changes. Often, we fail to recognise these shifts and find ourselves grappling with doubts about our resilience or capabilities, sometimes leading to impulsive decisions. This was my reality in my 50s.

After losing Tony and entering my mid-60s, I found myself on the other side of the menopausal journey. My confidence and mastery of independence had significantly improved. Meeting new men didn't unsettle me, as you'll soon learn. But finding lasting love and seeking "The One" proved to be my most daunting challenge yet.

If I were in my 20s today, it's anyone's guess where life might lead me. Yet, here I am, in my 60s, embracing a fresh start. Life is too fleeting to dwell on the past or ponder alternate paths. My past experiences have, without a doubt, shaped me.

With encouragement from my sister Kitty and my two daughters, I decided to look into online dating. It took me time to understand why anyone would want to sell themselves online. I was used to selling and presenting myself at conferences, so I found it daunting to write about myself to attract a partner.

It warmed my heart to receive compliments from friends and family. They said I look youthful for my age. Some suggested I looked to be in my 50s. I struggled to see it from my point of view. In the mirror, I saw a mature woman. She had lost a few pounds, so her clothes hung loosely on her. Her arms sagged, and her legs showed cellulite. Her hair seemed thinner than she remembered, the hairbrush on her dresser resembling a dog brush after a summer moult, confirmed it.

But, when I agreed to my sister Kitty's idea of a long shopping spree for a new wardrobe, my confidence in my allure grew. Skinny jeans, once a distant aspiration, now hugged my figure in all the right places. Off-the-shoulder tops and fitted T-shirt dresses were once overlooked in my wardrobe. Now, they felt like a natural fit for my evolving self. Even stiletto heels, worn for no more than an hour, now seemed to match my new mood and identity perfectly. All that remained was to showcase my new style. Dating provided the perfect stage for it.

At 66, I was excited about my new journey. Although, I didn't expect the rollercoaster of experiences and the many characters I would meet. I thought I would find a partner within six months!

So here I am, at 69 years old, reminiscing over the past highs and lows of my life and three years of dating. I'm at my kitchen table, my laptop on fire, reporting on some crazy situations, men, friends, and countries I've travelled to—all because a group of female friends insist I write about them.

Cajoled

At my local bar, I waited for my two close female friends. I reflected on our shared experiences over the last few years. All now single, they have had their fair share of love found and lost, tragedies and high points. What I love about them is their ability to bounce back. They stay funny and supportive when one of us is down. There are five of us now. My sister Kitty and my friend Maria are single. They sought our support to escape their loneliness.

Penny bursts through the door first, followed by petite Ann.

"Finish your wine, girl; we are all going to Ann's tonight."

Kitty opened two bottles before us once we settled at Ann's kitchen table. The conversation began with eager questions: "Who have you dated this week?" Aimed at me.

"Please do a blog," Penny and Ann implored me, both offering to be my editor/proofreaders. I shook my head, making excuses as my bemused friends shook their heads in return and kept filling my glass.

"I'm mildly dyslexic; no one would want to read it."

My excuses fell on deaf ears. "Better still, write a book. You're an amazing raconteur; I would buy your story," said Ann, slugging the last of the second bottle. She kept giggling over one of my past dates, a man with a prosthetic leg. Her hands were in her shaking head.

"I was so naïve when I married." The girls listened intently.

"I was 25 before I knew what a 'blow job' was. I didn't know what 'oral sex' or 'cunnilingus' meant. I didn't understand '69', either. See how green I was?"

The girls laughed, and Penny coughed and blurted out, "I did my first blow job at 15!!" Her face showed a sense of pride in her declaration. I was aghast and open-mouthed, and the girls laughed even louder at my expression.

"15? Oh my God, Penny!!"

Penny is one of my younger friends; she's my 53-year-old voice of reason. I love her to bits, but I worry too that she struggles to find "The One". She is elegant, intelligent, softly spoken, and 5'8" tall. With natural brown wavy hair that many women spend a fortune trying to replicate. She has never married or had children, which she has always regretted.

I always feel a sense of irony with Penny, as she is financially independent and gorgeous. She should be a catch for any suitor. But she struggles with anxiety about men. She's a thinker. She believes in fairness and honesty. Her 15-year-old "blow job" revelation was an amusing surprise. Sadly, her needs are unmet. I wish she could see herself as we do: a kind, loving, loyal friend. Unfortunately, she thinks men don't appreciate her. They either want one thing or are threatened by her intelligence and independence. While true in many ways, it's hard to know why there seems to be a lack of strong intelligent men out there who value her for who she is. She often says that all the good guys are married.

"Tony and I were your conventional missionary-position lovers. A quick petting session and five minutes of sex, then a shower, was our norm. It happened often on Sunday mornings or after a few drinks."

Penny softly responded, "No wonder you're making up for lost time now." We clinked our wine glasses together and laughed; I then continued...

"Just to add to that admission, my recent experiences as a widow have overshadowed those past norms enormously. I believe I had my first oral and first real orgasm by the first lover in my mid-

60s!!" Raising my glass, "so cheers, looks like I am way behind some of you girls."

"You have to write a book, please!!! From what we've heard already, you'll fill seven hysterical chapters."

"Women of your age will benefit from your stories. Oh, come on Jay, you said it yourself, it's never too late to live and learn." Penny, agreeing, poured the last drips of wine into her glass.

"Jay you're an inshhhpiration, you know that," slurred petite Ann, a year older than I with white hair in a soft bob style. I love her never-ending optimism. She had a shocked, quizzical expression on her face, waving her empty glass as if someone had drunk it for her. "What the fuck! No wine left."

"Think Costcutter shhtays open until 10." We all laughed as Penny mimicked her slurring. "Ann my lovely, I love you to bitshh, but for a five-foot woman, you are a walking, wine guzzling machine. Where do you put it?"

My younger sister, Kitty, sat back, sipping her drink. She choked with laughter at the table's hysterical conversations. Kitty was the only one amongst us working full time and finding it hard to keep optimistic about her prospects. She had been made redundant a few times, and each blow damaged her confidence. In her late 50s, she wanted to retire, but finances were not there to enable her to do so. She is my closest sibling. There is 13 years between us. We shared many highs and lows as we were both widowed by tragic events. Fortunately, we found strength through each other's emotional support. Kitty, like me, wanted to find love. But after a failed eight-year relationship, she had no incentive to start looking again. Dating sites made her too anxious. So, she declared she would rather be unhappy alone than in a stressful relationship. She said she didn't miss sex. She preferred our holidays and the company of our girlfriends of various ages. The youngest is 45, and the oldest 71. That seemed to be enough for her for the time being. And in a way, I could almost relate to her situation; however, I missed male company and partnership.

We changed the subject of my being an author and moved on to local gossip at the wine bar. "So, who is Jeremy shagging this time?"

A few days later, I spoke with my 45-year-old Spanish friend Maria. She had similar dating experiences, but was 20 years younger, with a fake tan and false eyelashes. She persevered and thought she had found her man. But he was dependent on drink, gambling, and drugs. I often listened on the phone to her dramatic stories and tears over this man. "But I love him," she would bawl. "You cannot help who you fall in love with." She tried to justify her constant boomeranging back to him.

I gave up trying to convince her that he wasn't good enough. He was known in our community for prioritizing his mates and habits over his girlfriends. Eventually, she did walk away.

When I had told Maria I was going to write my story, she had agreed, to my delight, that it would be a fun read.

My loyal friends and sister Kitty would be my dating story confidants, advisors, and shoulders to cry on. They were my Prosecco and Pinot Grigio buddies, my bosom pals. They brought the love and laughter of true girl friendships, especially in tough times. Yet, always at the back of my mind was my search for a romantic notion, a perfect man's strong arms, lips, and intimacy. At my age, is it too late for love? Surely not.

"69@69," I smiled to my cheeky self. Could I get away with that title, share my journey of sex, titillations, laughs, sorrow and my various 69 experiences LOL. Why not? So here goes... Sex in the City, eat your heart out.

I realised at 69 years old that number features quite often throughout my life. I was engaged to be married in the summer of '69. One of my favourite songs is Bryan Adams' "Summer of '69."

My first passport was in 1969. It was my first travel abroad. My first phone number ended in 69. Maybe this book will end with 369 pages. Who knows? AI wasn't around when I started writing; what you read is genuinely authentic.

This collection of short encounters, interwoven with some of my autobiographies, is a true-life story with names altered to respect their anonymity.

Within days COVID-19 came along. What better time to reflect on my experiences and the myriad of what I called "dalliances" during a break from dating websites, in self-imposed self-isolation? "STAY AT HOME" our governments worldwide are shouting from the rooftops. "SAVE LIVES, STAY AT HOME AND SAVE THE NHS." Here I am "at home" now pondering what would make an exciting book. No, it is not 50 Shades of Grey, but it will have some fascinating and, in some cases, erotic and embarrassing highlights. I will throw in a few poems inspired by some of my suitors.

Here is a list of the dates and flings that had the most impact and I don't just mean friends:

>	The professional online "Scammer"; 61
>	The "Daddy", deviant YouTube porn Therapist; 59
>	The shoe fetishist, toe-sucking narcissist; 63
>	The alcoholic, elderly father of twins; 69
>	The boring love lost engineer; 69
>	The gardener; 69
>	The ex-vicar; 55
>	The uncommitted, Viagra abusing, charmer; 70
>	The Toy Boy "friend with benefits"; 59 and counting
>	The obsessive climber; 65
>	The man who nearly died in my bed; 68
>	The teddy bears, back-breaking sex; 65
>	The 6'5" Man child, Big Foot; 60
>	The tour operator, motorcycling around Asia; 66
>	The handsome chartered surveyor, who turned my head;70

The lord of the manor eccentric; 67
The world champion cyclist; 69

These were the most memorable, funny, and hurtful of the many men I encountered. Some demand chapters of their own; not all were physical lovers. Watch this space.

My first dating poem was inspired by my online Match.com experience. It is so easy to think that once you are signed on to such dating sites, you are guaranteed the perfect match. It is a very complex experience full of pitfalls

DIGITAL DALLIANCES

Puzzled with digital dalliances?
Imagined keyboard romances
Behind the dating likes,
Tapping witty word delights.

Where the flirting rhythm beats,
A weak heart, beguiled, defeats,
Listening for playful comments,
Frozen in time-zone laments.

But does imagination want
A solitary picture taunt
Of a man in an Armani suit,
Or a lover playing his lute?

Vivid visions of creative minds,
Where truth should be defined,
Must question this digital reality
And online passion fantasy.

42 years of marriage did not prepare me for the crazy world of singledom. Protected by a matrimonial bubble and family life all

those years, I entered a new prospective relationship as if I were a 16-year-old before meeting my husband.

As with all marriages, we experienced ups and downs, and neither of us was perfect, but what I know is, that marriage did not fulfil my strong romantic, physical passionate side. Generally, he was a man of his generation, a great provider and father of our children; sex was more for his pleasure than mine. Maybe I was partly to blame for not communicating my sexual needs. To be honest I didn't know what my needs were. I was mainly led by him. Over the years I tried to make up for my strong desire for affection by devoting my loving nature to our two daughters. Showering unconditional love on my children brought rewards but this did not compensate for a lack of physical love, passion and romance in my marriage.

Why dwell on past regrets? I have found concentrating on past good times is the gift that keeps giving. If I make the most of the next 20 years, health willing, then, surely this is the key to my future happiness, reminding myself constantly that, "Life is too short, make the most of the life, and 'effing do it."

In my mind, ideally, I was looking for love, a companion who loved travel and a partner with whom I could share the good and bad times. Someone who would be my rock, watch my back when I needed it and cuddle up with me when we were content to have a cosy night in. Most of all I wanted him to love me for me. Was this too much to ask? Love at 66, I was not sure, and the only way to find out was to take the plunge and seek "The One" and love was the ultimate prize.

CHAPTER 3
ONLINE DATING
WEBSITE VIRGIN

At 66 years old, having emerged from grieving over Tony's death and a 42-year marriage, I treated this adventure with trepidation. Once convinced, however, and like most of my adventures so far, I threw myself into it with great optimism and enthusiasm, writing and re-writing my profile several times.

I chose my dating websites. Eternity, Match.com and Genuine Mature Singles.com and paid the subscriptions. Thinking to find my match, I needed to invest in love. It was approximately £100 a month though. I know, I laugh now since finding free sites like Plenty of Fish, where the same men appeared. Wondering why they didn't answer my cheeky notes, I soon discovered that many of the pay site individuals were long gone, though their profiles still appeared. I could, and maybe will, write a whole chapter on different dating websites, and how they operate. They are not all they seem.

I uploaded pictures showing my head, shoulders, and grinning face, full length in jeans, outdoors walking in boots, and who's that adventurous chick in a canoe in Alaska? Then, of course, there was the picture of me in my best dress, showing my shapely crossed legs and looking seductive with one arm draped over the back of the settee. That should cover most of the range of activities. Ah, wait a minute. No pout or glass of wine? No, I decided that is for 30-somethings.

Using my iPhone, I started to write a profile describing myself. I have written sales and marketing for products in my past life, but writing about oneself, basically a sales pitch, is a whole different ball game...

First draft:

"A young, spirited 5'5", vivacious, slim, natural blonde with a freckled face and broad grin, sometimes overconfident and sometimes insecure. My childlike sense of humour and pursuit of fun is part of my attractive nature. I giggle at my failings often. Creative, passionate and amusing poet".

Should I tell them I like sex? Hmmmm, no, probably not. Okay then...

"I'm tactile and love holding hands." That should be enough.

I cringe now at my first attempt, what was I thinking of, "childlike sense of humour and pursuit of fun" and "giggle at my failings often"? How stupid could I be? For men, this was a clear signal of naivety; I would be a pushover for the less scrupulous and disregarded by the kind of men I would want to attract.

Over the coming months, my profile was rewritten with various serious and amusing descriptions, depending on the responses I received from men. As time passed, I realised less was more, and most men were too lazy to read reams of descriptions. Therefore, I kept to smaller scripts.

I often receive bemused, inquisitive comments from family and friends thrown my way casually. "So, what you up to now?" It was not difficult for me to respond to their questions. I am not afraid of new technology and I try to make an effort to stay modern and relevant. My two 13-year-old granddaughters refer to me as their "cool grandma", something I am proud of. But in the same breath, I am a "potty grandma" too. One day, I turned up in ripped jeans for a family photo shoot in a bluebell wood. My modern attire was greeted with a mixed response; daughters raised eyebrows and grandkids poked their fingers in the holes. My son-in-law asked, "What possessed you?" looking me up and down.

"Maybe the devil in me," I giggled mischievously, my granddaughters giggling with me while my daughters dragged the boys away, pulling disapproving looks. I smiled to myself; if only they knew half of what I got up to in those jeans over these recent months.

My eldest daughter's husband insisted I told him where I was going, what time and who I was seeing, for the first few dates. I complied to begin with but fairly quickly, without any guilt, I decided it was none of his damn business. Quietly, I gave him a wide berth so as not to encourage his questions. Then, to my horror, at a family Sunday lunch, he informs me he has put a tracking app on my phone and asks why had I disabled it. Choking on my wine, I plead ignorant and fail to acknowledge him. I don't need to as my daughter glares across the table at him and shakes her head.

"Ignore him, Mum. He has no business tracking you; you are not 15." Relieved, I pretended the conversation had not taken place.

"Anyway, how's the dating going?" My daughter continued, trying to sound interested, I gave a polite nod and gesture that I had my mouth full of roast pork. The irony is not lost on me. I leave them to draw their conclusions.

JACQUELINE T. **MAY**

CHAPTER 4
DIAMOND MINE

David Lawrence is the first man to write to me. He was born in South Africa and, according to his online profile, was a doctor who lived in Cheadle Hume.

Not too attractive, average-looking, standing with a beautiful-looking, dark-haired younger lady, he made first contact. We exchanged a few sentences online. He suggested we come off the dating site immediately and move to email. He was travelling for work soon. I agreed immediately as his words and compliments hit every insecure cell in my brain.

```
"You are the most attractive, interesting woman I
have seen on here," ...etc. he texted to me. "I don't need
to look any further. Can we exchange email addresses
as I am not on this site often due to my business
travels? It would be nice to get to know you better."
```

```
"Of course,"
```
 I write in reply, almost instantly.

Oh my god, this guy finds me attractive and interesting. His life story is amazing and believable (well, to me). He trained as a doctor but now sells high-end, expensive medical equipment globally - MRI scanners etc. He has a house in Cheadle Hume, Lancashire, a very wealthy area in northern England (with an indoor swimming pool, of course – de rigueur in this millionaire footballer's county).

His writing is so romantic that it took me in hook, line, and sinker. I cannot get enough of his written word, and I look forward to his declaration of love for us every day and plans for our future. He said he loved poetry, a cue to me to start bombarding him with my first-ever romantic poems. "If ever I have doubts," he says, "let the angels guide us." I often write poetry to include his words.

US ONLINE

My love, we are flying so high,
Making wishful images of us,
A Pandora's box of pictures
Makes no sense or structure.

A future cannot be planned
Until our eyes have met,
Our chemical nuances felt
Questions and answers spelt.

It's hard to make a promise
On an imaginary dream of you,
The life you want to feel
With the one you think is real.

But as time goes by, going back
Now seems inconceivable,
Those doubts fall and fade,
Replaced by a path we have laid.

What will become of us?
Travelling an unknown destiny
We will put faith in feelings true
And let the Angels guide us through.

His only daughter was in Germany studying the language. His family owns a small diamond mine, which his uncle manages while he is in the UK. He is happy to leave the running of it to his uncle as David has no interest in the day-to-day running of the business, which is until his father kicks the bucket. He now struggles with removing this alcoholic uncle who was milking all the profits. He suspects that a rival neighbouring mine owner is trying to purchase his mining business for very little money and the wayward uncle would claim he owned it, selling the family's jewels. As the plot is thickening, I am getting at least four long messages a day and two phone calls. He is very charming in both and he appeals to my weaknesses; I'm a sucker for well-written messages. I send him more poetry, and in return, he sends me accounts of his meetings and his deals. Even when he was in Atlanta, America, on business, he would call at the right times, telling me of his worries and how he hated letting his customers down.

The most recent shipment, the biggest yet, is held up in Brussels in containers and the paperwork involved in releasing it has encountered problems. "The import tax needs to be paid Beautiful", he says via his mobile while walking to the bank. Then he says the bank teller is informing him his account has been frozen, he needs proof of identity, his passport is back at the hotel, or he needs access to cash from elsewhere.

"It's not as if I haven't got the funds to repay a loan, Beautiful." Without asking me directly, he sucks me in totally to the unfolding story. Then the telephone line goes dead. So, I don't know the outcome. I couldn't offer to help him.

In the nick of time, the doorbell rings; my eldest daughter, Zara, is popping in on her way home from work. After making her tea, we sit at the kitchen table. I ask her about her week, and she responds, "Never mind that that's boring; how's the dating going, Mum?"

In an excited state, I tell her all about David. Then, seeing her face drop, I know she doesn't approve. I think it was the "diamond mine" that did it!!! Did it sound absurd?

"He's from where? He does what? He lives where? Have you met him yet? He's in America? He has a diamond mine? Oh Mum!!"

I defend him, of course, my new romantic interest. Then she says, "Do you know where he lives in the UK?"

Being defensive and confident, I say, "Cheadle Hume."

Her response is, "Of course he does. That's where rich footballers live." Her cynicism causes me to start getting peed off with her. Why shouldn't he live there?

"Well!! Why shouldn't he?" I respond again in defence of him.

"Look, Mum, you need to know more facts about this man before you give any more information about yourself. If he is real, then he'll have no problem sharing it. We'll make up your postal address and say you are sharing this in return for his."

I'm appalled that she suggested I lie to my newfound romance, to whom I was already sending love poems and soppy music (cringing now). But she left me thinking I might not know if this person was genuine. So, as she suggested, I wrote, giving him my actual address and asking for his. He phoned straight away, querying my request. At the same time, I enquired if he managed to get the bank to unlock his account.

"I don't have a problem with it, Beautiful, but I do think the request is a bit random. What's it all about?"

I told him it was for both our peace of mind.

"Oh, I'm still fighting with the bank, and my customers are getting heavy with threatening cancellations, but don't worry, Beautiful, I will sort something out; I have a friend who might help me out."

He was convincing, and his knowledge of the shipping business and imports and exports sounded realistic. Investigating later,

I found that the details of the container port he mentioned all checked out, as did a specialist shipping agent he named. But still, my daughter's voice was nagging me, so I refrained from offering to help.

Within minutes, his home address was in my inbox, along with a picture of his house and a caring message: `"Hope this helps with your insecurities. I never doubted you, Beautiful, and cannot wait until we are both together once this shipment is sorted."`

There was my proof to convince my daughter, I thought. He is a genuinely caring guy. I told her the good news (oh, how I cringe now).

An hour later, she said, "Why is it up for sale? And why is it at a different address from the one he told you?" My stomach dropped; for the first time, I had real doubts.

I immediately telephoned him, telling him he must have made a mistake. He responded with, "Oh yes, it is up for sale. I'm downsizing to a cottage half a mile away. You see, Beautiful, I was proud of that house, and sadly, I have to sell to pay my daughter some of her mother's inheritance. I wanted to impress you." His voice was soft and reassuring. "Beautiful, I realise now that I need to be myself. You're not put off by my not having a swimming pool, are you?"

For now, I was happy to go along with him, believing him. Being called "Beautiful" was starting to grate on me, though. He explained that he had already bought the cottage and was waiting to move in once his business in Atlanta was finalised. It was that address he gave me.

"I'm so sorry about my vanity. I would have told you once the sale had gone through because, legally, it is still mine."

Of course, I would forgive him, for I believed his business pressure was unusually demanding, and his private life had taken a back seat. Reassured once more, I returned to my daughter. However, to my surprise, she did not comment; no more negative feedback. I felt confident I could continue and enjoy my daily romantic chats, hearing all about his challenges. I felt privileged that he was sharing everything with me; I was flattered when he asked my advice on occasion. I was falling hook, line, and sinker again! The shipment had still not been released, and his customers threatened to cancel within 48 hours; his money was locked in his account. I never asked why (now I cringe again).

And then ... my daughter pitches in again, this time with a phone call.

"I was in Manchester and visited the so-called estate agent he claims to have bought the cottage from. NEVER HEARD Of HIM!! The land registry doesn't list his name as the owner of the other property. I've searched, and no records show this man exists in the business he says he is in. Mum, he is a scammer. Please believe me. Have you paid him anything?"

I was shocked and almost convinced. Then, I suddenly remembered him saying, "Wouldn't we do anything for each other?" in a conversation about our loving relationship. Once again, I still started to defend him. "No one would go to so much trouble over six weeks making all that stuff up, surely? I'm not a rich woman after all."

In my mind, he wants to settle down with a "good woman" (I cringe). And **still**, I write him poetry.

SHAMEFUL DOUBTS

He's driving me to distraction,
I'm succumbing to his passion,
His words dance in my mind.

Will his love for me be kind?

He's getting under my skin,
I'm not eating, getting thin,
The life he paints is compelling.
My shameful doubts are telling.

His needs are all laid open,
A lover and walks in the ocean.
I want to trust his charm,
But my heart is afraid of harm.

I shouldn't keep him guessing,
He deserves better blessings.
I must keep my head,
And phone him instead.

"Mum, you need to block this man. And, by the way, his mobile was bought in Miami in a shop six weeks ago when he was supposed to be in the UK talking to you."

I'm speechless.

"The Crime Agency want to chat with you about him and, by the way, the online dating scam syndicate operates out of Miami."

Bless her. She had been beavering away as a detective in the background, and I was unquestioningly enjoying a phantom relationship.

I was reluctant to believe this man was a scammer, a man who had been in my life for six weeks and had made me happy to wake up each morning with romantic messages and go to bed each night with a good night kiss and soft words. No, he couldn't be a scammer. But my daughter's evidence was compelling. I eventually wrote to David and politely told him, "Your game is up." On reflection, I think the Crime Agency was perplexed by my actions. I eventually had a long chat with them, and they confirmed everything to me; the dating site blocked him minutes after I gave him my email address. Unlike me, they knew he was a scammer!

I wrote to Genuinesingles.com to complain and have my subscription refunded. After giving myself a couple of weeks to recover from my experience, I joined Match.com instead, another subscription site with a good reputation... or so I thought. I revised my profile as the Crime Agency advised, removing "widow" from my marital status, as scammers target us because, unlike divorcees, we haven't halved the family assets. However, within days of joining Match.Com, I was approached by other scammers. I was much more aware this time and have since reported many to ensure they do not approach other unsuspecting women. To give Match.com their due, they delete these scammer accounts immediately.

Red flags include professional-looking photos with immaculate hairstyles (photos sometimes copied from the internet, sometimes Facebook profiles stolen), almost model-like poses and lefthand-drive cars—overly descriptive, prosaic written profiles; God-loving, family-loving; looking for marriage and widowed. I started to realise that if they sound too good to be true, then they usually are. Often, the professions declared are doctors, oil rig engineers, accountants, physicians and lecturers.

It is common for scammers to start their first message with a very flattering compliment, such as "Hi Beautiful, that's a beautiful smile; where have you been all my life? Have you been on here very long?" a sign they are fishing to see if you are naïve or new to online dating like I was.

If I suspected they were scammers, I didn't answer their questions but replied with in-depth questions of my own. They often blocked me, knowing I was on to them. Then, I reported them to the dating site, and hopefully, the scammer should be removed.

CHAPTER 5
ONE SHADE OF ROLE PLAY

If I am honest with myself, it's a mystery how I fell for this one. Maybe I was desperate for my first physical experience, my new sexuality reawakening, after six years celibate, never expecting it to start with such a blast.

I certainly had no idea of what a "sub-dom" relationship was (submissive–dominant), which a 60-year-old Walter Mitty character Frank had to explain to me; he says he is a therapist.

I never considered myself sexually attractive; therefore, the attention I received came as a huge surprise; that's where my naivety ended, and my promiscuity started at the age of 66. I'm writing this book because I believe many people don't realise that women and men in their sixties still live an active physical life in the bedroom (and other places). In my case, I am still exploring and learning.

This therapist boyfriend, whose authenticity I came to doubt, was, ultimately, more psychopath than a therapist. There were too many tell-tale signs that he wasn't quite what he said he was; his story and reality didn't fit. It felt like he was from a deprived, uneducated background, and his text messages were written as that of a teenager. However, he had charisma and confidence, was fun and exciting, and undeniably spoke well; he was a refreshing change from some of my previous boring coffee dates. He told me many stories about his past escapades, including a short spell in prison for tax anomalies. That's where his nose was damaged, he said. I noticed on the first meeting that his nose was deformed, but his white smile and dimples won me over.

He bragged about how wealthy he had been in his 40s and 50s and his 17-year-long relationship with a woman with three children. Although he did not have children of his own, he boasted how he had given them everything as if they were his own. He drove an expensive classic car in those days and said he owned a five-bedroom house in Hull. According to him, making money was easy, but his tax declarations were not.

When he was released from prison, his partner had left him, and that was when he said he had trained to be a therapist. Now, he drove around in a beat-up old Ford. It all seemed very Walter Mitty. Still, I ignored my gut instincts and went with the flow. He was undoubtedly controlling, initially in a playful way, but I enjoyed his attention. Sex was good; in many ways, he sexualised me and made me feel confident in my body and image. It was exciting to take risks.

On our second date, I invited him for a walk by the river in my village. He said he wasn't much of a walker; golf was his interest, but he said he would come on the walk and take me out for lunch afterwards.

I'm not sure how we went from holding hands all the way to the river to ending up in my bedroom; it all happened so quickly.

I knew when I got dressed that morning and looked in the long mirror that I wanted to let a man see my body; I felt in good shape, and it had been three years since a man had seen it, six years since I had sex. I took time to choose my underwear, something I wouldn't normally do, making sure my pants and bra matched.

I remember when we arrived at my house on the second date, and, to my great surprise, I asked him if he wanted to go upstairs without anxiety. In retrospect, it was a dangerous thing to do, but I felt in control and had not even considered myself vulnerable.

He was very attentive and complimented me on my figure. "Wow, girl, I've dated 50-year-olds who would envy your looks and figure."

That was enough for me to disregard my inhibitions. We started slowly, and he stroked me all over, saying if we had body oil, he would love me to do the same to him. He started licking me between my thighs and then reached my vagina. I was succumbing to his mouth, crying out and shrieking at every stroke of his tongue.

"Well, who's a very wet girl then? And very ready, me," he crooned before penetrating me with his penis. It was such a relief that I wasn't dry after such a long time since I had sex.

I noticed how verbal he was, constantly talking his way around my body. When the intercourse was in full swing, he kept changing position, asking me all the time, "Is this good?" I would groan back, yes. Then, after a few minutes, his language became forceful; he started saying, "Come on, make me cum bitch."

I froze. "Please don't use that word." He ignored me and carried on, saying it several times. I suddenly found myself feeling very vulnerable. What was I doing with this complete stranger in my bed? I wriggled away from him and told him to leave. I was scared and shaking.

"I'm not a dog, and I find your insistence on calling me one offensive. Frankly, it's a turnoff. Please leave now."

I could see his face turn to thunder while he was dressing. My duvet wrapped around me while I didn't take my eyes off him, feeling ashamed I had put myself in this position.

"For your information, I'm not being offensive; the word excites me. It's only a word, but if you're going to kick a man out of your bed over a word, then, my lady, you have a lot to learn about men. You're a fucking tease."

He left without another word. I shook for about an hour, wondering what I had gone through. Was I still excited? Did I have a lot to learn? Was I a tease? I know this man turned me on, an experience I hadn't had for as long as I could remember.

I didn't sleep well that night, repeatedly thinking I had been unfair to Frank, leading him on and then kicking him out over a word. But I knew how I felt then; my gut reaction was that I felt unsafe. My inexperience was calling me loud and clear.

I decided to send an apology to him. Within minutes, my phone rang. He seemed to think I was rubbing in my rejection of him. When I tried to explain that I felt vulnerable and hadn't taken any precautions, it was a knee-jerk reaction to my fear. He responded that I should never leave a man with full balls as it was asking for trouble, and I was not very sexually intelligent. He said I needed to learn some lessons. He was shouting down the phone at me, saying I was a privileged, spoilt cow who didn't live in the real world. He finished with, "I don't have time for you," then hung up on me. I was in a worse state than before. Why hadn't I left things alone? I blocked him on the dating site and WhatsApp.

Going through my head for the rest of that day, I shouldn't leave a man with full balls. What the hell was I playing at? That was just bizarre.

For a few weeks, I couldn't concentrate on talking to men on the dating sites. Frank had affected my confidence. Perhaps the teenager in me was still spellbound by the attention he gave me, and my sexual desires had been reawakened. I unblocked him, thinking my initial response had been immature. He quickly made contact.

"Have you stopped sulking?" It was a WhatsApp message with a smiley emoji.

"It's hard for both of us at our age. You're not a bad lass, and I'm not a bad lad. You need to talk and not overreact, me too. I've been thinking about you".

"Me too." I couldn't resist responding.

"Fancy a chat? I can meet you somewhere?" Another smiley emoji. "This afternoon if you're free."

"Okay, I'm free after three" I was shaking at the thought of hearing his deep, rich, sexy voice. "Text me first".

"Great, speak then."

I paced the bedroom floor repeatedly, looking at my bed, remembering how I felt, the excitement and fear all overwhelming and so different to anything I had experienced. And I had had sex for the first time in six years. This man had an intoxicating charisma, and I loved his dominance. I should have run a mile, but he was like a magnet.

We met and talked for two hours. He told me much about his life experiences, being abused as an orphan at a home run by nuns, his difficult career choices, and mixing with the wrong boys. He had no problem attracting girls but admitted he had little control over his sexual urges, with little consideration for their feelings.

"I've been a bastard, but I became a changed man when I hooked up with a divorced mother of three children. I enjoyed the responsibility and encouragement from her. She showed me the rewards of loving someone unconditionally. I couldn't do enough for her. Our age gap became more apparent, though, when I reached 30 and she hit menopause. Her moods made me mad."

He swallowed and seemed remorseful. "You see, the selfish bastard in me came back; I was just interested in making money. She became needy, and I felt I could do better." He coughed nervously. "How wrong I was; I missed her and the kids as soon as I left. She wouldn't forgive me, though, even when I apologised and begged to come back."

Looking at me, he reached for my hand. "You, however, seem the forgiving kind."

I wasn't sure how I felt about this statement.

He went on to talk about other relationships, but it was clear that his divorcee had gotten away.

Over the next few weeks, we were intimate again, always at my house, and he showed much more consideration, refraining from using offensive language. Our daily texts and telephone calls were fun and cheeky, sometimes affectionate.

It wasn't long before he started to encourage me to look at sex beyond what I was already familiar with. He showed me some porn sites and asked me if I had done role-play. Did I know what sub/dom was? I hadn't and didn't.

"From now on, you will call me Daddy."

This made me feel uncomfortable initially, but I didn't refuse, excited to experience anything new.

Here is one of our "Daddy and Little Girl" days. I have been in denial at the ease with which he manipulated me, or perhaps ashamed at my willingness to participate; it felt like a dream at first. This is not happening to me:

—

It's Daddy time! I glance at the clock in panic, rushing to tie my second pigtail. My thoughts now turn to how I look as I stand back to admire my outfit.

"Oh my God," I cry

There in my bedroom stands a woman in her mid-60s dressed in a girl's school uniform: a little grey pleated skirt from Sainsbury's, nearly black hold-up stockings from M&S, cute white ankle socks, black pumps and a white shirt she already had ... with the biggest smile on my face I have seen in months.

"I can't believe this is me," I mutter under my breath, feeling a little guilty. Who is this woman, this adventurous, turned-on woman?"

I continued musing. I never believed someone would encourage me to do this willingly. I try to put this man's influence over me in the back of my mind, but my gut keeps prodding at my conscience.

"I know I'm a mature woman, but this feels so good," I say as I reach down under my skirt to feel the dampness between my legs, triggering butterflies to fly around my stomach. I consider for a while whether to wear my new lace panties or none at all. Momentarily, I smile at myself.

My mobile phone pings.

```
"Wait at the bottom of the stairs with your legs
open. You know the script," he commands in text.
```

Followed by another. `"I will let you know when I've arrived. Daddy X"`

I'm half an hour early and, all of a sudden, standing in a school uniform seems stupid. Plus, I am starting to feel a little nervous and apprehensive; if I don't go through with this, he could get angry with me, and I know what that feels like.

I pose sideways looking in the mirror, reassuring myself that my legs and figure can carry it off, but I decide my blonde hair, barely long enough for pigtails, would look cute on a younger woman, not me. While I pulled the two bunches out, I noticed my reading glasses on the bedside table. I put them on when I finished wiping them clean with my shirt. "Oh boy! now the look is complete. I feel more comfortable playing a studious little girl." This situation was feeling weirder by the minute.

Gazing out of the window at the frost-covered lawn, I start to feel under pressure. "How is he expecting this little girl to speak?" I tell myself it's only role play and not to think that this represents anything like a paedophile drama.

"This won't be natural for me," I say out loud, remembering his comment last time. "You gotta get more vocal girl," now ringing in my ears. He had tried to persuade me for some time about the benefits of role play in the bedroom, but I was too cynical to comply, and it caused quarrels. However, here I am now, determined to do anything to save my relationship because he meant the world to me. Or did he? Was it manipulation, and was I too desperate for attention of any kind? I made an effort to block those thoughts from my mind.

"What would a 15-year-old say to a Daddy figure?" As I look in the mirror again and practice my coy look. Horrified at the image reflecting at me, I stand rigid.

"What the fuck do I say?" the thought of role play tormented my usually logical, pragmatic nature... after all, this successful businesswoman had presented to an audience of a hundred plus in my career. Yet, the thought of acting out a sexual fantasy made me tremble and feel sick.

"This is ridiculous," I groan, and with that, I remove the skirt I barely got into in the first place. However, I would have succeeded a minute later, but the telephone pings with a message.

```
"Daddy is here x."
```

Panic sets in as I fasten the tight-fitting skirt meant for a 13-year-old, the zip getting stuck and mumbling to myself, "You stupid old woman." I see he is already striding up the garden path out of my bedroom window. I am so glad I told him to come through the back door, as the latch was left off.

Then, in an adrenalin-fuelled instance, the school girl at the top of the stairs suddenly becomes my character, although, praying he wouldn't be annoyed, I cannot bring myself to be legs apart at the bottom of the stairs.

The familiar sounds of the back door closing and his keys landing on the table are her cue to wait on the stairs. He arrives and stands back in the hallway to study me as I pose on the fourth tread, biting my lower lip, one knee bent and foot rested on my toe. I give him a coy look, the one I was practising earlier, without the grimace.

His grin says it all. "Wow, look at you, Daddy is pleased. Look what I've created," he says with pride as he beckons me to come down the stairs. He takes my chin and kisses me with a deep-throated groan.

"Oh, Daddy is very pleased, my little girl," as he takes me by the hand, and I float up the staircase in an air of expectation and delight. I cannot remember the excitement on this scale before, convincing myself there is something to be said for role play. You can forget your age and all responsibilities or negative influences around you.

He climbs the stairs behind me and gently taps my bottom on the stair turn, making me escalate faster, exhilarating my excitement with every step. Once in my spare double-bedded bedroom, nicked named by him the "screaming room", he places his hands on my shoulders and sits me on the bed, slowly stroking his lips against my ear. I can feel his hot breath and hear approving sighs, my hands trembling at the thought of where this role-play is going.

Sitting beside me, he puts a hand on my lower thigh and asks. "How has your day been, my lovely girl?" He looks at the floor while gently sliding his hand over my leg. "Have you been thinking of daddy?" His voice is deep and convincing.

I am so nervous and yet excited now, almost squeaking out the words, trying not to sound too submissive. "Sort of." I dare not tell him I have been preparing all day for his arrival.

"Daddy," he roars with a commanding voice.

I had forgotten to address him as he wished and felt my face reddening.

"Daddy," I respond in my adult voice.

"You are a disobedient little girl aren't you, and you know what that means?" He points to his knees. "Now, don't pretend you don't know what happens to naughty girls."

I know too well, for I have been there with my birth father, only he didn't have sex with me, thank goodness.

Shaking at the thought of his intentions, I realise I need to place my body over his knees.

He pauses for a few seconds, enjoying my submissive position. Slightly traumatised but tingling with anticipation, I can feel his hard bulge against my side. Then his hand slides up the inside of my stockinged leg, his fingers gently reaching my fleshy strip. In one quick movement, he raises my skirt to reveal my lace panties and proceeds to move them to one side, exposing a white, expectant cheek.

"Oh, naughty girl," he exclaims. He raises his hand and strokes my cheek. He raises his hand and strokes again, only rubbing as if polishing my cheek. He raises his hand again and strikes hard!! I'm taken by surprise now and shocked; I squeal loudly. And before

I took another breath, he struck me hard again!! I gasp, but his hold is strong and keeps me in place. While I catch my breath, he admires the pink mark.

He bends over me and kisses my hot cheek gently. "Mmmm, pink," he says with pride. "Don't forget the other one is there if you misbehave again. What do you say?"

He sits me on the edge of the bed, my cheek stinging. Nearly forgetting my manners, I blurt out. "Yes, Daddy. Thank you, my Daddy."

His soft smile is my reward as he runs his fingers through my hair and bends down to kiss my waiting lips.

"Now undress me", he commands.

Lifting his arms, he stands to raise his T-shirt above his head. No word was spoken, just a soft smile. My knees are trembling as I sit down to unfasten his belt. With one fast, almost aggressive move, he slides the belt from his trousers, studying my reaction, then places it gently on the floor, teasing me again, I know. He takes my trembling hand and puts it in his trousers front. Gosh! I am so wet now at the thought of revealing his hardness, his bulge so warm and throbbing, coming through his boxer shorts.

When the remainder of his clothes are removed, standing before me is an olive-skinned man, 5'8" tall, with a youthful body for his age. His hair is thinning, his mouth is kissable, and his white teeth grinning with lust. He tells me later that his eyes do not appear to move in unison; they were damaged in a fight in prison. Somehow, this physical abnormality doesn't affect my attraction to him.

"Bend over the bed", he commands, then lifts my school skirt and rests it on my back. My soaking wet panties and very hot cheeks are revealed now. He kneels to kiss my pinkness again, his fingers exploring the edges of the lace, working their way down to the dampness.

I am overwhelmed with excitement. As he uses his tongue to take me into further ecstasy

Turning me over, he whispers, "Okay, little girl, it's time for you to please your Daddy. You know what I like." He stands in front of me, his hand holding his erect penis.

I stand then, kissing him deeply, tasting my own juices in his mouth; I work my way down his body, kissing, licking and sucking each hard nipple. As I arrive at his erection, he groans, "Don't make me cum yet."

"Okay, Daddy," I say, allowing him to resume control.

He tells me to stand while he undresses me slowly, unbuttoning my shirt, telling me I am a good girl; he leaves my stockings and socks on.

Cupping my breasts, he stoops to kiss and then suck each one, raising me to another groaning high. He sucks my nipple hard, almost taking the whole breast into his mouth. My wetness and excitement are ready for anything.

Falling backwards on the bed, he beckons me towards him; this is my cue.

I feel him pull my thighs up further to envelop his face in my swelling lips and clitoris, his mouth moaning deep within me. His tongue penetrates; he pushes hard, greedy for more. I'm screaming with each high, arching my back. Oh, how new this all is, making me pant and cry as I climax again and again, quivering and shouting expletives, grabbing the headboard as if my life depended upon it; I am totally out of control. Finally, I relax and enjoy every stroke of his tongue.

"Well, how good was that?" he exclaims proudly. I love exciting you, my little girl. Now come to Daddy. I want you to ride me. Oh, how lovely you are. Every man should have someone like you."

I sink deeper into him. Thinking this is a rare compliment. Daddy only does commands, so far, not compliments. This role play is starting to feel real. He raises himself in a rhythm, penetrating further, making me concentrate on the moment. And then ... his moment comes. He cries out, calling me 'a bad girl' for making him cum so soon.

All of a sudden, this phrase puts me in fear mode. Reminding me of our first attempt at sex at the beginning of our relationship, where I rejected him for calling me a "bitch". I then return into submissive mode and kiss his face and lips to appease him; somehow, it seems the natural thing to do. We both lay in each other's arms, panting. He always insists I put one leg over his body and my other arm wrapped around him. He starts to reminisce about his past life, of a deprived and abused childhood. Then, without explanation, he jumped out of bed, bending down to his clothing and produced his belt from the floor.

"As you made Daddy cum too soon, I'm going to punish you and stripe you," he proclaims gleefully.

Now I'm fucking scared. I sit up immediately, thinking this is a step too far. I plead with him not to hurt me.

"Look, Daddy," giving him the pleasure of his roleplay name but using my grown-up voice. "I'm not into S&M, thank you. That is not me, okay?"

He continues striking his hand with the belt, making a slapping sound, smiling softly. "Don't worry, little girl. I'll not strike you. It excites Daddy to see little stripe marks on your lovely white bottom. Only two." Still smiling, "You can manage that, can't you for your Daddy."

His voice is starting to feel creepy. I regret the whole Daddy business. However, it seems crazy that I did trust his word. He is desperately trying to make it sound fun; I can see the excitement in his eyes. And still, I am struggling to find an excuse to escape the situation.

"Shall I get us both a drink, a cup of tea, maybe?" I say in a high-pitched, nervous voice.

"You trust me, don't you?" He uses his more serious voice. "It's only a bit of fun; you won't feel it much. Trust me, it's exciting". He stops hitting his hand with the belt.

Under pressure, I agree that I will trust his word, yet inside, I'm terrified, trying my best not to show weakness.

I am tense, in anticipation of the first strike of his belt, taking my mind back to the little girl I was when my father did the same over some misdemeanour I cannot even remember doing now. How I would sob, and he would say things like,

"This hurts me more than you for me to do this, but I did warn you." My father would lecture me for what seemed forever and then ask if we were still friends. He would give me one of the best lingering hugs.

I realise now that my memory of him hugging me and giving me any loving expressions was on the back of those beatings and at no other time. Therefore, I never considered him to be abusive; I deserved it, and the natural positive outcome was his love for me. Perverse, really and here I am again playing the victim with the benefit of attention,

The memory of that sting was still in my head from childhood. But what a relief; on this occasion, I only feel a little bit of a sting; his swift flick of the wrist as the belt lands on my bare buttocks leaves the desired marks he wanted. After the deed, he kisses both my cheeks and then takes a photo of them on his mobile phone to show me.

A few weeks later, he bragged about his other belt conquests and showed me their photos. That's when I no longer felt special; this man set out to have trophies. He insisted I was "The One" and wanted us to be "best buddies forever," but I didn't feel comfortable with this anymore. I knew this relationship was going to end messy. He wouldn't let go easily, and I knew my feelings for him were starting to sour.

He became more aggressively demanding. On top of that, I was shocked to learn he ran a soft porn site on YouTube, once again bragging about the number of followers he had. I started to worry. Had this man posted anything of our antics on his porn site? He was offended when I suggested it; then he became verbally aggressive. I backed off and said I was not comfortable with his pornography and not to show me again. I think he realised I was starting to be disillusioned with him.

We seemed more like an average couple for a short while, but there were signs of him trying to distance me from my family and friends, saying they didn't care for me.

"Name what they have done for you. Are they as close as you think? It's time you woke up to reality, my girl," he is preaching.

I distanced myself from them without realising what I was doing until my daughter questioned me one day. Why had I been secretive about Frank? Maybe because of my mistakes with the scammer. I didn't want my children's disapproval or worry again, so I kept a low profile.

"How come you have seen this guy for six months, Mum? You are planning on going on holiday with him, and we haven't met him yet? Have you met his family or friends?"

I kept quiet for a minute, realising I hadn't even assessed this as a problem.

"I know how it seems, but he's truly a nice man. We're taking it slowly." Realising this is the response of a mother trying to reassure her child.

"Oh Mum, are you sure this man is for real? Have you visited his home?"

He had two properties in Manchester. One he rented out to his daughter and the other was left vacant.

"Mum, please tell me more about this, Frank. I'm sure he is a very nice man, but don't you think I'm bound to be concerned about your secrecy?"

Trying to keep my composure, as I was genuinely worried about Frank's position, I started to tell my daughter that he was managing a very criminally delicate project.

Looking back, I had no evidence of his work position besides finding him on Google. For a year, he was the club member of a golf club. He also had a LinkedIn profile that didn't appear active.

I was mainly in denial about his more than dodgy persona. I even struggled to mistrust him, yet a few nagging doubts would occasionally surface. He would say he was travelling to Ireland for a meeting, then would tell me it was for golf. He only ever stayed over one night at a time and had no weekends off.

He started probing more about my marriage and past, trying to convince me that I was a victim, in need of therapy and that I ought to keep my daughters out of it until I was healed. He started undermining my confidence and affecting my self-esteem. Towards the end, he had me in tears at every visit. Eventually, he encouraged me to write down all the negatives in my marriage and the secrets of my past. I wonder now if Frank hypnotised me. I agreed because he was so convincing and because he convinced me I needed therapy. I liked the idea that my past torments would be behind me.

I wrote a script and arranged to read it to each daughter, which he approved. His last words were to not involve his name in my actions (one of my biggest ever regrets involving my daughters in his pseudo-psychology games).

To say that the reaction from both girls was traumatic would be an understatement. I was besmirching the memory of their father and our past family life. They were distraught and rightly cross with me when I had naively believed that they would be sympathetic. They quizzed me as to why I felt I needed to tell them about their dad and the past issues I had. I told them Frank, a therapist, advised me that I needed it and it would bring me closer to my daughters. It would be a healing process and help me recover from past hurts.

NAGGING DOUBTS

Please hear me out
Your story's bold
A life that's on hold
No solid ground
Your value unsound
Evidence lacking
No proof or backing.

You play a friend part
But aim for the heart.
Is a fragile victim your goal?
You don't show your soul
And take what you need
No respect precedes

To use where you can.
Are you an honest man?
It's time for the truth
Put aside the abuse
The game has died
We loved and lied.

There has to be trust
Or say goodbye to lust
I hear a secret employer
Alarm bells, destroyer.
You threaten you'll leave
Yet it's not I who deceive

I've too much to lose
If I'm about to be used
Like a toy abused.
You have a short fuse
So, tell me it straight
Or it's all over dear mate.

My 'investigator daughter' returned.

"Mum, as a result of the revelations from you in the last few days, I've done some investigating on Dr Frank; I hired a detective to research his history." I was speechless.

I sat down to hear what she had to say, feeling weak after yet another disapproving phone call from Frank, which had left me in tears yet again.

"I'm sorry for prying Mum. It's not something I'm proud of, but you've given Louise and me a great deal to be concerned about."

I listened carefully to her words.

"I don't believe he is what he says he is. There are no records of him being a registered therapist nor of reporting to the Crime Agency. No records anywhere. However, he does have a criminal record and has spent three years in jail for embezzlement. This man has no fixed abode, possible flitting from one widowed female to another." At this point, I remembered his belt-striking images of other women; I might be one of many.

I felt sick and stupid at the same time. How could I be foolish again? Then, suddenly, I remembered him bringing his dirty washing for me to put in my machine. I'd been appalled at the state of his clothes back then. And when he asked me for money towards his petrol, as driving from the North East was draining his weekly budget, I should have known then and there that he was a fraud.

My daughter put her arms around my shoulder and hugged my shaking body. "Mum, I understand this stuff is hard, but you must take more care. There are some very clever deceitful men out there."

I nodded as I wept. After a few minutes of self-pity, I then stood up and paced the floor. I could not tell her everything, but I knew I had to listen to her now.

"You're an extremely desirable woman for some of the 'low-life' out there, Mum. I'm trying not to be overprotective or judgemental, but you've lived in a relationship with one man, our dad, since you were 16; I know he wasn't perfect, but he was honest. It's time to wise up now you're single."

I sobbed, with self-pity and loathing of the man I trusted. But did I? Actually? Deep down? It was yet another example of not taking notice of my gut instincts. I doubted him very early on, but his charisma was irresistible and I was pretty sure that many other women fell for his cheeky charm and 'striping'- I cringe even thinking of his belt and the photograph of the stripe on my pink cheeks!

After a sleepless night, I wrote to him to finish our relationship. I did not want to hear his excuses and refused to answer the phone or text messages; his bleating messages came thick and fast. He was pleading with me to talk to him in one message and then accusing me of pushing him under a bus in the next. Then the aggressive name-calling started; words to belittle me eg simpleton, cow, mug, fool, pathetic, insecure and finally "bitch", which he knew I hated.

The seesaw of pleading and abusive messages over the next few days arrived via various means; WhatsApp, mobile, email and Facebook Messenger. He tried everything to contact me, all bar snail mail. For days, I kept my curtains closed as I was petrified that he would turn up at my home. One of his messages had a threatening tone "I know people, you know that?" I remembered he had been in prison, this felt like a veiled threat. Again, my stomach turned over at the thought of someone watching me. I kept my fears from my daughters, as I didn't want to worry them too.

Eventually, I did respond to his text messages saying…

```
"I am a woman alone protecting my life and family;
I take my responsibilities seriously; for a while,
I did you too, even when you described me as a'
fuck buddy' to gain a reaction and put me down.
Whatever you think I did to you I didn't deserve your
vitriolic response. I am sure, if you refer to your
words again, you will see a surprising behaviour for
a therapist. Plus, I feel you will always believe
you are right about everything, opinionated and
disrespectful. I can no longer tolerate an abusive,
controlling relationship. I blame myself for not
ending us sooner and admit to enjoying our intimate
moments at the beginning. But let's be honest, we
are very different people, and one of us was bound
to walk away eventually.

Take care, Frank, I will not write again. And I
want to reassure you neither my family nor I will
interfere with your job, it's not in our interest, I
just want to put the last 7 months behind me.

Jay"
```

So, now you're wondering how a reasonably intelligent woman can allow herself to be groomed and controlled by an individual such as this. I am desperately ashamed now of my part in this sick roleplay he persuaded me to participate in. When I know there will be those who have suffered actual child abuse reading this and would rightly chastise me for making such traumatic memories for them into a fun role play, particularly as an adult. I imagine some will be disgusted at my inclusion of this "Daddy" experience in my book. I wouldn't blame them for throwing it across the floor and stamping on it and throwing it in the bin. Yet it happened and I feel the need to show the light and the dark of meeting men, as well as my stupidity, as painful as it is sometimes.

I know now I should have checked my motives and his more, instead of focusing on the sexual highs promised. I would be lying if I didn't feel some excitement. However, my shame has overshadowed that feeling now.

I also realise that he found most of my insecurities and used them for his gratification. My daddy issues, wanting to please men, feeling unworthy of male attention, my body shame and, most of all, my sexual and creative imagination. I was an open book, and he took pleasure in reading it and taking advantage of it; maybe I was hypnotised (a cop-out, I know), or maybe I was desperate for love and attention, irrespective of the cost to my self-esteem and principles. Frank was not my finest hour but for the most part, one of my most memorable and shameful ones for not listening to my gut instinct:

Getting away

I took a trip to London with my sister Dawn, originally planned for Frank; he had always wanted to see Les Miserable the musical, so we planned it together. I paid for tickets and the hotel, and he would drive us down to London. I invited my sister instead, as I needed to get away and forget him. Frank had done an excellent job of getting under my skin and frightening me, too. I remember crying as soon as the Curtains opened at the theatre; this was supposed to be my and Frank's first trip away together.

On the day of the musical, he wrote, "This is a tough day for me, and I know you will miss me when the curtains open."

Like a mug, I had booked not only the London trip but also flights for Frank and me to spend a week on vacation in Spain. I invited Dawn again; I needed to get away from this man for good. I was in bits emotionally and struggled to eat and make decisions. I was glad of her company; she kept me focused.

Dawn and I had a hilarious day in Spain when we walked a mile to the nearest restaurant for Sunday lunch, Spanish style. After a large lunch, we left a little tipsy, I think the two bottles of wine had something to do with it; we then called in at a wine bar where live music was playing. The guy who chatted to us both offered to buy us a cocktail. Big mistake! We had no idea what was in it, but we drank it anyway. We also drank the Aniseed drink we had at first rejected earlier, too pissed to know the difference. So, to say we were legless when we stood up would be an understatement.

Dawn fell into the rose bushes on our way out and was rescued by some regulars. We staggered towards our accommodation, and she fell into a ditch at the side of the road. We were both laughing uncontrollably. I couldn't lift her out and landed on top of her. By now, we were both screaming with laughter, as we two middle-aged women in dresses, with legs flaying in mid-air, were too inebriated to get out of the dry ditch.

Within minutes, a man in a van stopped to assist us; he was the drummer from the band; he first helped me to my feet and then physically lifted my sister out of the ditch. Insisting he drive us to our digs. As we neared our accommodation, a moment of reality hit me, and I asked him to drop us off at the end of the road, for it was then the realisation that getting into a van with a strange man wasn't a good idea. (I know, a bit late to come to that conclusion).

My sister and I staggered the rest of the way when, all of a sudden, she fell flat on her face; I couldn't catch her! Once in the apartment, I put her on the toilet, went into my bedroom, collapsed on the bed, and fell into a deep sleep. Not sure how many hours later I woke up with a start. What if Dawn was unconscious? Staggering into the bathroom, I found her still slumped on the loo, her head between her legs, her sunglasses at an angle on her face, and no sound coming from her. What a relief when she lifted her head and slurred.

"I think I'm drunk." I found the strength to put her to bed and left her fully clothed. And fell back into my bed.

To my surprise, at 6 a.m., she arrived in my bedroom with a cup of tea, bright as a button. "Morning Jay, it's a gorgeous sunny day out there, " she said as she opened the curtains.

With horror in my voice, I said, "Dawn, have you looked in the mirror?" She shook her head. There she was, displaying two of the blackest eyes I had ever seen! Her sunglasses must have smashed against her face when she fell. We laughed all day about us two 60-plus women behaving disgracefully.

Getting away and having a good giggle was the therapy I needed and helped me to find the strength to ignore Frank's messages and telephone calls. I blocked him on everything from then on.

For two years, he would send me occasional messages from different telephone numbers, telling me how he was and how much he missed us. One of his last text messages was, `"We were meant to be best mates forever, you know. Are you coping okay? Please let me know. Just a 5-minute chat, girl?"`

I could hear his voice in his writing, which still disturbed me. I couldn't see a therapist saying "mates forever" either. Despite my blocking him, he found ways to get messages to me.

Eighteen months now since the last message, but I have since learned that his porn site is doing well; a friend's boyfriend had mentioned to her about this crazy guy on YouTube who uploads short porn video clips while he laughs and jokes over them. He has his own merchandise with regular sayings on them. My friend's boyfriend bought one of his T-shirts with his logo. Maybe I'll keep that logo description to myself. I felt sick when I saw it.

Writing this and the process of remembering him still gives me shivers down my spine. Shame and the fear of a video popping up of him striping me also.

FUCKER

You're fucking with my head
Sleep-filled eyes sore 'n red
My brain noise deafening
Early insanity threatening.

You're fucking with my life
Cutting my world with a knife
The controlling words I fear
With false phrases of love I hear.

You're fucking with my security
No comfort blanket or purity
Hard language and role play
Always having it your way.

You're fucking great in bed
Considerate lover, gives head
Arms enfold in moulded pairs
So natural is this toxic affair.

You're fucking too addictive
My life options are so restricted
I've succumbed to attraction
For this girl craves affection.

Are you fucking wrong for me?
I've fought a cul-de-sac destiny
My pride has taken a cruel blow
You'll no longer fuck me I know.

JACQUELINE T. **MAY**

CHAPTER 6
AWAKENING

It took me months to get over the Frank/Daddy experience. Actually, I didn't fully recover, as he left me with a mistrust of men, their fake persona recreations, and untruths about their past. I lost weight and confidence over it. It made me realise that dating in my 60s was not something I could instinctively cope with.

Still determined to pursue my dating journey to find "The One", I sought advice from dating experts on YouTube about what women and men want in their 60s. I learned that many women are embarking on a new stage with a different status, coming to terms with what that means, having more freedom of choice, financial independence, and enjoying the many experiences available. Many are retired and looking for companionship and, hopefully, love. I indeed identified with that. Then I had to ask myself, did I want love? And I cannot identify what that meant to me. Of course, I wanted companionship and being with someone who appreciated me for who I was, not what they wanted me to be. A partnership of equals. A lifestyle similar to that of Tony and me. My need to fill the void he left. Now, all I could think of was 'trust'. I needed that quality more than ever. Many of us fall foul of our future quest because we fail to trust again.

Also, I have to find more confidence in myself. My average build, average looks and freckled face have kept me looking youthful, so I have been told. Yet I focus on silly things like my poor skin quality, which bruises easily, and my uneven teeth. Most men would probably not even notice these things. One told me I had lovely eyes and a smile, not that I ever noticed; I was too busy worrying about how I looked in the nude and the state of my cellulite and skin. Then there is the fact that, at my age, I have health weaknesses like late-onset asthma.

I read once that to love someone else, you need to love yourself first. It sounds like a cliché, but the fact is that many of us have had our self-image damaged in past relationships and overcoming that is a painful process. I must forgive myself for past mistakes if I am to move on; stop thinking it was my fault all the time. Anxiety, gosh, most of us suffer one way or another; summoning up the courage to make that first phone call to a stranger to discuss who we are, what we want and that all-important question, "Shall we meet up," putting the phone down and kicking myself that I haven't asked this and that. Or I talked too much and gave away too much too soon.

I need to realise that there are more eligible women than men out there, and while that is so, I tend to think that men have the upper hand when it comes to deciding whether to date you or not—flirting, for instance. I was out of practice and forgot how important relaxing and having fun is. As I progress through this journey, I will discover if men have the upper hand and if it is always so.

However, you cannot keep an adventurous girl down. Armed with my new-found knowledge of sex and the pitfalls of trusting too soon, I embarked on a new profile on the online site, removing the "Widow" status again and keeping my information minimal and controlled. Many conversations ensued, and a few pleasant coffee dates were held. Most lasted an hour, rarely two. Afterwards, where appropriate, excuses were given, the "sorry cannot see it working for me" message, either from me or to me. I became a little ruthless, I admit. Many men were truly genuine, but some clearly were not. You see, dating sites enable people to create a false persona easily; they make up their own fantasy characters to attract a potential date; some are obvious, and some are scammers. All the time, I was learning and gathering more knowledge about men I had been sadly lacking.

John Lewis Cafe

I reminisce now about my coffee rendezvous at John Lewis in November, and with Christmas shopping on my mind, I meticulously plan a series of dates. Some days, I meet one in the morning and another in the afternoon, while others, I allow myself a day's breather. We usually agreed to meet at the foot of the escalator leading to the first-floor café at John Lewis. I'd casually peruse the store until spotting my date waiting as arranged, and then I made my approach. Greetings exchanged, we proceed to the café, usually with him ordering the coffee while I stand with him in line. Once our order is placed, I sit at a table, awaiting our drinks. This routine plays out with several different men over nearly two months.

Before long, I notice the regular café staff catching on—two in particular, one with a comforting roundness to her middle-aged frame and a slim, blonde girl in her thirties sporting a ponytail. After about five dates, they began to exchange knowing glances, usually when I approached the counter. Once, a wink; another time, a discreet thumbs-up, especially when I arrived with a distinguishing tall, silver fox of a middle-aged man. All that seems lacking is the holding up of numbered cards from these intrigued café observers.

One day, I arrive solo. On this occasion, after my final big Christmas shop, they jokingly inquired if I had been stood up. Chuckling along with them, I assure them that I haven't. At this point, I said to them I would seek out new meeting spots in the New year, and they laughed out loud.

Then, their almost disappointed expressions were tempered with well wishes, Christmas greetings, and "Please come back, won't you?"

The creep

The holiday season has passed, and I am determined to diversify my rendezvous locations. Meeting in the daytime halfway between our residences seems sensible. Today, I am on my way to a Bedale pub. Leading up to today, John sent me engaging and intriguing messages. My eagerness led me to agree to the meeting without the precaution of a phone call, breaking one of my own rules. I hope he is worth the journey.

He sits there with his dark beer. Calling me over, "Here, lovely lady." And stands up, offering me to sit near a roaring fire in the corner of the bench seat. He shuffles up to be close to me.

His eyes say it all immediately. I feel like they are undressing me. He is wearing a quilted gilet over a denim cotton shirt and jeans and has the look of a farmer with his pink weathered cheeks.

For several minutes, he paws at my knee and thigh, creepily telling me I am the sexiest lady he has met. (How I regret wearing a skirt now). I remove his hand from my leg without a smile. I know he is not my type, and his breath smells, it's not hard to miss; he is so close. I immediately feel uneasy in his presence. My skin is crawling as he continues pawing my arm with the back of his hand and then my leg, asking me personal questions about how many sexual encounters I have had during my online dating experiences. I push his hands away again whilst I try to slide closer to the fire. Feeling overwhelmed by this man in my personal space, I cannot wait to finish my coffee, but he has hemmed me into the corner sofa, fireplace on one side and him on the other. As simple as this creep is and how overt he is with my personal space, he refuses to read my obvious frozen demeanour. "What a creepy twat", I wanted to say to him but was too scared to say so.

He makes me realise that a lack of chemistry, being physically molested and listening to one's gut are not to be ignored. The courage to stand up and say, "This isn't working for me," or "Feck off, you weirdo, creepy twat," was tested today. However, I opted for "Sorry, I have to go; I am feeling uncomfortable." His response was instant as I tried to move around the table to leave.

"You are a tease, do you know that?" With an unapologetic mocking tone in his voice.

I responded, "I'm sure you know there are boundaries on a first date, so a woman feels comfortable and not threatened." I gestured with the back of my hand to him to allow me to pass. "What's more, you didn't respect my personal space when I signalled you to stop".

I am glaring at him now as he hasn't moved. It seems like forever before he slides down the corner sofa to let me out, muttering under his breath, "You are a fucking stuck-up bitch and shouldn't give out the wrong signals", and added, "It's women like you that give the dating sites a bad name." I translated that to mean he couldn't get what he wanted on the first date. I can imagine him wanking in his car to get over his frustration; he was that fired up. Ugh !!! I will block him as soon as I return home. Wildly, whilst shaken by this, I'm proud I had the courage to kick the creep into touch.

I constantly evaluate my experiences and do not always understand how I put myself in ridiculous situations. This made me ask, "Did I tease men, or was this their way of responding to rejection? I have a lot to learn," I tell myself.

I still struggle to understand what I truly want. Tony, my late husband, was a hard act to follow in many ways, although he had faults too. He was an honourable, honest, well-mannered man who dressed conservatively and had a fantastic work ethic. His hygiene practices were not bad either. I know I loved him. I think I initially set out to look for a similar type. One thing I know about him is that he was respectful and dependable and would never have treated women the way this creep did.

Many of my dates put me off with their appearance: beer bellies, bad teeth, how they dressed, how they talked, misogynistic behaviours and health issues. I sometimes feel shallow with my distaste for these things, except the misogyny and bad teeth, of course. Some have troubled relationship histories, family feuds and money matters, making them bitter. It can be as simple as, can I see myself kissing him? Or how would my family see him? One made it clear he doesn't want to travel; that is a non-starter. Another said his late wife used to do everything for him, and he is lost without her; he needs a replacement. Woah, no way! Nor the man who said he didn't want anything to do with grandkids, his or mine, well that said something about him

Nice guy

Patrick turned up at our agreed destination, a hotel eight miles away. It was an early spring day, and blossoms were blowing around the car park like confetti. He has a walking stick, the type of stick that has three prongs at the end; he clearly should have been in a wheelchair as he struggled to start walking towards the entrance. His sway was almost painful to watch and very slow. I cannot help but admire his determination to walk to the bar, which I could see was tough work for him. He points to two wing-backed chairs in the corner of the room; I imagine a higher chair is more accessible for him to rise from.

Once he has caught up with me and settles into the chair with his stick propped up by his side, he smiles and asks me what I would like to drink. I couldn't bear to see him go to the bar, and I offered to go for us. To which he announces, "I have a prosthetic leg", almost immediately, "hence the stick." He chuckles, patting it like an old friend. I decided to do the right thing and order our drinks. While standing at the bar, I wondered why he hadn't warned me when we chatted on the phone.

I felt very uncomfortable at first as he described his injuries after a significant car crash. He told the sad story of his fiancé who abandoned him and how forgiving and understanding he seemed when describing her; clearly, he loved her very much.

"It wasn't her fault as I was very affected mentally at first; being sporty and independent most of my life, to depend on others was even worse than the pain of the operations I went through; that's all finished now; this is the best I am going to be from now on." He grinned again, punctuating, "I haven't given up finding love; if Steven Hawkins can do it, so can I." The twinkle in his eyes was captivating.

I felt such overwhelming empathy for him, and I had to suppress the urge to hug him. I was desperately trying not to be patronising and wanted to treat him as if he had no disabilities.

But now I sit back and relax, deciding this lovely man just wants to talk. I know it is only fair to listen to his story. He had been successful in his career, well-travelled, and played golf and five-a-side football before the accident. You could see he didn't take his hardship too seriously and made fun of it. He didn't have children, and I didn't pry into his past relationships. He didn't offer any explanation. Judging by the car he arrived in, he had no major money worries, but little comfort for him. I suppose when most of the things you loved have been taken from you, a fraction of a second incident and his world has changed.

We agreed he wasn't in a fit state to join me on my travel plans, but he was glad I turned up and was delighted that we had a lovely conversation. He paid for our coffees, and we both strolled to his car. On arriving at the driver's side, he put out his hand, I thought he wanted to shake mine. Instead, he pulls me towards him to kiss me. There is a surprising amount of strength in his arm and it took me by surprise.

I laugh with embarrassment as he cheekily says, "You can't blame me for trying. There's life in the old dog yet, hey?" and then winks.

He has a lovely warmth in his smile, and I imagine it's very difficult for anyone to get angry with him.

I feel very humbled by this amazing man who wouldn't let his disabilities get in the way of romance.

There was still a smile in my voice. "You're very cheeky, and no, I don't blame you for trying; there is no harm in it. You're a nice man, and I wish you all the best."

On the way home, I pondered what it took for a man to be suitable for me. Was it the physical or mental qualities? Compassion, humility, reliability, passion, and humour are essential, as are honesty. This man has almost all of the qualities I was looking for, but not the physical, which was a huge hurdle. I decided I had to be honest with myself and keep focused on what mattered to me. Stay strong!

Please Sir

Keith, 62, the Comprehensive School Deputy Head Master, was someone I regretted turning down.

He is a keen cyclist, caver, climber, and canoeist, slim and, of course, fit. He is a single parent to three teenage daughters. We wrote to each other over several weeks before arranging our meeting. I thoroughly enjoyed our correspondence; his banter was my kind of humour. His stories were fascinating; I have rarely come across such a fellow adventurer, and I was intrigued by his travel and sporting activities.

When I arrived, he was already at the pub. He turned around when he noticed me walk in and gave me a huge smile.

"I'm having a small glass of wine; fancy joining me?" as he points to his. "Oh, I don't mean it has to be a small one."

I reciprocate with a big smile too. "It's fine, a small one will do nicely, besides I am driving."

We found a cosy corner in what I assume is the lounge bar, and he asked me about my journey. I already had a nice feeling about him, and I felt relaxed immediately.

We talked and laughed for three hours; he was a great listener and interested in my career and family history. I feel more comfortable opening up to him than I had during my first meetings.

Knowing he has children at comprehensive school, I ask him how he copes with being a single dad of three pubescent girls, telling him how my girls were at that age? He laughed, "The honest truth?" shaking his head. "They are more of a bother to each other, squabbling and competing over everything and anything. I stay out of it, put on my headphones with my favourite rock band and hope it's all over when the music stops, at the same time praying they haven't committed murder."

Taking a sip of his wine, he said, "I love them very much and cannot imagine my life without them." I admired his loving commitment to them, and it was a refreshing change from the men who had lost all contact with their children, leaving the parenting to their ex-wives. He matched my values when it came to supporting and being a role model for our kids.

However, all the time he talks about his dependent three daughters bothered me. As he describes each one of their characters, they begin to feel like a huge commitment, and I cannot see myself as a stepmother, for my own daughters were in their 40s; my grandchildren were my priority now. That awful feeling of being shallow overcame me again.

On my return home, I decided to write to him, saying how much I liked his company, but that his personal circumstances would make it difficult for me to pursue a relationship.

He responded the following day. He said he was disappointed with my shallowness (OMG that is what I feel) and, after having such a good meeting, he finds it difficult to comprehend that I am not willing to give him a chance.

My rejection hurt him, and I felt I had not handled his feelings very well.

I wrote to him a few weeks later, saying I regretted what I had done and would like to talk again; I missed our correspondence. His response "I could never go back to someone who rejected me. My heart has already been broken once, and therefore, I am not going to put myself in that position again."

We wrote a few times after that, and he said he was happy to meet again, but each time we planned something, he cancelled. I eventually gave up.

Often, online dating is given a poor reputation by women, who cite sleazy characters, scammers, users, gold diggers and stalkers. And whilst those sorts are there, I discovered from men that there are also broken hearts and hardships. On many of my dates, I came across (their stories) of women mistreating men. However, I have to say that women come off worse in many cases because they do not have the ego men have and are more willing to walk away than fight. Or try to balance being a mother and singledom; they usually suffer from conflict avoidance, a trait I recognise in myself. It is too easy to generalise about people seeking romance, company or sex. Loneliness is the key driver for many.

Salute you - not

Peter, a retired engineer from York, met me in my local bar. I was immediately attracted to him; in fact, I was blown away by how the chemistry affected me. He was an ex-military officer too and had a very upright posture with impeccable manners, opening the door and gesturing me in first, finding a chair at a table for two and standing behind it to help me get seated. I was happy with the location; as you can imagine, after the "Creep", I'm acutely aware of my potential escape route now.

He was dressed smartly casual in a green jumper with his white shirt collar sitting on top of his neckline, dark blue jeans, and smart walking shoes. We had a lovely chat about the area, his career, and my family—nothing heavy, just comfortable.

When we parted, he asked if I would like to join him that next weekend for a walk around the York City walls. Of course, I agreed, and he said he would confirm the arrangements by text later.

I was ecstatic and phoned Kitty straight away with the news. I told her he ticked many boxes and couldn't wait to meet again.

That morning, I woke with a start. I haven't set my alarm on my phone! I rushed to wash my hair and get ready. I am 10 minutes late meeting him in the car park too. This isn't a good start, but he politely accepted my apologies. Then my nervousness kicked in; my giggling state must have been unbearable. I could even hear my giddy voice, and my brain cringing inside. Oh no, he is looking at me quizzically.

"What are you giggling at?" I pathetically replied, "Everything." I tied up the laces of my dirty walking boots and noticed his pristine boots opposite me, and I was dying of shame inside. And at this moment, he kneels down on one knee and fastens the second boot for me. "Thank you," I try not to giggle.

"Thought I'd better help, or we will be here all day." He laughs this time. "Follow me; I need to lock up my apartment. His place overlooks the river and is four floors up in a relatively modern building.

"Wait at the bottom of the stairs. The lift has broken. I've reported it several times, but no one has come to fix it. I would fix it myself if it weren't for insurance ramifications." Showing me where the lift is. "I'll be back in a jiffy." He then runs up the stairs, two treads at a time.

On his return, we set off on our walk. He walks at quite a pace, and I'm doing my best to keep up with him, sacrificing conversation for breathing.

The daffodils are in bloom this time of year, and the banks of the walls are covered with various shades of yellow and white. It is such a lovely time to see York.

He did his best to keep me entertained with his knowledge of York and its walls. Taking me into two ancient public houses and telling me of their history and the famous people who have drunk there over the centuries; after two glasses of lager he recommended, I relaxed and giggled less.

At the final part of the walk, he calls into the toilet of one of the pubs. On his return, he sits next to me on a picnic bench and says, "I've enjoyed your company, Jay, but I don't think there will be any romantic future between us. I'm very fussy about what attracts me to a woman; it could be something as simple as her hair. Unfortunately, I have to be honest: I'm not attracted to you the way I would like to be, I'm afraid. You are a nice lady, and I wish you all the best in finding your match." There is an air of superiority in his tone.

I am speechless when he stands up. "Oh, your car park is just around the corner, to your right; thanks for coming and spending the day with me, Jay. Safe journey home."

In a nervous giggle, I blurted, "I understand, thanks for the guided tour," as he started to march away, but I'm not even sure he heard me; he didn't look back.

Realising that I now feel the same rejection Keith felt, I sit in the car shell-shocked and then check myself in the rear-view mirror. My hair!!!!? It is like a frizz ball. No wonder he mentioned hair.

The bastard, I think to myself. Now, who's shallow? I was not too fond of his grandad jumper anyway. The 16-year-old me coming out. I have to admit I hurt myself as I punched the steering wheel, screaming out loud, "Stupid bitch." As a young couple passes in front of my parked car looking at me, then at each other, the stupid situation made me giggle again… aagghhhh!

There are red flags, which I realise as I drive home. He loves cycling and is a member of a very active group, while I don't cycle. He was ex-military and probably liked to be in control. I cannot see myself saluting him and saying, "Yes, sir," whilst I am on top.

"Fussy, well, I am too," I shout.

NEXT !!!

JACQUELINE T. **MAY**

CHAPTER 7
COME IN VICAR

After months of meticulously planning to meet numerous men at various venues, usually within 30 miles of my home, I grew weary of the coffee dating scene. The initial excitement gave way to a sense of fatigue, prompting me to become more selective in my choices. Rather than proactively seeking new encounters, I became more reactive, only responding to those who approached me. I felt more in control. While the earlier chapters of my journey are marked by intense learning and sometimes painful experiences, the next phase carries a bittersweet undertone.

Neil, a 55-year-old, was extremely polite, modest and quietly charming. At 5'11", he was the tallest man and the youngest I had dated. What I have learned about men in their late 60s is that they are not very tall, 5'6" to 5'8" is quite normal (I am 5'5"), and many admit to adding a couple of inches on their dating site profiles as well as reducing their age by up to five years. What is the point, you may ask? We all have to come clean eventually. It's all to do with ego; many think women are only interested in taller and younger men than themselves. If they find a woman interested, they hope to get around the little white lie with their charm.

The irony is that women put more credence in truth and will lose respect for men who lie. Women lie too, so I am told by many men, remarking on old and photoshopped photos on their profiles and looking nothing like their photos when they meet face to face.

One man said that when he waited at the railway station for his Naomi Campbell-look-alike date, a huge woman tapped him on the shoulder, saying she had recognised him from Tinder. She was his date! When he remarked on her appearance and said she didn't match her photos, she shrugged her shoulders and said they were of her younger sister. He turned on his heels and left the station without another word. Who could blame him?

My new suitor lived half an hour away and was very determined that I was his kind of woman. I pointed out our 11-year age difference, but he was insistent that age for him didn't matter; it was just a number; he had always dated older women, and his ex-wife had been seven years older than he. His most recent lover, however, did not fit his average profile. She had been only 40. It all ended badly, as he realised that she had mental health issues and, though he tried hard to fix her, he couldn't. Neither could God, by the sound of it.

All the above was discussed between us over our first phone call. After an hour, I agreed to meet him in a pub in the next town the following day.

I decided to wear my new blue slim-fitting trousers, rolled up at my ankles and a pair of bright patterned, high-heeled shoes. Feeling classy and almost sexy in them, if a 67-year-old can get away with sexy but a little unsteady; walking from the car park to the pub was as much as I could manage. I pray he doesn't ask me to show him around the town.

I felt hopeful about this one, based on his seemingly enthusiastic chasing. Why shouldn't I have a younger suitor? And he certainly impressed me on our first date. He was pleasant-looking and had excellent manners. Being a maths and religious history teacher, he had some amusing stories to tell. His first comment was about how sexy my shoes were (result). The date lasted an hour, and I made my usual excuses, though not because I didn't like him. On the contrary, I was worried I would like him too much and it would not be requited.

To my surprise, he wrote a beautiful message that night, saying he wanted to see me again and that I had made quite an impact on him, notwithstanding that I looked many years younger than he expected. He was, he said, both physically and mentally attracted to me. Gosh!!! Gosh!! And the shoes? I giggled in amusement. Once I had got over his eloquent message, I decided to sleep on it. The following day, I had a message.

```
"Good morning. I hope you slept better than me?"
```

```
"Do you fancy meeting again?"
```

Of course, I responded that it would be nice to meet again, though still a little wary of his intentions.

He impressed me again with his choice of venue: a medieval mansion hotel for coffee on a warm summer's evening. We agreed to meet at 6 p.m. When I arrived, he was there, opening my door and taking my hand as I stepped out.

"Oh my, chivalry is not dead,"

He responds with his dimple smile. (I am in trouble now).

"How was your journey? I'm so glad you could make it." He takes my hand and leads me up the ancient stone steps through huge, ornate oak double doors.

We order our coffees, which arrive on a silver type tray. Every action of this man is distinctly considerate and gentlemanly. His clothes are casual-smart but classy. His dark, thick hair, showing grey highlights and brushed to one side, is longer than most men his age, but he suits it all the same. His broad smile and full lips are mesmerising. All the time, I think that this is too good to be true.

What is the catch? We chat about our past dating experiences (excluding Frank). Then the catch. He is in the process of being separated, still living in the family home in separate rooms. It is up for sale, but he isn't in a position to move out yet.

I felt disappointed. "Therefore, you are still married and living together, am I right?"

He holds my hand again. "I am an honest man; I wouldn't lie to you to impress you. And I also must tell you I am an ex-vicar," coughing into his other hand. "I lost my vocation four years ago when I had an affair with one of my parishioners; she was nine years younger than me. When the affair ended, I decided to leave my post as a vicar. My wife never forgave me for leaving the parish, with its beautiful home, social life and charity work; that affected her more than the affair. Her life revolved around the church, you see. She was a key vocalist in the choir, and before long, I found out why she never made a big deal of my affair. She was fucking the choirmaster! Excuse my French."

He turns away. His head is in his hand now. "It's been such a mess for the kids. We live in separate rooms; I cannot leave unless we sell the house."

He goes on to tell me how he delayed leaving the church, getting a divorce and selling the house for the sake of the children. However, he knew he had to make changes, so he applied for a job as a lecturer at a local college. He didn't tell his wife until after he had been accepted. That was when the final breakdown had started. Up until then she was in denial.

Multiple bombshells in one sentence! Dumbstruck for a while, I then tell him I am not judgemental but find it challenging to trust men because of my past experiences. He holds my hand again and kisses the back of it. I'm totally disarmed.

After our coffee, I suggest we walk around the hotel grounds. All the time, he holds my hand and clears his throat as if he is about to say something important. I feel a sense of longing for him to kiss me, but I refrain from giving any hints. He describes a little more about his two children, now at university but still returning home for holidays and when they need their washing done.

When we returned to my car, he opened the door for me and asked if he could see me again, holding onto the top of the door as if he wouldn't let go until I answered.

"I don't see why not," I say, unphased. "Let's chat later, see when is best for both of us".

His dimpled smile says it all. He's keen.

Honestly, I was a little confused and disappointed at the new revelations. Too good to be true, I kept telling myself, and if it seems too good to be true, it usually is, but will my gut instinct listen? How much of what he had told me was a deal breaker? God knows! I laughed at myself. Anyway, there was another potentially tricky situation I could find myself in. The other woman, maybe?

I had visions of him knocking on my door, looking dejected, his suitcase and a couple of bin liners on my doorstep, telling me he was homeless and couldn't think of anywhere else to go, that I was the only thing on his mind. Yes, if he came looking for a roof over his head. I might be weak enough to let him over the threshold. So God forbid it doesn't happen!

Considering the potential of a dependent man in my house made me anxious. Surely this would be a deal breaker? I started to imagine having to be tidy, putting my clothes neatly away at bedtime, no more dirty knickers and socks on the floor, having to flush the toilet at night after my regular bladder releases, not to mention tripping over his socks and underpants. Would I have to start planning mealtimes instead of trawling through the fridge and freezer, putting together weird concoctions because I cannot be bothered to cook? What about my family gatherings, my daughters with their practised skills in detective work? Poor sod wouldn't have a chance of being accepted and I would be looked upon as the careless, desperate old mother who hasn't a clue about men. I decided to sleep on it.

The next day, I received a text message at 7 a.m.

```
"Good morning. I couldn't sleep last night, Jay. I
hope you will see me again. I have a free day on
Friday. Can we meet somewhere?"
```

I hesitated for an hour, making myself a cup of tea and gazing at my computer. I told myself the company would be nice and there was no harm in seeing him again socially, but my weak will was starting to take over.

We decided on Yorkshire Sculpture Park. I love the large open spaces, the views of woodlands, the lake and lush pastures, and the enormous sculptures adorning the landscape. We chatted more as we slowly strolled around the lake. He put his hand on my back as he directed me through the kissing gate, cheekily remarking that he had resisted. However, I felt a surge of electricity go through my body and giggled nervously. I could not sleep that night and spent an hour writing a poem about the kissing gate moment.

ELECTRICITY

I recoiled at your touch,
A sudden electric shock
Shooting through my core.
Did I imagine those eyes,
The corner of your smile,
The crease in your cheek?

The tone of conversation
Mellowed in my ears,
Not wanting to awake,
As your hand reached out,
Enveloping mine,
And the small of my back
Burned with your touch.

Tell me, did electricity wrap
Our receptive bones,
Creating imagined sparks
Of desired passion?
The future flashing by
As we hold our mood.

Will life's distraction invade,
And that dying moment be
A ghost of a passionate hold
And parallel chemistry?
For only time has certainty.
If our paths cross again,
Let the lightning bolt
Strike twice in a heartbeat.

We enjoyed a lovely lunch and never stopped talking about our life experiences, where we would like to travel and how. It was easy to talk to him and holding his hand felt natural.

We said our goodbyes with no mention of seeing each other again. I felt a lump in my throat as he stood by my reversing car, grinning with that dimpled cheek and waving. How could this be so good? Like a nagging finger on my forehead, my age kept reminding me that I didn't deserve this feeling.

Two days passed. I kept my cool, though desperate to write to him. All the other messages from other men on the dating site seemed so unexciting; I didn't respond to any of them.

On the second evening, a message pinged on my phone. Remembering the online dating advice, not to appear too eager, I waited for a few minutes. It should have been at least an hour, but I couldn't wait that long.

"What you up to this weekend? Fancy a walk? Neil". At the end, he puts on a kissing emoji. Oh feck, I said to myself; I was in trouble now!

"Well, yes," I responded. I had lost all rational thought about keeping my distance from him. I said, "Come to my house, and we can go for a walk locally. The weather forecast is beautiful."

What harm was there in enjoying the company of a nice man? Besides, if we do end up intimate, it might help me get over Frank's trauma. I decided not to second-guess where this might go. I would just enjoy the moment and savour the chase while keeping an eye on who was available on the dating sites.

When he arrives, he keeps apologising that he cannot reciprocate by inviting me to his, but that might change soon as he has sold his house as someone is interested in buying it. I am encouraged by this news and by some of the deep conversations we had on our previous date, reassuring myself that he likes the same music, is a lover of the arts, he doesn't like football and boozing in the pub. He loves to read and can talk about books he has read all day long. Yet I am always concerned about our 11-year age gap and signs that his serious nature could be a problem for me.

While we are resting on a bench at my favourite beauty spot by the river, he turns to me and asks if he can kiss me. Memories come flooding back of my first kiss with my late husband Tony, he was my first boyfriend; we sat at this very bench.

I watch the river running at a high level, not typical for this time of year. The distant summer storms of the Dales are throwing their mighty weight around upstream, causing an unusual volume of water; this is evident by the ripples stroking the waist-high grasses of the embankment opposite us. The clear blue sky is broken only by the cloud of insects rising from their larvae on the water. Fortunately, they waited until dusk before dining on my arms and legs, but still, I avoided wading through them. This beautiful, dappled-shaded clearing overlooking the river is my favourite place to sit and take in its serenity. It never ceases to calm my well-being, gazing at the craggy limestone cliffs and verdant pastures on the opposite bank. I have often sat here, listening to the music of the wind in the trees accompanied by birds, the robins, blackbirds and thrushes, usually overshadowed by noisy jackdaws nesting in the craggy cliffs.

My husband Tony was my first love, and neither of us had real experience kissing anyone. Our intimacy had been awkward at the beginning, but we soon got the hang of where our noses should go and how to keep our mouths open, not clammed shut. This setting had been probably the most romantic you could find for two innocent teenagers in the 1960s. Beyond the clearing were tall grass banks adjoining a neatly sown field of bright green new shoots. We had returned to these grasses a week later and lain down, kissing furiously, both innocent and in love, or was it curiosity and youthful lust? It's hard to believe our skinny frames had been capable of those intimate moments where we entwined for hours.

We would tread precariously down the narrow tree-rooted paths, with him holding out his hand for mine at the tricky parts; I would feel safe in his presence. The towering cathedral-like tree branches shaded us from the hot sun as we swung our arms in unison, singing our favourite song on the way home. He was always pitch-perfect. Me? Well, his face had told me that I was not so perfect.

Before opening the door to my home, Tony stopped me, removing the straw from my straw-like hair, the evidence of our youthful affair. I remember my mother's quizzical look. Tony had winked across the room and I had blushed, knowing I was no longer a child.

"Jay, you have been driving me wild during this walk. I have to kiss you." Neil's words break through my reminiscing of Tony and I. However, his politeness comes through, as always, making me smile.

"I will understand if you think I'm being too pushy. Please don't be offended."

Before he can continue, I put my lips on his. Immediately, I felt regret for betraying Tony's memory. Why did I bring this stranger here to our special place? To say this 55-year-old man in front of me is eager would be an understatement. He practically devours my face, his hands all over the upper part of my body. I keep looking over his shoulder in case anyone should walk by. I was feeling a little ridiculous, imagining my 16-year-old self, seeing a couple of old folks having a rampant snog on a public bench.

"I'll tell you what, Neil, let's go back to my house for coffee, and we can kiss in private there."

He nearly pulls my arm out of its socket when he grabs my hand to lift me from the bench. Thankfully, we are only half a mile from home, for I swear he is so excited all the way that it can't be comfortable for him in the trousers department. Escaping my beautiful riverside Crag and all its memories is a relief.

Hardly through the front door and he is already pawing at me. I give in to his advances because I, too, am turned on by the idea of us getting together. We head straight up the stairs and go to what Frank and his leather belt called the "screaming room."

I close the blinds as my bedroom overlooks the road; I would hate to traumatise school kids at 3 p.m. seeing a couple of wrinklies naked. We slowly undress each other; he is hairier than I expected, black hair covering his white torso. It's not my favourite feature on a man, but at least it is soft and not like wire wool. I cannot seem to get Frank out of my head; his smooth olive skin and hairless body were features I admired. But what is a perfect body?

Neil runs his soft hands over my back, then my breasts, then holds my shoulders gently, lying me on my back on the awaiting bed. Why do random thoughts like, glad I have washed the sheets, invade my mind? Within a minute, he is straight on top of me, his kisses frantic and his mouth like a very wet suction pump. Suddenly it is all over; he ejaculates on my stomach. As I lie there with his warm, sticky mess in my belly button, I am also disappointed that I had no time to have an orgasm, yet I am also relieved it is over; I have realised that, in the rush of the moment, we forgot about protection. He was so eager that I came to the conclusion it had been some time since he had had sex. He keeps saying, "Sorry". Rather than massage his ego, I take myself to the bathroom, silently washing myself.

I stayed in my dressing gown and returned to the kitchen; he was already sitting at the kitchen table, looking like a sad puppy. I squeeze his shoulder as I pass and pretend not to acknowledge a man troubled and tormented by his feelings. He sits before me and I'm not able to offer him consolation, a solution or a future. He has so much personal unfinished business to tackle before embarking on a new chapter in his life. I know without any doubt that I would never be part of it. Our fling was a fleeting distraction for both of us. We are fighting our tigers in life and sometimes we feel overwhelmingly caged, and he looked caged. Yet I now understand widowhood has benefits, a finality that divorce rarely has. That person who shared your life and reared children with you for years is still around. Sometimes, the past continues tormenting you through your children and other commitments. I'm grateful for my independence and the opportunity to spend a "special moment", guilt-free. Today, I am with an exciting and passionate man, much younger than I am. However, I wish his kisses were less devouring.

"Would you like a coffee or tea or something stronger?" I give him a broad smile.

He grins back, "Bit early for something stronger. Do you have caffeine-free?"

Caffeine-free tea? I repeat in my head. Bloody hell, an old blue Yorkshire Tea caffeine-free box is at the back of my cupboard. I have no idea how old it is. I grin back, wondering whether to subject him to mouldy teabags.

"Sorry no, but I have coffee or green tea," pointing to a box and a jar.

He spots the Yorkshire Tea decaf at the top of the back of the cupboard. "There it is at the back, I will reach it for you."

We drink our tea silently for the first few sips; then he breaks it with a coughing fit. Oh, heck, is it the decaf tea? I think the last time I used it was when my friend Penny visited months ago.

"Is it okay?"

He coughs once more. "Gone down the wrong way."

Thank goodness. I would have difficulty finding his family to explain how he's died on my kitchen floor after mouldy tea and hasty sex. I realise how little I know about this man. Calling an ambulance without even knowing his surname or address would be tricky, to say the least. "Jay, you need to be more careful", I shout in my head.

"Are you okay, Neil?" I asked, using his name to remind myself that I know that much, as well as his age of 55.

I reach out to hold his cold hand. "I've been thinking Neil. It's been lovely having time with you, but I feel the 11 years between us will cause us problems in the future. I don't think it would be wise to get too involved. We'd be in danger of hurting one another if we don't face reality now."

He nods solemnly and coughs once more. "Yes, you're sensible. But, all I know is that you turn me on. You're so passionate; I've not had that before; not many women have that effect on me. Still, it's your choice and I respect you for it." He pauses for a moment to think. "There's no harm in us continuing, though, in my book. After all, we are adults." He holds my other hand. "It's your choice, Jay. I won't pressurise you."

I refrained from telling him he needed to finish the process of his divorce and leave the family home before embarking on a relationship. It's life and I understand his need for friendship and intimacy, no need for me to lecture him.

I thank him for his understanding, and before he leaves, he insists on giving me one of his hoover suction kisses. I can't help myself, wiping the moisture from my face as I shut the front door.

The following morning, I decided to make myself clear, reiterating my feelings from the day before.

Dear Neil,

I delayed writing to you until this morning to give us both breathing space and time to reflect. You are certainly a very charming man; any girl would dream of walking with her hand in yours. You are intelligent, good looking and a great listener. You also have a sensitive touch and a kiss that makes a woman feel very special. It is such a pity I am not younger. I cried at the sadness of our dilemma. I came to the conclusion that we crossed each other's path for a reason; two lonely people were very happy for a moment and I will always value that. It will make me smile when I go for my regular river walk. But I know in my heart that it wouldn't be fair to continue seeing you. You deserve more than I could give.

Yours fondly, Jay xx

He responded to me within minutes. It had taken me an hour to compose mine and he responded with a thoughtful reply, which told me I had done the right thing, with no hurt feelings.

```
Dearest Jay,

Thank you so much. I couldn't have wished for anyone
with more maturity and understanding than you. Your
insight into me and into my situation was laser-
like. I am sad to say the conclusion you have come
to is confirmed in my own thinking too.

We certainly 'enjoyed the moment' and for once in
our lives said 'sod the consequences'.

But consequences have to be faced and we both know
it's not right to go on. You are a wonderful woman at
every level and from any angle Jay. It will surely
only be a matter of time before you find someone
worthy of you. Drop me a line from time to time. My
sincerest and very best wishes go with you Jay.

Love and fondest affection. Neil xx
```

I enjoyed my time with Neil. Moreover, it was the first time I felt in control of a relationship situation and listened to my gut instinct. However, is being in control of a relationship the right thing, shouldn't it be mutual respect, understanding, sharing and consideration. I'm still confused as to what makes me happy.

I often updated my sister Kitty and friend Penny on my progress with the new men in my life.

"An ex-Vicar Jay! There has to be a story there. Did you shag him?"

Both girls were enthralled by this revelation and insisted I told them more. All agreed I did the right thing. They usually laughed at my final word; a sign I had moved on.

NEXT!!

CHAPTER 8
THE NARCISSIST AND HIS SHOES

Peter, 62, was still working full-time for a furniture supplier. He was typical of a salesperson, or should I say a director, with charisma and the gift of the gab. I immediately liked his voice on our first phone call; it was a deep, warm tone; I always find this alluring. We laughed at a few things, mainly our first dates disasters. His dating site profile read very well and confident, with a little humour thrown in. Better still, he only lived three miles away. He wasn't shy, as you would expect from a man who worked in sales—knowing what he wanted from a woman, even down to her smelling sweet and dressing well. Little did I know then that he had a particular interest in shoes.

I'm beginning to understand that men have many excuses for why their last relationship failed and how hard it was when she did the "dirty" on them, often over money. Peter was no exception. Despite hearing his woes, I eventually decided it would be good to meet each other. He was five years younger than I then, but I didn't feel the same pressure that I felt with Neil. He loved music, particularly my era. We often exchanged YouTube links to our favourite songs.

We met in the car park next to the church; he preferred it there because it was less busy. When I saw his car, I understood why—a very well-maintained Mercedes sports car. He said cars were his big passion and that he loved F1 racing.

He immediately grabbed my hand, and we walked down the high street together. This felt awkward at first; I even remarked, "Hey, you are a bit forward," punctuated with a little giggle of approval when I accepted that I was enjoying the experience.

Besides, he is nicely dressed and looks good in his crisp white casual shirt, waistcoat and jeans. I cannot help but notice his brown, shiny, brogue-type shoes with square, almost pointed toes.

We walk towards the heavily buttoned maroon Chesterfield settee in my local wine bar. He then goes to the counter and orders our two cappuccino coffees. We talk for two hours nonstop. I suspect our body language says a lot as we laugh at similar things and gush about our music tastes and who we have seen perform live. I observe his very animated face, a neat goatee beard, his deep wrinkles deepening on his cheek when he smiles, his ice blue eyes sparkling when he expresses something that pleases him, and his nose often twitches too. I find his expressions fascinating.

It wasn't long before he asked me, "What are you looking for in a man, Jay?" I hate that question; for the last few years, it hasn't got any easier for me, perhaps because I want to present myself as someone desirable; that's the pleaser in me again. Whilst I was hesitating, he frankly said, "I'll just come out with it; no point in beating about the bush. Sex is very important to me; I have a high sex drive."

His eyes twinkled as he gave me a quizzical look. "How do you feel about that?"

It didn't take me long to answer. "Yes, it is important to me too, with the right person," I stuttered. "I have had an uncomfortable experience with a previous relationship, which I would not want to go through again, so forgive me for hesitating." He held my hand; I could see he wanted to know more.

I continued, "I need to know if a man's intentions are honourable."

He chuckled and sat back on the sofa.

"You sound like someone from our parents' generation, Jay... honourable?" He patted both of his knees as he laughed. "Of course, I would want to respect you. I'm not one of those men who eats, shoots and leaves. His eyes twinkle as he grins. "I want a long-term relationship with mutual respect."He then leant forward to hold my hand in his. I asked myself if this was going too fast. However, what he said was music to my ears; he was certainly growing on me. Maybe my gut was getting scared of the speed at which this date was progressing. There was a hint of his self-centredness when he talked of his breakup with his partner; it was all her fault and not his.

We ordered more coffee; we didn't want the afternoon to end. But eventually, it did, and we walked back to the car park, hand in hand, more naturally now, laughing at nothing, it seemed. Once we were next to his car, I took the opportunity to admire it. I could see him enjoying the adoration, so I continued to inspect, walking all around his highly beloved, polished machine. He gave me a deep kiss, which at first took me by surprise. At least it was enjoyable and not a suction pump this time.

"Well, Jay, have I treated you honourably enough to see me again?" Holding both my shoulders, he gazed at me with blue sparkling eyes; the deep creases in his cheeks seemed deeper with his smile.

I laughed straight away, trying to look away, but he grabbed my chin.

"Is that a yes? If it is, I will cancel my next date, which is tomorrow."

I was taken aback. Next date? Was he trying to make out that he had women queueing up for him? I nodded and gave him a wink.

"Now, who's teasing? I like that." His face became animated again. "Sunday okay with you? Let's meet for breakfast somewhere nice; I'll let you know where." I loved his assertiveness.

"Yes, that would be lovely. Let's see how we go. I'll wait to hear from you." I do not want to sound overly eager.

"Great, I will be in touch soon."

He jumped in his shiny car and drove off at speed, beeping his horn as he left.

I walked home slowly, reviewing everything that had been said between us. Was Peter too full-on for me? Could I see a long-term relationship with him? His last lady gave him a hard time and returned to her husband. Before considering being intimate with this man, I decided I needed to know more about his past.

He made contact that evening, saying he hadn't forgotten his promise of breakfast; he still needed to organise it, but wanted to say how much he had enjoyed the afternoon with me. I was a lovely lady who looked better than in my photos, and he liked how I dressed, too. On reflection, I should have guessed we were both more influenced by our appearances rather than our personalities and interests. This relationship was only going to go one way to start with.

He called me on Friday saying, "I've decided to make you breakfast at mine. Is that okay with you? I will understand if not, but it will allow you to see where I live and whether I'm honourable or not." He giggled down the phone.

I replied, with a smile on my face, "Okay, cheeky. I'll put on my chastity belt."

I felt comfortable enough to say yes. After all, I am getting more confident at saying no. Some women may consider my impulsiveness and taking chances because I am desperate. And whilst there might be a little truth in that, I also need to learn to trust.

Sunday came, and I arrived at 10 am at his four-bed detached, 1980s brick house with mock Tudor eaves and a block-paved drive. Welcoming me with one of his animated grins, wearing Ugg slippers, he took my coat and directed me into his kitchen. I remarked on the house being quite large for a single person. He told me he had rented the house with his ex-partner. She had returned to her husband, leaving him to pay the rental for the remaining contract period. He couldn't wait to move out to his father's old house in Wakefield and rented out to his brother. I could tell he was very bitter over the circumstances this woman had left him in.

"Ah, I see; you won't be living here for much longer then," I suggested, disappointed that the convenient three miles would be no more.

He had laid out the breakfast bar with croissants, muesli, and a fresh fruit cocktail, plus a beautiful rustic loaf that, I could smell, was still warm, with jams, marmalade, and butter to accompany it. Plates with napkins neatly folded were on the kitchen table. He offered me fresh coffee and asked if I wanted a warm croissant. So far, I was impressed with his hosting skills.

We sat down and ate breakfast, interjecting with questions of one another's past. Peter spoke mainly of the process of changing his home and how he would buy his brother out of half of the house; he was annoyed that Jan had left him in the lurch to pick up the outstanding bills. He also talked about his successful role as Sales Director, although he didn't people manage others. I started to feel that this man had quite an ego and it could be easily dented.

We started talking about passions, likes, and dislikes. He said he had a passion for shoes, particularly Italian shoes. I had never heard of these brands of shoes.

"Would you like to see my collection?"

I politely agreed, although this was the first, new slant: "Come to my place to see my etchings."

We climb the stairs, and he explains that if this were his house, he would get rid of the 1980s and 90s décor, lots of swagged curtain pelmets, and fancy border wallpaper, which is so outdated. His bedroom, however, is painted cream with silk finish curtains and bedding, red dried poppies in the window, and small red cushions nicely placed on the large pillows. He says he couldn't stand to sleep in the dark blue floral room as it was before, so he agreed with the landlord to paint it.

He beckoned me to sit on the bed. At the same time, he opened one door of his fitted wardrobe to reveal shoe box after shoe box, probably 15 high in two towers from floor to almost the top of the wardrobe. One by one, he opens them, explaining what range they came from and their individual designer names. Most are pointed or square-toed, which makes them look enormous; they come in various colours, and some are three-toned. He also explains how much they are valued at and how he manages to get some in the January sales or Black Friday deals, looking out for specific ones to add to his collection. He tells me they often retail from £300 to as much as £500. I have seen enough by the time we get to the tenth shoe box. He stops, registering that I am glazing over. To be fair to him, some are very artistic and well-made, but how many shoes does a man need? Obviously, a lot. It's an obsession in his case. We eventually moved downstairs. I'm not ready for intimacy yet, and I am pleased he doesn't pressurise me.

He told me that he had to go to his late father's house to meet with his brother Jim, confiding that he was not looking forward to having a difficult conversation about buying him out of his inheritance. Peter was the older sibling by 12 years, losing his mum while his brother was five, and had felt responsible for him for most of his life. The property had been Peter's responsibility after their Dad died when his brother was in his teens. He had given the property a modern makeover after his brother left to live with a girlfriend, then rented it out for a while. When Jim's relationship broke, he returned and paid a low rent to cover costs. Now Peter felt he had done enough to support his brother, who was 50 years old, and it was time for him to take over the property.

Peter had only one son and a granddaughter with learning difficulties. He told me she was the apple of his eye, sweet but demanding, and he didn't mind; he loved spoiling her.

We arranged to meet the following Friday for a walk; he had the day off. He told me he had taken very little holiday that year. We met at his house again; I didn't mind as I wanted to know him better before I invited him home. The walk was cut short because the brand-new boots I was wearing were killing me. Stupid on my part! We went back to his for coffee and chatted.

When I returned from the toilet, he stood by the kitchen door. Grabbing my hand, he took me into the sitting room.

"Do you think I'm honourable now?" he said, directing me to the sofa. He bent over me and kissed me. I responded willingly.

"I'm a patient man; my last girlfriend insisted we both had tests for STIs before we made love. If you want us to get intimate, let me know, and I will happily get tested first."

STI's? It took me a few minutes to work out what he was saying, thinking this was something that easily tripped off his tongue. How many sexual partners had he been with in recent years? Well, I had never considered being tested and didn't even know that was the name of the clinic, but it seemed to make sense at the time, and I told him I would think about it. He brought in two cups of tea, and we chatted briefly, discussing his interview for a new job.

"Shall we go somewhere more comfortable? I know the very spot, no pressure." He waited for a response from me. I knew what he meant and what he wanted. After the last conversation, the decision of sex or 'STI test 'came around very quickly, in fact, all of 15 minutes.

I let him lead me upstairs. It is midday and his bedroom curtains are very lightweight. Even when closed, the sun shines through. He undresses himself first while I sit on the edge of the bed and watch him fold his clothes, putting them on a chair. He puts his Ugg slippers together tidily under the chair.

Then, there stands this naked man whose first words are, "Well, what do you think?" his hands on his hips as he swings his (larger than I had experienced) penis before me. Worryingly, it appears semi-flaccid, more like an elephant's trunk than a hard, erect penis. His skin is as white as snow, as is his pubic hair. I doubt either has seen the sun in years.

I sit, embarrassed at first, then he comes over to me and starts undoing the buttons on my blouse while kissing my neck. His hot breath is pleasant, but all I can think of is his penis, close to touching my knees. I then notice his extremely hairy back, the hairiest I have ever seen, but, as with the rest of him, white and soft. I still feel embarrassed at this naked hairy man with his swinging dick before me, wondering what sexual experience is in store for me. Will it fit me when erect?

He finishes undressing me and then pulls down the duvet, slipping into the bathroom to collect a large towel, placing it on the bed and smoothing it out. He informed me he had just changed the bedding that morning and didn't want it soiling.

Oh my god, **soiling**! Suddenly, I feel dirty, and the passion is lost for me in that moment, standing there in my altogether, starting to regret being there. He takes me by the hand and lies me on the beach towel, with a print of Betty Boo on it! It seems he didn't want his best towels soiling either.

I cannot imagine this man having much empathy for me when my weak bladder leaks on many occasions as I am putting my key in the front door on arriving home. What is that about? I am convinced there is such a thing as doorstep incontinence. Once the door is unlocked, I find myself flying to the bathroom, desperately trying to pull my trousers and knickers down in time before the floodgates open. No, I cannot see him understanding my lack of bladder control. What if I were to wee on his Betty Boo towel? I'm starting to panic now. Anyway, I digress.

Finally, he gets down to business, starting to give me pleasure between my thighs, then kissing me down the inside of my legs to my toes. He then explains, "I love sucking toes. Do you mind?"

I say, partly bemused, "I don't know, I haven't had it done to me before. I cannot guarantee they are not smelly," laughing at the thought of it while I watch him take a condom from his bedside drawer and puts it at the side of me.

"No worries, I like them that way."

His grin was wider, and the creases in his cheeks deeper. I close my eyes, anticipating the squirming at the tickle of his tongue.

This afternoon is getting weirder by the minute. Peter grabs one foot and starts sucking my toes, one by one. I do my best not to be ticklish, biting my tongue every time he sucks each toe. Once he has had his fill of my toes, he starts tearing the condom cover. Phew, at least the toe test bit is out of the way, not to mention the all-important STI test, as he takes precautions. When he penetrates my vagina with his large penis, it is uncomfortable at first, he takes it slowly, and eventually, I cum quickly, and so does he. Shouting, "Oh God, that was good".

Holding me in his arms and stroking my body, he asks, "Are you okay". Surprisingly, I am. It wasn't unpleasant, and I felt quite relaxed; however, stroking his hairy back was like being alongside a rather large teddy bear.

"Do you like Rod Stuart, would like to go to a concert in Hull, including a night in a hotel?" I didn't take long to answer, and I said yes.

TOO GOOD TO BE TRUE

I feel a beautiful warmth
Has entered my being
Penetrating the core of me
And fibres of my heart
From a stranger,
his love-praises streaming.

Is there really a new world
Of love and sharing?
As the third quartile of my life
Fades to distant memories,
My optimistic mind needs
to believe you are caring.

Could this beautiful warmth
Be treasured by us two,
A romance where hearts
And minds are insured
Protecting us from life's
Hard expectations and view?

This shivering willow,
Naked in all her glory,
Stands before you
Patiently awaiting her time,
Hopefully, in your strong arms,
Are you too good to be true?

For several months, we went out together, dining out and visiting nice places like York, Harrogate, the South Coast, and London.

Shopping—oh boy, did he like shopping—clothes and new things for his house. We attended a couple of gigs: an Eagles Tribute band and a soul band.

One afternoon, he had an appointment with the optician in York, and he telephoned me to see if I could join him for a quick lunch. I was free so I agreed to meet him at the market. Bumping into Kitty and Maria at the market, I told them I was waiting for Peter.

"Things are getting serious then. How long is it now?" said Maria, hugging me simultaneously. She looked gorgeous with her long, dark, wavy hair and huge brown eyes. She was wearing a fur-collared coat, which, while not expensive, looked so. She often bragged about her TK Maxx and charity shop bargains.

"Kitty, so glad you are here." Knowing Peter wouldn't be long and we were already under the clock where I planned to meet him, I was hoping I might have a chance for my sister to meet him. On cue, he arrived, a full grin across his face. He grabbed my shoulders and kissed me on the lips before the girls.

Maria, who is not shy, took the opportunity to introduce herself before I had a chance. "So, this is the mysterious Peter our Jay has been hiding from us. I'm Maria." Peter put out his hand to shake hers.

"Yes, Jay has mentioned you and your wild parties." He laughed out loud and looked straight at Kitty. "Kitty, I presume. I can see the family likeness; you both share the same beautiful genes." He stepped forward to hug her. I could see her expression as she looked over his shoulder at me; one of those, 'Is this guy for real?' moments.

I had little chance to speak when he immediately asked the girls what they were doing for lunch. "Come and join Jay and me for a quick bite somewhere. Have you a favourite place nearby?"

I agreed with him and nodded my approval. The girls looked at each other and nodded at the same time.

We sat outside at a table for four in the sun. The town was bustling with shoppers, giving it a Mediterranean feel. Peter dominated the conversation with the girls, and I spent most of it listening. Then his phone rang.

"Sorry, do you mind if I take this? It's a customer of mine. He's a pain in the arse if I don't answer. I get loads of voice messages from him."

The girls nod. He puts his mobile phone on the speakerphone and talks as loudly as the voice emits from the phone. To say there was an element of showing off would be an understatement. Eventually, he stood up and walked down the pavement to continue the call, pacing up and down. The girls continued to eat their salads in silence. When he returned, he commented on how quickly they had finished their food. He was a slow eater, he said; eating fast upset his stomach.

Kitty leaned over to me and made excuses; they must go. Can I pay their part of the bill? She and Maria left £20 each on the table, which more than covered it. I said I would make sure I paid them the change later.

Peter was surprised they were leaving, but he stood up and said he hoped they would meet again and that it was nice to put faces to their names. At the same time, he was taking the notes from the table and putting them in his wallet. Unsurprisingly, the girls looked puzzled. I was even more surprised that he didn't tell them to keep their money so that he could settle the bill. After all, he did invite them.

"Look Peter, I'll pay for the girls and myself and make sure I give them the change later." I could see the arrogance in his face.

"Don't be silly; if they had stayed longer, they could have settled their own bill. More fool them for leaving." His attitude was not good, and I was starting to see another side to him I didn't like. I didn't want to make a scene at the café, so I dropped the subject.

There were also times when I didn't feel totally convinced of his fidelity. When he shut himself my bathroom, whispering to someone on the phone, it sounded like he was talking to a woman, arranging when they were meeting next. I was desperately trying not to be paranoid, but it did make me wonder if he had another woman. On reflection, there were other signs of him seeing someone else. He sometimes walked outside to take phone calls, whispering in a low voice. But I put those doubts aside when, on one occasion, in an Italian restaurant, he told me he loved me and couldn't see himself being with anyone else. Of course, I believed him and felt elated that night.

He eventually convinced his brother to take the money for half of the bungalow's value. He took me to visit it before moving in. Then, his brother's solicitors said he could not move in until Peter had paid all the money. His financial arrangements and loans were taking time to process. In the meantime, he had to find temporary accommodation because his lease on his present rented house had ended. He found another house to rent not far from the bungalow but was highly stressed about it all. I tried consoling him, but he seemed obsessed about things out of his control.

In the hope that I could distract him from his worries, I organised a weekend away, staying with friends in the Yorkshire Dales. They had a lovely self-contained cottage that they let us use. We joined another couple one evening; I had known these friends for years. The weekend started well, and he seemed to get on well with everyone; he enjoyed the walk, too, albeit he had to walk in a pair of his Jeffry West shoes because he had forgotten his walking shoes. That evening after the meal, the six of us played a Pop Trivia game; Peter was knowledgeable about music and musicians, but his lack of tolerance and competitiveness spoilt it for the group. He also lost his temper when he got a question wrong, yet mocked others for doing so too. I started to see yet another side of him when wine and competition met. He became an embarrassment, and our hosts decided to bring the game to an end. I made excuses we were tired and made a hasty retreat to our room.

We drove home in silence the following morning, but I could tell he wasn't happy.

Sex was good in the morning, I thought; however, he seemed more withdrawn than usual. We arrived back at his house, where my car was parked. He sat at the steering wheel, staring into space, without a word. I asked him what was troubling him. He opened the door and took my case from the boot, leaving it at the side of my car. No words were exchanged, and he walked into his house and shut the door. I was left standing on his drive, confused and upset, not knowing if I had done something wrong.

The following day, he called me: "Jay, sorry about yesterday, but I was not in a good place and didn't know how to tell you that I don't think this is working for me."

He coughed. I remained silent.

"Are you still there?" he asked.

"Yes, but I don't know what to say." I was struggling to hold back the tears. "I thought we were doing well, but I suppose you have to do what is right for you." I was puzzled. What on earth had gone wrong? I silently broke down.

"I'm moving out tomorrow. Can you put the slippers and shirt I left at your house on my porch? You will find your kettle there." He spoke with no emotion, like a stranger. I cried and tried to analyse what had happened for the rest of the day. Why was I upset, he had been an arsehole this weekend in front of my friends? I was confused about my feelings for him. Was it hurt over being rejected?

No reasons were given, and for days, I kept asking myself what I had done. Did he not like my friends, had I said something wrong? Was it the pressure of purchasing his brother's half of his father's home? Work worries? I realised it could have been because I didn't offer for him to move in with me temporarily, or a combination of all those things. I was another responsibility. No, I had been deluding myself all along, yet still in denial, this man was never going to be suitable for me, and I was using my fear of being alone and filling that void that, I couldn't accept it was inevitable, if he hadn't finished our relationship, I should have,

But I decided to have the last word; I would write to him about my feelings, how hurt I was, and how unfair of him to leave me for no reason. It was a long email covering all the nice things we did together, that latterly we had told each other our loving feelings, meeting my family and friends, meeting his too. His cold treatment of me had really hurt my feelings. I couldn't go on wondering what went wrong and eventually concluded I had to let him go.

He responded:

```
Hi LOL!

Want you to know in the words of a famous band:

"I'm already gone."

Thanks for the war and peace covering our last 8 months.
I don't know why you feel it necessary to write chapter
and verse and include every sliver of conversation and
exchange of various experiences we have had in our
lives, but I guess that is just your way.

I could respond, but just don't see the point. It's
a pity I'm not perfect, but neither are you. Let's
just forget each other and move on.

Peter
```

I was devastated by his cold response. And in a moment of rage, I wrote to him saying.

```
Hi,

What an immature response Peter.

You are a cold, cowardly, narcissistic, TWAT! who used me. I hope I never see you again. Plus, my son-in-law says he hopes you never cross his path.

Jay
```

I asked the girls to come round to mine for coffee, wanting to give them the change I owed them from the lunch in York. I had already poured myself a pink prosecco. They could tell from the moment I opened the door how upset I was. Kitty embraced me and said, "He was a twat anyway, Jay; you could do so much better. Maria and I didn't like him; he was arrogant and disrespectful, and we didn't like his shoes."

Laughing I add. "And he looked a prat with his shirt tucked into his underpants. His dressing routines were without doubt weird, he would walk around dressed with his shirt sticking out of the bottom of his 'Y' fronts, have breakfast and at the last minute put on his trousers before leaving the house as he didn't want to mess or crease his clothes. OCD was his middle name." The Girl Tribe were in hysterics.

"Weird but practical" screamed Ann through the noise.

I should have spoken to them earlier, but I suppose I was ashamed of my weakness, letting such a man get to me. I suppose another car crash was avoided.

"NEXT!!!" shouted Maria, already topping up my glass of prosecco and the others.

GOODBYE NARC

I didn't see your intentions
Nor how obvious, I sigh
The coercion so clear now

As crystal as the blue sky.

How did I not see real you?
A victim of others you played
With such theatrical precision

A drama fit for a BAFTA hey?

I was that empath sponge
You took into your bed,
Cancelling my choices,

Often messing with my head,

Gaslighted, muting my voice,
My spirit and self-esteem,
To feed your hungry ego

And your pleasure it seems.

You devoured all the good
Under your micro control,
Degraded all the love

To win was always a goal.

A victim you played me
With the evilest pretensions,
I'll no longer be manipulated.

Now I see your intentions.

So, take your narcissistic head,
I'll no longer be your toy
For I recognise your game

And its toxicity you employ.

I'll be so happy without you
Without criticism and control,
Travelling my own path
For I'm now strong and whole.

Now fuck off you narc!!

Lessons and emotions

I did it again! I was deeply hurt, letting myself believe I had something special when all I had was a sexual relationship with occasional outings. Peter, the "narcissistic twat," had given me an insight into my own perceived failings, blindly thinking everything was going smoothly when clearly it wasn't. I felt naïve and heard my father's words in my head, succumbing to "stupid and thick, you will never come to anything". Lack of worthiness and imposter syndrome haunting me as usual.

Peter was a narcissist though. For example, he had more toiletries and cosmetics than I had in his bathroom. It took longer for him to get ready in the morning than me. He was fastidious about his appearance, especially his shoes, in every outfit. He constantly asked me if he looked alright when he appeared from the bathroom. Never complimented me and controlled everything we did together. He also had a tendency to belittle me in front of his friends. When I told him that he was disrespectful, he would gaslight me and say I was over-sensitive or it was my fault for letting him down with my attitude. I never seemed to win arguments and came away feeling stupid.

I was devastated all the same, realising the pleaser in me had given too much; I over-romanticised, like giving birthday presents to your best friend that you know you would love to receive yourself, yet the friend forgets when it's your birthday. You are hurt, but you say nothing. They wonder why you don't respond enthusiastically, keep making excuses, and don't accept their invitation to a night out to celebrate their birthday. I've always forgiven, but sometimes I quietly protest and still feel bad about it. And still say nothing.

In Peter's case, I had given too much: poetry, songs that reminded me of us two, presents, wearing stockings and suspenders and a lovely dress when we met, making candle-lit dinners with his favourite expensive wine, washing his clothes when he was busy. He used to turn up with flowers and wine in the early days, but that stopped, and stupid me carried on. I suggested we go away to Spain, as I had friends there who were asking me to come over with my new man, but I should have heeded the signs then; he never responded with enthusiasm. He said, "You know I'm busy with this new job." In fact, we never talked about the future either. These should have been red flags.

But no, I kept blindly on being the pleaser, sending good morning messages, `"I hope you have a lovely day, thinking of you,"` good night messages, `"Sleep well Darling, I hope things went well for you today and work is getting easier, miss you."` Lots of emojis; he introduced me to emojis, and at the beginning, I was showered with heart and kissing emojis. But then, when our relationship was waning, he finished his messages mostly with xx.

I was a fool. I started to understand what the phrase 'lovesick' means, that fear pit in your stomach that stops you from eating. I knew something wasn't right, why I didn't acknowledge it? I was basically smothering him, or was I? So many questions. He didn't feel the same about me. Maybe I took the chase away from him. My head was spinning with doubts and questions.

Reading online dating advice mentions that men should have some space to chase, to keep them excited; otherwise, they give up. He was still a TWAT, though; it was all about him and how badly he was done to by his ex, his brother, his job, and his hair falling out.

He once told me to shave myself below, bearing in mind I hardly have anything there to begin with. My teasing response was to ask him to wax his back first. It didn't go down well and he didn't speak to me for the rest of the day. Then he said I was insensitive. I wish I could say I learned my lesson from this experience. Hoping I don't go there again and recognise a narcissist.

I OWE YOU

I owe you my thoughts today,
If only in a positive way
Words and actions intended
Once mattered, now resented,
For you left that stamp in my head
A reminder of things you said.

I owe you my life today,
Negative opinions portrayed
A constant critic never deflected,
Confidence scarred and rejected,
For you put that stamp on my life
And for this I now value the strife.

I owe you my courage today,
Jealousy and hate displayed
Has driven me to greater things,
The strength of new beginnings.
You will no longer stamp on me
For its never too late to be free.

CHAPTER 9
ARMANI MAN

After a few weeks of getting over the toe fetish lover experience, I decided, once again, to trawl the dating site, reading profile after profile, mainly swiping left (not interested). Maybe it's me, but there is a sort of window shopping experience manifesting itself on these sites. Resembling purchasing a new dress online, there are those you would love to wear but know they wouldn't suit you, and there are those that do nothing for your figure and are less alluring to the opposite sex, but you love the colour. Constantly looking for the right match but not satisfied with the fit.

Standing out, there was "Armani MAN", clearly very well-dressed and, on the surface, a man who didn't have worries about money. He was my age and, from reading his profile, he was used to younger women, stating his ex-wife was 20 years younger than him. I wondered if she was more of a trophy wife, why would he think otherwise? It was stupid of him to say that on a dating site; it obviously didn't work out, so why should it again? Another narcissist I thought. However, after Peter, I felt this would be a challenge, and I couldn't resist making the point to him and telling him that many 60-something women are very fit, sensual, and attractive. They have the added benefit of not being menopausal and are often self-sufficient. If he were heading for retirement, someone free of child responsibilities and employment would suit him better.

He thanked me for my message, which he said made a lot of sense, and he had felt very bruised after his ex and left him for her personal trainer. She was his third wife. He could not understand why she would leave him when he gave her everything she wanted. He had four children from his previous marriage, and suddenly, she announced she wanted children at 46. He didn't want that. My thoughts were she probably took as much out of him as she could to start a family with a younger Mr Fit.

We started corresponding. Because he often confided in me, I felt like an agony aunt. I used to call him Mr Armani. He kept reminding me he was Andrew and then admitted he regretted his profile name; he was getting a lot of stick from women. He lived in Leeds and owned a commercial property agency, hoping his daughter would take it over soon. All the time, I felt how familiar this was to me. Still, I felt that he was a challenge. I would tease him daily with things I thought would appeal to his vanity. One day, he said I was making fun of him, and he wasn't sure he liked being ridiculed. I told him to toughen up, women like banter, and not to take himself so seriously. I left him for a few days to sulk. I learned from Peter not to pander to sulks; they come around eventually, and I give them space. I told myself that he would return if I meant anything to him. Then I received a message on Monday morning.

`"Have we fallen out?"` Smiley emoji.

I left it for a few hours because I was busy. However, I don't like playing games or disrespecting people, so I responded as soon as I could.

`"No, not fallen out, just busy, how are you? "`

He responded immediately.

"I guess an attractive lady like you has many dates to attend. Are you busy this week? Fancy a coffee sometime?"

Yes!! Now he was interested. I laughed to myself and punched the air. I never saw him as a possible relationship candidate. And yes, I was playing games. Was it a sort of revenge on Peter? Maybe deep down, I am happy to turn this arrogant man into a conquest. Perhaps I was trying to improve my self-esteem after Peter, proving that I could still attract so-called high-value men.

"Do you know Rodley Park Hotel?!"

"Yes, I know it."

"When are you free? We could do dinner or, if you prefer, just coffee and see how we go."

"I am free Wednesday, shall we say 11am?"

He replied a couple of hours later.

"That's great, see you there. I'm driving a large silver Mercedes, AMG." Smiley emoji.

Why was I not surprised that he would want to brag about his car? He has three: a 4x4 and a sports car, too.

On Wednesday, I dressed casually, wearing a nice loose blouse, slim-fitting black jeans, and knee-length boots. I knew Rodley Park Hotel was posh; I had been there a few times for work conferences during my Internet career days, so I was not overwhelmed by the place. I wasn't surprised he chose it, trying to impress and be cool, Mr. Armani.

I arrived in the car park on the dot of 11, and as I was looking for a parking space, a silver Merc pulled into the only vacant bay close to the front. I had to drive down to the next level, which meant walking to the hotel.

He spotted me walking up and, as I expected, he was dressed from head to toe in black Armani, with Armani sunglasses, but what I thought were dark trousers from a distance turned out to be tight leather trousers. He had slightly bandy legs and a little stoop; honestly, I wasn't that keen on the look on a mature man. He at least apologised for taking the last bay, and if he had known it was me, he would have gladly given it up. He did score a point for that gesture.

We walked into the foyer, and he was immediately greeted as Andrew. We followed the Maître d', who took us to a pair of Chesterfields opposite each other. This was beginning to feel like déjà vu. He asked if I wanted coffee to start with. I agreed.

For the next hour, he talked mainly about his ex-wives, his business, and some of his recent dates from Match.com. He seemed little interested in my pastime or interests; I listened.

"What are you looking for in a relationship, Jay?"

Oh no, not that question again. I started to think about Peter and his comments about sex. I didn't want to go down that line of conversation with this man, whom I couldn't see myself kissing.

"I'm not sure; I have no preconceived ideas; I just know when it happens. I'm quite self-sufficient, really. I had a few flings and disappointments, but it's all a learning curve; I was married to the same man for 42 years and met him when I was 16. He died unexpectedly on our way home from France four years ago."

He started to nod and seemed interested in what I had to say, but he lacked empathy and those all-important questions, making me feel he was genuinely interested in me. When an hour passed, and I felt more like a counsellor again than a date, I didn't want to spend any more of my emotional energy on Mr Armani. He looked ridiculous in his leather trousers, lacquered hair, plucked eyebrows and massive gold chain. He was definitely not my type, and I felt empowered to stand up, thank him for the coffee, and wish him all the best in his search for a partner. He stayed seated and looked puzzled.

"Aren't you staying for lunch? I'm having some," pointing to a nearby dining table, laid with napkins and wine glasses, with an expectant waiter standing next to it. "On me, of course."

I smiled sweetly and said, "Thank you, Andrew. It's been a pleasure meeting you, but I must go now."

He stood up and shook my hand. "I will be in touch," he said, still shaking my hand. "I will send you a link to that film; let me know what you thought of it," he said as I turned away, then looked back in acknowledgement. I waved and walked past the grinning waiter. I bet he knew I was on a date, and I wasn't the first to come here to meet Mr Armani. I probably broke the format, walking out before lunch. It was amusing that he stood there expecting us to sit at the table together. All the same, I felt a little guilty too.

I walked out of the hotel feeling a sense of control that I didn't need his *kind* in my life, but I felt confident again that a man desired my company, albeit as a counsellor. Perhaps a bit childish of me, but I laughed to myself all the way home. It was a gorgeous late spring day, so I travelled to the Dales for lunch at a lovely old café in Malham.

Unexpectedly, I met some of Tony's old walking palls fresh from a walk they had finished on the moors; they gave me a lovely welcome and hugs all around and wanted to know what I had been up to these last few months. Was I coping okay, and when would I join them at one of the regular curry nights? They all listened intently and asked how my family were. I promised I would join them next time. What a contrast between meeting them and the man I had recently spent an hour with. It reassured me that existing friendships are more important than fleeting coffee dates for my well-being and self-esteem and spending meaningful time and energy with people who love and value you. I spent the afternoon around the village and drove home feeling content, enjoying the long shadows as the sun disappeared in the sky. The drystone walls snaked over the lush green landscape, young lambs skipping towards their bleating mothers; everything looked perfect. Spring is here.

CHAPTER 10
TOOTHPASTE AND MORE DATES

After Mr Armani, I continued to speak to several men at a time on the dating sites. I had given up on exclusive conversations that often came to nothing, being ghosted because they, too, were talking to several women, hoping one would develop into a date, many resulting in one-off coffees. Some weeks, I would have two to three dates a week; on one day, I had two dates. I almost feel ashamed of my multi-male conversations, but as I said, these sites are like sweety shops, with lots of people looking for the same thing. Many decline a date for various reasons: too far away, money, family commitments, work or lack of transport. One man rejected me because he didn't like freckles when I told him. Well, I don't like shallow men with tattoos, I told him. Sometimes it's like being back at school. I so wished I hadn't stooped to their level, but it's hard not to bite back.

A retired accountant I had agreed to meet in a pub walked in armed with a briefcase; he hadn't looked in the mirror after brushing his teeth and had toothpaste running out of the corner of his mouth spilling onto his chin, like a baby having his first feed. I thought this was going to be interesting. He was smart, shirt and tie, very stocky, with a round face, the kind of man with short legs and broad shoulders who should be careful about the choice of jackets;

double-breasted looked like a box on him. He seemed nervous and admitted I was only his third date in nearly a year. I felt humbled that he was nervous and not practised at dating, and he was open enough to tell me. I tried to reassure him that it isn't easy meeting strangers.

We started off well, and he suggested we eat. He hadn't had breakfast and really recommended the fish and chips. After we ate, he put his briefcase on the table and produced an orange file. Was this developing into an interview or a sales pitch? I braced myself for the latter. He started telling me he had no children in this country but two in America whom he hadn't seen for ten years.

"I have no dependants, you see," he sniffed and pulled out his handkerchief. I watched, hoping he would remove the toothpaste, but alas, he missed it, and I didn't want to interrupt him in case his nervousness came back. As he opened his folder, he started to smile for the first time, and the damn toothpaste looked even worse. He looked ridiculous, poor man. I was transfixed but tried to concentrate on his words.

"I own my own house, I have a good pension, I also have a commercial property which I rent, that gives me good income, and I have a part share in a factory. I have three cars, a property in Portugal, which I visit at least three times a year, and two racehorses. In other words, I am very comfortable and looking for someone to share my fortunes with me."

He started laying out his portfolio and photos of all the items he had listed and discussed partnerships in various ventures. Short of producing his bank account, he shared everything. I thought this man could be very vulnerable to unscrupulous women, otherwise known as "gold diggers". I tried to be diplomatic and say that he didn't need to share so much on the first date and that he could attract the wrong person.

"Sorry, I know what you mean." He closed his files quickly. "It's only that you seem sincere, and I want you to know I would look after you, and we could do some great things together. There's no point in being on your own."

I smiled. And he continued.

"I know what you mean about gold diggers. My first experience on the dating site, I spoke to a beautiful Asian lady. She had problems with her computer and said she couldn't send me a photo because her camera wasn't working and she couldn't afford to replace it. I sent her the money to fix it, and she sent me a photo. I was surprised at how young she looked. After a few messages, she said she had always wanted to come to the UK but couldn't afford the ticket. Like a fool, I sent her the money for the ticket and enough to buy a new suitcase and a few clothes. It wasn't a fortune, but after a few weeks, her hardships became more intense: a baby brother who needed medical treatment, etc. After reading an article in the Guardian Newspaper about online dating scams, I realised she had a typical scammer profile."

He looked ashamed. "You must think I am stupid," he muttered, putting his portfolio away, "but I'm an honest man and obviously not streetwise when it comes to dating crooks."

He excused himself to go to the toilet. I felt sorry for him and wished I had told him about the toothpaste now. He returned, grinning, with no toothpaste and closed his briefcase. "I cannot believe I have sat opposite you all this time and you didn't mention the toothpaste on my face. I'm not doing very well, am I?"

I couldn't work out if he was cross or still embarrassed.

"Sorry, I didn't want to distract you when you seemed to have so much to tell me." Bearing in mind that I had little opportunity to talk about myself, I thought to myself. However, I was not going to say that. I had already decided he wasn't for me. He was very intense, particularly about his wealth, which I am sure he had worked hard to accumulate. Being an accountant, he probably did not have time to enjoy it. I didn't want to ask about what happened to his wife. He mentioned briefly that she had been paid off and he didn't have any other commitments.

I went Dutch with the bill, which I might add he didn't object to. As he held the door open for me when we were leaving the restaurant, he asked if we could meet again. Rather than hesitate, I said we had much to think about and probably best to sleep on it. He gave me a hug and off he went with his portfolio briefcase. I didn't even look to see what car he was driving. I felt confident that money was not my driver for finding a man that suited me. I truly hoped he would find someone kind and not a gold digger, but I cannot help feeling that would be his likely outcome. I dropped him a text the following day thanking him for seeing me, and I hope he finds his lovely girl to share his life with soon—my best wishes.

—

I had quite a few dates after this one, mostly one hour of listening, often feeling disappointed with the fiction of their profiles, the years subtracted, the inches added, or, in some cases, that they were still in their 'loveless marriage' and needed someone to have fun with, no strings attached. The latter usually received short shrift from me. I told them it was bad not to disclose their situation before meeting a woman. One guy said,"We all deserve happiness, and I have been a carer for my wife these last five years. I can't just abandon her." I must admit I felt sorry for him, but not enough to accept such an offer.

Some of my dates disclosed far too much on their first date, leaving me little time to discuss myself. In fact, 70% of men would offload all their history and problems, leaving me feeling like I had been through a washing machine of stories, with no matching socks, sometimes aghast at their self-centredness. Their lack of concern for their family and ex, who they believe shafted them somehow. They had very little interest in me. I concluded that many had decided we would not meet again so they used the time to talk to someone about their life. You could say, why didn't you walk away? Well, I thought about it many times, but I felt everyone had taken the trouble to meet me, and it was only fair to give them an hour of my time. Maybe I have helped them in some small way.

I was once asked how long I had been dating, and I wasn't ashamed to say, "About two years, I think." I had already decided in my head that he wasn't for me and I think he suspected that.

He responded, "You are one of those serial daters then?"

I laughed, partly out of embarrassment. "I cannot say I had thought of being one; I did not find my match, I suppose. I have had short relationships, but they haven't blossomed for various reasons."

He stood up and walked out, leaving me with the coffee and cake bill. To say I was a bit pissed off would be an understatement as I had travelled an hour to meet him; he only travelled 20 minutes. I never heard from him again. I laugh at that date now.

NICE GUY

He was a nice guy
Said the right things
Bought me flowers
Chocolates and ring

Opened doors for me
Listened to me moan
Paid for my latte
Jam, butter and scone

He's been so attentive
Rings me every day
Friends say he's a nice guy
Yet I wish he'd go away

JACQUELINE T. **MAY**

For who dates a nice guy?
I couldn't tell him so
It's not that he didn't try
But nice guy has to go

Oh, to love a nice guy
Pampered I would be
Ah, it's always the bad guy
Who gives you an STD*

*Sexual transmitted disease

CHAPTER 11
THE MUSIC MAN

The week after meeting the 'toothpaste accountant,' I met a musician from nearby Selby at a quiz night run by a singles social group in Harrogate. I needed a change from online dating sites; I needed to get back to everyday situations and meet someone face-to-face with no preconceived ideas and lies. His name was Jim. He told me he was a singer-songwriter, a little younger than me. He was handsome in a rugged way. I liked his confidence when he beckoned me to sit next to him at a table of six.

"Are you new to the group? I'm Jim, by the way." He held out his hand to indicate the chair next to him.

"Come and join this motley group. You can only improve on our performance; in the last few competitions, we have come near the bottom." He had a big grin and I had warmed to him straight away.

"Hi Jim, It's Jay, and yes, I am new to this group. Thanks for inviting me to join your team." I smiled back and sipped on my lager.

"I see you managed to fight your way to the bar. Not many survive the first test of getting noticed by the bar staff; you must be over 6ft to stand a chance. I'm 5'8", and if I don't get here early enough, I miss out on half the quiz." He chuckled and lifted his glass to chink against mine.

Jim was warm and friendly; it was a great start to my evening. I only managed to contribute two questions. One was, how many Pope Pius had there been? For some bizarre reason, I knew the answer. Unbeknown to me, it was a bonus question and came with a free bottle of wine. That was it; I had earned my place in the team. Jim was delighted. I asked for six glasses to share the wine and felt I was accepted as one of the crowd/best of pals, promising to return the following week.

I wasn't expecting anything to come of that evening with regards to romance, but it was a lovely experience, and I patted myself on the back for having the courage to go there alone and have an impact. However, the following day, I looked on the Meetup website, and three people on the quiz team had written to me saying what a pleasure it was to have me join them. And there was Jim, one of them. His words were, "Get to the bar early. Mine's a pint." It made me laugh out loud. I loved the banter and decided I would write to him directly.

I started to write and then suddenly stopped. He might be taken and have a partner or a wife. I didn't want to flirt too much, just in case. After an hour or two, I told myself, what harm would it be? I kept thinking I would love to meet him again, but I must be patient. I started introducing myself as if we were starting from scratch, describing my circumstances as a widow trying to expand her social life a bit more. I missed the company of men; meeting him and having some banter made me realise how much I did. I started writing.

"I had such fun the other night. Thank you for including me. This is a cheeky message to say if you would like to show me how to get attention at the bar, I would be happy to join you. I would understand perfectly if you are married or have a partner." But you don't get if you don't ask, I'm saying to myself.

I left the note for an hour and tweaked it a few times, telling myself that there was no reason to beat about the bush; I'm in my 60s, and there is no time like the present.

I went to bed without sending it, sleeping badly, and regretting not sending the note. I knew I couldn't send it in the middle of the night, as he would guess I'd been troubled by it. Also, I didn't want him to think I was an insomniac.

Come 10 a.m., I decided to send the note. My stomach turned over at the thought of some kind of humiliating rejection. Swiftly, the phone pinged; it was the Meetup App. Message from Jim on the header.

```
"You must be a glutton for punishment if you want to
see me again. And no, I'm not committed to anyone.
I'm in the middle of a difficult separation at the
moment, so you might want to think twice, but I'm
happy to show you how to get attention at the bar.
By the way, best chat up line ever lol xx."
```

"PS. Where would you like to meet? Beers are on me."

I was elated. Such a simple response yet so hopeful. I was going to meet this man one to one.

We met in Selby Market Square. His car was in for service, and he asked if I minded meeting him there. He would take me to his favourite pub. On that Wednesday, I already had a meeting in the morning, so had to suggest early evening. It was a very traditional old pub off the square. My dad would have loved it, a real ale type of place. I walked in a little apprehensively. I knew nothing about this man, even less than the dates I had been on previously. At least with them, you have spoken by email and probably had a phone conversation before the meeting.

The bar was immediately in front of me. As I scanned along it, I noticed the barman grinning and nodding towards the far corner of the room as if he was expecting me. Jim was there with a pint of beer on the table. As I approached, he stood up and offered me a chair opposite him; no handshake, no hug.

"Hi there, you found us okay. What would you like half of?" as he pulled the chair from the table for me.

The aroma of his aftershave was intoxicating. I hadn't appreciated how fit he looked on the quiz night. Then suddenly, I thought, he doesn't know my age, and I don't know his. This could be a tricky conversation. I commented on how my father would love the pub, and I would be happy with half a lager as I was driving. He joked with me that the car service was a ploy so he could drink. He then winked and gave one of his broad grins.

"What kind of music do you like?" He was straight in with questions to break the ice, it was a refreshing change,

"I like most music. If it's good, it's good."

Waiting for his reply, I remembered from his Meetup profile that he was a singer-songwriter.

"Hah, not a bad answer, but do you like country rock?"

He told me about his gigs and writing music, how his ex-partner used to duet with him; apparently, she had a lovely voice, but a bad attitude. They were successful in the pub entertainment sector, along with a few festivals each year. He regretted them moving together into his house, which he had spent years modernising.

"She came with a few bits of furniture and £20,000, which she spent on putting a new kitchen in because she didn't like the old one, which was perfectly fine, I might add," taking another sip of his beer.

"I've not had an easy life, Jay, and I've worked hard for what little I have. I was a single dad of twins, a boy and girl. Their mum left me when they were two years old to go to America because she'd always wanted to. She even cadged some money from my poor old dad so she could pay for a flight. He didn't know what it was for then; she said that we were broke and needed to pay some bills."

He continued, "I've raised my beautiful kids on my own." He sipped on his beer, and I saw a sadness in his eyes for the first time. "My career choices have had to adapt so I could care for them. I have been a teaching assistant in the early days and a specialist care services manager in later years. I owe nothing to anyone."

He sighed and took another drink. I noticed a small scar on his eyebrow, and his eyes were green.

He shook his head. "As I said Jay, I have never owed anyone, except apparently the woman who only lived with me for five minutes, only paid for a kitchen, made no contribution to the running of the home and has now sent me a solicitor's letter demanding 50% of the value of my home, my children's home."

I could tell he was fighting a very emotional battle. "I'm so sorry to hear all that Jim, you…"

He interrupts. "No, it's me that is sorry. I shouldn't be loading you with all this stuff. Anyway, I've always wanted to live in a croft in Scotland and write music, me and my dog."

What happened to the funny man I had started talking to initially? I was beginning to think this was a mistake, yet another man with ex-partner issues. I was increasingly finding that men of a certain age come with baggage, emotional, financial, physical, and sexual. He was no different. We exchanged some historical facts, travel stories, and the all-important ages. He was 65, and I was 67. Phew! Despite my reservations, I was attracted to him and loved the idea of him being a music man. This appealed to my love of music and I couldn't wait to be invited to one of his gigs.

I met Jim five times over the coming weeks. I cooked two meals for him. I arranged a couple of walks and took him to a gig to see my daughter, a lead vocalist in her Funk Rock band, which he loved. He, in turn, invited me to do one of his gigs the following month. We never kissed, although he did put his hand around my waist at the gig. I felt warmth in his touch, or was I being optimistic? I wanted things to go further, a kiss at least. Later, we sat outside my house in the car and I asked him if he would like to come inside for a coffee. He declined and told me he was still too emotional about his ex to subject me to his problems or any commitments. I said it was okay, but, in my head, I was disappointed because I really liked him and was happy to continue our chats without any physical expectations. The kiss could wait, I told myself. He opened his door and looked back at me, putting his soft hand on mine without a word. I then watched him walk back to his car, his head hung low. He seemed to hesitate, and I was praying he would change his mind, but instead, he opened the door and left.

Two days later, I texted him to say I understood his dilemma, but he hadn't shown me any intentions or indicated to me that I was potentially a future girlfriend or special friend. If I didn't hear from him, I would put myself back on the dating sites. It wasn't meant to be a threat; it was my frustration, and I wanted him to know I wasn't going to hang around waiting for him to decide if I was worth a chance.

Jim came back to me. He agreed it was better I went back on the dating sites as he was in no position to have a hold on me. He said I was a lovely lady, with a happy disposition and generous nature. He even said that he could have fancied me if circumstances had been different. However, he had already suffered a broken heart, and he couldn't risk another. He wished me success in finding someone. He said it wouldn't be long as he considered me an attractive lady, a real catch. I was furious with myself for being impatient. This truly was an honourable man albeit one with lots of emotional conflicts.

I had a few G'n'Ts with my Girl Tribe and, as I do with all gin cocktails, I started to be morose, crying on their shoulders.

"Come on Jay, Jim wasn't meant to be. Can you not see he was still wallowing in self-pity? You would have had the heartache of always consoling him and comparing yourself with his ex; you deserve better than that. He sounds weak and embittered anyway."

Kitty, my sister hugged me as I sobbed, "I can never get it right; why is life so complicated?"

"There are worse men out there, I must admit," said Penny darkly.

As I poured a glass of water, I noticed the chip in it. My luck. Even the glasses have it against me. It had taken me three years to pluck up the courage to seek another mate. Now after more than two years, I was wondering why. Was it worth it?

"You've no physical bruises, only emotional ones; you will get over him." Ann was still getting over the loss of her beloved second husband. However, she showed great interest in my attempts at dating but had no interest in herself. Well, not for a while anyway. "Anyway, he's a big baby. You need a proper man, who wants to get into your knickers," she giggled into her gin glass.

The sad thing is, I knew he was a thoughtful, sensitive man, and I put him in the same category as the rest, the getting into my knickers brigade, whose priority and agenda was firstly for sex, a relationship second. Not his, he clearly loved deeply and couldn't risk being hurt again.

I got very drunk that night and must have used every expletive I knew several times. The F word, the C word, the W word and even the B word. Penny suddenly stood up and shouted at the top of her voice in our corner of the wine bar, "Fucking **NEXT**!!!!"

We all fell about laughing. Just what I needed.

THE ROMANCE FARE

No-one tells of the negativity of devotion,
For some people a thin veneer of emotion
Covers a deep-rooted mistrust of romance.
For their experience ended in grievance

The weight loss and sleepless nights,
A grip on your stomach, incredibly tight.
Irrational behaviour of the obsessed,
Feelings of insecurity you cannot address.

We give this malady credence in names,
Referring to it as love sickness and games.
Absence makes the heart grow fonder,
Making the agony worse, no wonder.

What about the lust and love expectations,
Worries over rejection and humiliation?
Who should next communicate or call?
Do you chase or hang around at all?

It is no wonder once Cupid's arrow
Has pierced the heart some follow
A melancholy journey of painful sorrow,
Only to repeat again and tomorrow.

To all you lovesick souls out there,
You pay the price of the romance fare,
Taking the emotional rollercoaster ride,
Hoping love appears the other side.

Chapter 12
Dancing Stew and Heather Paul

Stew from Malton, 65, had retired at the start of the year and decided he was bored and needed a part-time job. He began as a maintenance man at a local hotel and progressed to working in reception. He sounded very content and happy with the outcome of his first year in retirement.

6'1" tall, with thinning blond hair and an uninhibited smile with uneven teeth, we met at an out-of-town shopping centre near York; he arrived on a motorbike, wearing leather with red trim and red shoulders. His bike was almost coordinated with his leather gear. After initial introductions, we chose to eat at Nando's.

I asked if his bike was his main form of transport, which, on reflection, sounded like I was disapproving of his bike. Defensively, he informed me he had a nice car but took the opportunity to ride his bike on beautiful days.

"Do you like motorbikes?" he asked. I think he anticipated my answer without letting me reply. "I imagine leathers are not part of your wardrobe." He started to laugh. "It's okay; I'm not expecting a future partner to ride a pillion." My mouth was still open from trying to answer his first question.

He winked and waited for me to respond, as he browsed the menu.

I closed my mouth and laughed, almost nervously; I quite liked his cheekiness. "I'll have you know I used to ride pillion on a BSA for several years. It started when I was nine." Pretending to read the menu, I was still laughing behind it, I couldn't concentrate on choosing.

"Gosh, you started dating early. Were you a child bride?" Looking straight at me, he seemed very self-assured as he ran his fingers through his helmet-flattened hair. Then, he returned to browsing the menu.

A waiter arrived, and without hesitation, he asked him to give us five minutes.

"Pillion on my dad's motorbike, cheeky." He nodded in recognition. "Ah, still young, though. My dad wouldn't let me on the back of his until I was at least nine and a half."

We laughed and chatted about past relationships and our careers, which was becoming a standard process for me on the first date. However, Stew and I were more relaxed and less serious, finding humour in most of our past predicaments.

I eventually decided on a chicken wrap, and he had a pizza. I struggled to finish mine and asked if he wanted it. He waved with a dismissal. "Don't do meat?" he said with a mouth full of Margarita pizza. He never mentioned he was vegetarian. Not that it bothered me. But it is interesting, as most vegetarians tell you almost immediately when looking at menus.

Our conversation flowed nicely, but I felt he wasn't quite into me. Eventually, he asked for the bill which was delivered to him. He threw £15 on the table, which just covered his meal and drink, then passed me the bill. I added another £20 and said that should include a tip.

"Oh, I don't pay tips, particularly in these chain restaurants," he said. "Ask for change," he said assertively, as he rechecked the bill.

"It's okay if that is your policy, but I think restaurant staff are poorly paid and rely on tips," I interjected. This was when I decided he was what some people would describe as a tight Yorkshireman. His comment shouldn't have mattered too much, but somehow this didn't sit well with me.

Still, everyone deserves a chance, and I decided that if he wanted to see me again, I would agree. We arranged a second date at a local dance hall, where we attended modern jive sessions occasionally. He didn't turn up! No note to say he couldn't make it. Fortunately, I met some friends there, so the evening wasn't wasted. It was pretty fortuitous that I sat next to a lady who was also single. We spoke about online dating, and Stew's name came up. She used him as an example of dating men from the dance classes. She warned me he had dated many women and not to be fooled by his charm. She called him a user. I smiled to myself, remembering his refusal to pay a tip. Yes, I could now see that this man was not for me.

He wrote the day after we were supposed to meet, saying his car had broken down and he had to get the AA to help him - sorry he didn't let me know, hoped I had a nice evening all the same. I replied, thanked him for letting me know and wished he had a good week. I didn't follow up after that, and neither did he. It was meant to be.

I saw him a few weeks later at the dance hall, and he asked me to dance. I did so, only once; his style was wooden and not very pleasant to dance with. He seemed distracted anyway, and I believe he asked me out of courtesy.

NEXT!!

Paul – the landscape gardener.

Deciding not to be put off dating younger men, I started talking to Paul 60, the landscape gardener, on the Plenty of Fish dating app, a new free app I had been trying. He lived in Keighley. We met only three miles from where I live for a coffee. He proved to be yet another man who was still getting over his last girlfriend. I'm beginning to think I have a relationship counsellor written on my forehead. All the same, I did find him very attractive; liked the way he presented himself and his considerate ways. Fit too! Like many men who are desperate for love or sex, he was probably too soft on his previous girlfriend who took advantage of him. Not that I need a man to take advantage of, I want an equal relationship, a man who has his own shit together. We agreed on a second date. I liked him and wondered where things would go between us. Besides, my garden could do with a makeover. I seriously did think that was a consideration.

We met again, nearer to his home this time, at a shopping centre, as I needed to buy a warm coat for my up-and-coming Canada trip. He was a very patient shopping buddy. We tried three different shops and, as usual, I went back to the first shop and bought the first coat I tried on. He treated me to lunch, still talking about his girlfriend and how she was pestering him to start again. He was clearly hurt and wanted to move on, emotionally, but he wasn't there yet, I could tell. We parted company in the car park where he gave me a very tender kiss. I could feel myself twitching in my knickers.

"I'm probably not what you are looking for," he said quietly, "but I love spending time with you. You make me laugh, and I cannot remember the last time I did." He was sweet in his way.

"Well, I have enjoyed our day today and thanks for helping me choose a coat. Let's meet again soon and see where we go."

He nodded and kissed me again. Oh heck, I'm in trouble, I thought to myself.

I set off in my car, still feeling the sensation of when he kissed me. This could be dangerous, so I put on the radio to distract myself. After a mile or so the car was stationary in traffic; the queue of cars crawled for a few yards then stopped every five minutes. After a few hundred yards I saw a sign for his village, a right turn. I was dying for a pee and had another half-hour's drive ahead. So, I dialled Paul's number and asked if he was in, told him my situation and asked if I could possibly use his toilet.

He responded immediately: "Yes, of course. Let me direct you. It's difficult parking, so ring when you are on my road, and I will help you park."

He sounded lovely and pleased to hear from me, and there he was waiting outside his cottage on a steep incline; I had to use second gear. Once I arrived at his house, I did as he said. I could see what he meant about parking. He directed me to reverse into his tight drive, trying to avoid hitting a beautiful dry-stone wall. I noticed beyond the drive was moorland, covered in purple heather. What a glorious day to see this amazing location. When I eventually parked, after three attempts, I stood and looked at his spectacular view, the Aire Valley below us. We talked about his location and I could see he was very proud of it, telling me he had a choice of several walks from his cottage.

Paul invited me into his cosy lounge with an open fireplace and log-burning stove. He had removed an adjoining wall to open up the kitchen dining area. The kitchen was in keeping with the cottage, in light oak. It was all beautifully renovated. He guided me to the narrow, steep staircase, and, as I climbed, I was struck by his choice of tartan carpet, wondering if he was of Scottish descent.

I found the cute white bathroom with black and white floor tiles. The cottage was tasteful and very tidy throughout. Returning to the kitchen area, I found that Paul had already put out two mugs on the table.

Yes, he does show me around the rest of his cottage, including his bedroom, which is again tartan-themed. We undress without a word. The sex is tender and silent, which is unusual for me, for I often sound like I'm screaming and laughing at the same time. He cums quietly too. I can feel myself trembling as he holds me. It's almost as if I am not allowing myself to enjoy the moment and the effort is making me tremble.

"Are you okay? You are trembling. Are you cold?"

He rubs my arm and back. I suppose I am a little, but it is a feeling I haven't experienced before. Indeed, I have to admit to myself I conceded to pure lust.

"Do you like anal?" he says out of the blue. "My last girlfriend wanted nothing else. It was the only way she would cum."

I am unsure where this is going. Anal is something I have avoided, thinking it is more a man's thing than a woman's. Besides, in my mind, it could be very messy. I am surprised a woman would prefer it to vaginal sex. This statement would stay with me for a long time, along with my curiosity. Not quite as fast as it started, the trembling stopped. He rubs my arm again and suggests I could use the bathroom first. I quickly get up out of bed and take my clothes to the bathroom. I then wait for him in his lounge.

Gazing out of his lounge window onto the purple heathered moors, I wonder what had happened. Am I becoming addicted to sex with anyone? Or is this an experimental phase? I know it excites me. However, I might be feeding on the attention and addicted to men desiring me.

We say our goodbyes a little awkwardly, and he helps me manoeuvre my car out of his driveway. The journey home goes smoothly, and I smile to myself most of the way.

It was several months before I saw Paul again. I assumed his ex-girlfriend had got her way. He sent a cheeky message on Plenty of Fish.

```
"Hi, Jay. Gosh! I'm surprised to see you are still
on here. You probably guessed I went back to Sophie.
Predictably, it didn't work out, so here again."

"Remember me? Don't suppose you want your bush
trimming?"

Paul xx"
```

He did make me smile. We chatted for a few days and agreed to meet as we both hadn't found anyone yet. I was still convinced he wouldn't settle with me but it would be nice to have his company.

He turned up with a massive bouquet of pink lilies. I told him to park at my house, and we would walk to the village for a meal at the Italian restaurant. We consumed a bottle of wine between us, and we finished off with Limoncello. I considered asking him if he would like to stay the night, as I was concerned that he would be over the drink-drive limit, but I decided not to and offered a coffee instead. It was only 8.30 p.m., so the night was young.

We were no sooner through my front door when he grabbed my arm and pushed me against the wall to kiss me. I pushed back. To my mind, we hadn't had coffee yet, and he was being presumptuous. He hung his head low and apologised for being pushy and offered to go home straight away. His iron-grey hair was very short and all I wanted to do was rub my hand over his head.

"Don't be silly, we haven't had coffee yet," giving him a wink. "We don't get anywhere if we are too hasty, do we?"

He laughed and leaned against the worktop in the kitchen, rubbing the soft bristles on his chin.

"Must admit it's been a long time for me, bit eager, hey?"

I was warming to the idea of having sex with him, but felt I needed to be in control because it was my home.

As we both finish our coffee simultaneously, he seems to be more relaxed. Without a second thought, we headed to my bedroom, where, again, we didn't speak. This time, he undresses me first and I sit on the edge of the bed, waiting for him to remove my stockings. Yes, I am prepared with stockings! I stand up and unbutton his shirt while he undoes the belt on his jeans and kisses my neck. He has a very toned body for his age. His chest hair is soft, and he has a lovely heart shape around his pectorals. This time, I really appreciate his body, hoping he isn't studying my body too much; a few ugly bruises from my daughter's very boisterous dog, the cellulite on my thighs; I know... at my age, what do I expect?

This time, he is much more in control, and I feel he is leading our intimacy. At one point, when he turns me over, all I can think of is his ex-girlfriend's anal preference. I take a really deep breath and brace myself. What is someone supposed to do to prepare their anus for sex? Gel maybe, douche, or hope there isn't a messy outcome, although I imagine the most likely outcome would be breaking wind. Oh my god, what have I let myself in for? I don't need to worry; he only penetrates my vagina. What a relief, because if I were to consider such an experience I would want to be consulted first.

We cuddle for about an hour, discussing the last six months since our last encounter. Of course, the girlfriend drama comes into our conversation. I am disappointed, but WTF, I have at least had my vagina serviced. Sadly, I feel that this won't be repeated again.

After we dressed, he felt comfortable with the idea of driving home, which relieved me. We were less awkward this time. I'm sure he felt the same way... for me it would be a one-off.

CHAPTER 13
TESTICLES, HIV & STIs

After casual sex, I find many men would go quiet the following days with no messages or phone calls. With their testicles discharged and hormones released, they are contented to go about their daily lives without thinking about what happened the night before or any prospects for the future. I am sure I am not alone in feeling this; I am immaterial to them. Until the urge between their groin becomes difficult to ignore, they seem to go in search of their last sexual partner, expecting lonely women like me to be waiting, willing and able. And whilst I am eager some of the time, as I do enjoy sex, I also feel as if I am leaving myself short. I shouldn't say 'used,' as I suppose I use them too, but I am a woman of my generation who was brought up to not 'be easy' as our mothers would say. As I have matured, this feeling has become less so. Now, I enjoy the fuck moment and move on. It took a few heartaches to get to that point.

My daughter's generation is much more adventurous and considers sex as part of any kind of relationship; it doesn't have to be committed; it can be casual, fun or part of an adventurous relationship. Being used is rarely a statement they make. Experimenting with different genders and bisexuals is not unusual either. University relationships are often a period of finding their sexuality, with many coming out and realising their preference.

My generation suppressed sexual preferences, and sex was usually a taboo subject. The films of my day showed the leading man taking the initiative and kissing the leading lady. But you never saw what happened next, and definitely no same-sex couples. I know my mother believed Rock Hudson (a famous American film heartthrob of the 1950s) was a victim of malicious rumours when he admitted to succumbing to AIDS and being gay. AIDS or HIV was the turning point for society to acknowledge the gay community. However, Aids is now more prevalent in heterosexuals. Carelessness in using protection, at my age, is becoming even more common. I will admit to the occasional hasty unprotected moments, regretting not using a condom afterwards and hoping I don't catch anything.

I will admit to visiting the STI clinic more than once. After Peter was my first time, I suspected he had another woman in his life, and I couldn't risk passing a disease on to a future partner. Besides, his ex-girlfriend's request didn't seem so implausible now.

The STI clinic

I walked into the clinic wearing sunglasses and my hair behind my ears, trying my best to be incognito, sitting in the waiting room full of late teens, 20 and 30-somethings, all using their phones. In the seats in front of me was a young couple, clearly into each other, her legs over his knee and him stroking her thigh, both on their phones too, sharing images as they giggled and kissed. All I could think of was 'get a room'. It made me laugh; oh, how lucky they are being so comfortable with each other and their bodies, even in public.

I spotted a giant black arrow on the wall pointing to a basket with the words 'take one and wait to be called' printed on it. I took a number from the basket and waited for my number to be called. I estimated there were at least six in front of me. It seemed like an age. Thankfully, I was seated by the window so I could gaze out, trying to keep my composure.

"Number 24," the receptionist shouted from behind a screen. That was me. I walked past the remaining group and around the screen. To my horror, I knew her! Too late, I couldn't turn away. She was concentrating on her computer screen, preparing her 'new client' form.

"Name and address?" in a monotone voice. I remembered where I knew her from as she looked up.

"Hi Jay, how are you?" Her voice raised an octave, giving me a grin. She looked at me over the top of her glasses; her blonde-dyed hair showed her grey roots.

Oh shit! This was really difficult as I remembered she was in the local drama group I joined briefly two years ago. This was turning into a bit of a drama too. I was one of the Three Bears in a pantomime; as Mummy Bear, it was not my finest hour, but my sister and I laughed, particularly over the fact that the choreographer couldn't get the two of us to dance in synch with each other. We would both start on the wrong foot and fall into giggles, the lady teaching us tutting constantly. As it happened, we brought the house down on the night; the audience loved these two middled women in bear costumes making a tit of themselves and not caring. Sadly, some of the cast felt we were upstaging them. We had the biggest cheers and applause at the curtain call. For goodness sake, it was a pantomime, and unfortunately, the principal boy/girl was as stiff as a board. We took the pressure away from her. How ungrateful.

Kitty and I were not forgiven by the older members; the lady in front of me was one of them. We did apply again to be in a future production and turned up for play readings, but we were never given another part. As Kitty said, "Their Loss."

There I am, in front of this drama woman, wanting my vagina and blood test for Herpes, Syphilis, Vaginal Warts, HIV and Gonorrhoea. When I listed it like that in my head, it made my skin crawl, so, I decided not to mention the list to her. I answered her questions. Thankfully, all she needed was my address and telephone number, and the nurse would discuss my medical concerns. I returned to the waiting room haunted by my mother's words. "If you sleep around it only leads to diseases and pregnancies." Well, I was past the latter, thank goodness.

The nurse was lovely, probably younger than my eldest daughter. Oh my god, what if my daughter found out? Would Mrs Drama, a busybody who lived in the same village, say something? I tried to compose myself.

The nurse asked me what concerns I had. As she directed me to a special chair with straps and things I didn't recognise. She placed my ankles in the stirrups and lowered the back of the special chair.

Her head and surgically gloved hands appeared between my knees, and I began to feel awkward and vulnerable; I found myself apologising for troubling her; "As a woman of my age concerned about sexually transmitted diseases, I'm extremely embarrassed."

With a very sympathetic voice, she said, "Sex isn't just for the young, you know," as she prodded my vagina. "You have taken the brave step of coming to the clinic and the rest will be very simple." She then took a blood sample and vaginal swabs placed in a tube and reassured me. "Everything looks okay, and you should know the results of the blood and swabs in a week."

As I stood up, still apologising, she passed me a white envelope.

"You can have more of these if you need them. Pop in and see us if you have any doubts about your sexual partner."

Reassured by her kindness, I left, avoiding the reception desk.

Then, to my horror, I realised I had left my new sunglasses on the nurse's desk. I needed to go back in, but I knew she had called the 'in love' couple straight after me. Kicking myself, I braced myself to see Mrs Drama again.

"Sorry to bother you again. Can you contact the nurse? I realised I left my sunglasses in her office."

She dialled the nurse's office. There was no reply. "You will have to take a seat until Nurse has finished with the clients in her room."

I felt stupid, reluctantly thanked her, and sat back with the 20– and 30-somethings, all gazing at their phones.

New people had arrived this time, and no seats were left. My age was conspicuous, to say the least.

I stood up against the wall at the side of the room and noticed two girls whispering to each other, giggling and looking at me. It was hard to make out what they were saying, but I am sure I heard, "Aw bless do you think that old lady has come to the wrong clinic? Or how gross, you don't think she does it, do you? Err wrinklies in bed together."

Within minutes, Mrs Drama shouted out the next number and, immediately after, shouted my name and asked if I could return to the desk. I was livid. She used my name. What happened to discretion and anonymity? I didn't say thank you or goodbye; I quickly picked up my sunglasses and made a hasty retreat.

I was absolutely sure I wouldn't be coming back but was reassured that I had had my sexual organs checked. If my bloods were OK, I could sleep easy. The envelope had six Durex condoms in it. Maybe one day they may come in useful. I will put one at the bottom of each of my regular handbags and two spares in my bedside cabinet drawer.

BAG OH BAG

Bag oh bag, where is the bottom?
Hiding there, something forgotten.
Memories of past buys, their old receipts,
Evidence of weakness, you know, sweets,
Pennies poured of an upturned purse,
Looking for change you know and curse,
As you rummage through emery boards,
Pens that died, not saying a word,
The yellow curled up post-it-note,
Whose list had a purpose and hope,
A utility bill to give as evidence of address
Months ago, to get you out of a mess,
A hairbrush woven with a year's strands,
Children's hairclips and Alice bands.
But hiding there, a hope never forgotten,
Was a shiny condom sitting at the bottom.

The blood and swabs came through negative, and I considered myself to have learned a valuable lesson. At least the condoms were a bonus. I only confided in Maria this time. She was so surprised I went through the whole thing alone.

"Can I come with you next time? I'm not sure how many sexual partners Jeremy has had. I don't think I could do it alone."

Regretting my confession, I responded. "What next time? I don't think there will be one, ever. Besides, I've no appetite for seeing your bits and legs in stirrups."

I was still reeling from seeing Mrs Drama.

CHAPTER 14
DATING APPS AND OLD ROCKERS

After several coffee meetings with men, I learned much about others' online dating app experiences. Questions on which apps my date had joined and whether paying gave a better result than free sites. It felt weird at first, but I realised this was part of a common theme: sharing stories of scammers and how the companies that run the sites deal with them. We all seek reassurance that you are conversing with a genuine dating prospect. Therefore, hearing others' experiences saves you the trouble of doing your own research.

I have to admit, by the second year, I had tried a few apps, starting off with the paid sites Match.com, eHarmony, Genuinematuresingles.com, and Ourtime and then moving onto the free ones Plenty of Fish, Tinder, and Bumble, realising that many of the same profiles appeared in most of them. It wasn't long before I discovered that some of these companies shared databases because they were part of the same corporate organisation, sister companies, only a different brand name.

I thought I would give the free ones a go, unashamedly thinking that men are inherently tight and avoid paying to meet women. To be honest, some do treat the apps as a hook-up tool; they meet, shag, and drop women to amuse themselves. However, that applies mainly to those in their 40s, and I am sure some women treat men the same. Then, when it comes to men over 60, 'game playing' is less prevalent. Many are looking for companionship, a listening ear, a cook, and a cleaner and many want nothing serious, yet they want exclusivity. Some even admit to wanting a "quiet life" and "no drama" whatever that means. Their profiles read:

"What you see is what you get" (my observation being, one photo of head and shoulders and very little profile is not much of a clue about "what you get")

"I'm not looking for drama" (however, often they want you to listen to their life's misfortunes and miseries.)

"I am laidback and honest, looking for a nice lady I can trust" (yet they lie about their age by at least five years or their height by five inches)

"I am looking for a wife" (rare, this one, but usually recently widowed and his late wife did everything for him, cannot manage alone.)

"I am not into one-night stands; looking for a long-term relationship" (Oh, how many women fall for this one? It's a ploy to win your confidence; if you give the benefit of the doubt, tread carefully.)

"I am not rich, but I have a nice life" (probably one of the most honest, but usually terrified of gold diggers and the online dating scene)

"I love animals, outdoors and walking" (often genuine but beware of scammers who use this to try to win your confidence)

"I'm confident God will find me a good woman" (this has SCAMMER written all over it! Any profile written with "God" in it often originates from America, beware!)

"I'm tactile, enjoy a good cuddle on the sofa with a glass of wine" (of course, most of us do, it usually means sex is high on the agenda though)

Just looking for something casual"(Sex is definitely on the agenda, friends with benefits and certainly not love)

"I'm sporty and active; a gym member, looking for similar" (Again quite honest, wanting a fitness buddy that understands their gym obsession and can keep up with them in bed)

"Looking for someone active; I'm not a pipe and slippers man" (usually a man who has had experience with an older partner or is new to being single. Wants to enjoy an active life but not alone and prefers a younger model)

"Please, no time wasters" (often a sign they have dated many times, been rejected or some women have ghosted them. To me, this shows either arrogance or an insecure bitter man)

"GSOH, looking for someone who doesn't take themselves seriously" (we all love a good sense of humour, but beware of amateur comedians. Or those who think teasing is fair game in a controlling narcissistic way. Can affect your self-esteem)

Working out what GSOH was took me a while (good sense of humour). Other profiles are so wordy that you end up swiping left (you are not interested) before you get to the end.

Free apps such as Plenty of Fish and Tinder have been around for a few years now and are flooded with scammers. After my near scam experience, I soon learned to spot them, using the old adage, 'If it looks too good to be true, then it is.'

Professional model photos - with just left the barber's hairstyle look. Copied from someone else's model photos.

Wearing sunglasses in most of their photos, posing in exotic places or leaning against an expensive car

American-style clothes are usually not from the UK; check out the wording on T-shirts.

Age declared sometimes evident that they have reduced their actual age by five years.

Left-hand drive car showing the seatbelt on the wrong side, often shown in photos in their car mirror.

Flowery wording in their profile "God-fearing" with over-the-top principles and promises. Love phrases from the outset.

If a prospect insists on coming off the site too soon to use email or WhatsApp, refuse; because a) they could be scammers or (b) sometimes the unexpected "dick pic" (a selfie of their penis) arrives in your inbox soon after. If you share your personal contact information, scammers have your attention; they then cancel their own account so that the dating sites don't pick up their scammer language on their algorithm and warn others or block them. It is all about the speed in which they operate that catches the dating novices and lures those like me into a romance trap.

Often scammers move on to their next victim quickly. Genuine men will respect that you do not want to rush into moving off the site until you have had more conversations and feel comfortable with them. I always recommend that a phone call, withholding your number, is one way of establishing if that person is worth getting to know. Again, a genuine man will not be pushy and happy to meet on your terms. It doesn't harm to explain that you want to take things slowly.

And yes, I have had dick pics sent to me, not from scammers. It is a complete mystery that men think this is something women are waiting for to appear in their inbox, that it will be a dead certain attraction. That the sight of their white pubic hair and flabby sausage is going to drive a woman to date them. They are delusional, well, I think so.

Regarding free apps, most Yorkshire men, for example, don't waste words on their profiles. They are succinct. "Young at heart, fit, good sense of humour, solvent, honest and romantic."

Sadly, they are let down by their photos. They put no effort into them. Let's face it, the initial attraction for most of us comes from the photos. And, oh boy, do many men get that wrong. Slouched in their armchair, taking a selfie from somewhere near their knees, showing several double chins, a droopy mouth and, to cap it all, the mound of a giant beer belly in a vest supported by the waistband of a grubby tracksuit bottom. Old and fading tattoos.

Honestly, I can only think these men believe their profile is honest and therefore, women should 'take me as you find me'. It is sad, I know, that we put so much importance on appearances and men don't do themselves any favours, thinking their big smile behind a 20lb fish is attractive. I dated a fisherman once, obsessive about the weather and when he could next sit by any mass of water hoping to catch the 'big one'. I certainly was second best in his world.

Overall, the profiles of most men could be improved vastly if only they would smile, drop the sunglasses, the large pint in more than one photo, take group photos with mates (which one is them?), untidy house in the background, grandkids, meals they cooked, pictures from more than ten years ago and their ex stood beside them. I don't mind that their adult children's appearance beside them shows they are proud of their family, and that sits well with most women.

I continued for a while on the two leading free apps and then discovered Bumble. It was started by one of the ex-female executives of Tinder, Whitney Wolfe Herd. She changed the 'first approach' dynamics, allowing women to control who they wanted to interact with first. Men had to wait for women to decide on their terms. I love this idea; there is less chance of being hounded by scammers, too. As with many apps, there are charges for extra features. It's business; I get that. Compared with Match.com, eHarmony, etc., you are dealing with a monthly subscription service, and men can contact you as many times as they like. It's up to you to block them if you don't want their attention,

More recently, I discovered the Facebook dating section, which is totally free, and more men live locally with me. Many other apps are geographically southern-centric, and I am not interested in long-distance dating. It is easy to use and features most functions on other sites: liking, texting, blocking, and plenty of room for profile photos and text. As with others, scammers are still lurking, but follow my advice, and you will not waste your time on them. I have reported many, and sometimes, if I am bored, I string them along and then report them. It is satisfying knowing that they have wasted time on you instead of targeting some innocent person who has newly started using dating apps. All the same, I would recommend the Facebook dating facility as it will give most people a taste of the process and who is out there looking for love, companionship, etc.

Mean machine obsession profiles.

Let us talk about men who show off their mid-life crisis motorbike or sports car purchase, posing, wearing tight leathers on a machine that many women would run a mile from, not to be their pillion. Besides, a 60 something man in leathers does nothing for me. As I said previously, Dancing Stew turned up on his motorbike and looked great. I cannot help but feel that men who have invested in purchasing their 'dream machine' expect us women to be impressed with their choice and wish to jump on the back of their throbbing beast at the slightest invitation as if it's an exciting extension of their manhood that we cannot resist. Well, they should think again. I admire that they are reliving their youth or the chance to fulfil a long-wished passion, and why not? At my age, the idea of cold knees and relying on some elderly gentleman to keep his balance, particularly when stopping and having the strength to hold the machine upright with me at the back, praying he makes the next corner, fills me with dread. Then there is the possibility of heart failure, arthritic hands and failing eyesight. Did he take his pills? My imagination would not allow me to foster any trust in their control of two wheels at 60 miles an hour on Yorkshire country roads. It all seems absurd and a risk I will not take.

Don't get me wrong, I think there is something healthy about a man having an interest, belonging to interest groups, as it shows an ability to commit, communicate and to some extent shows passion, makes them more interesting than couch potatoes, even if it is for a piece of metal on two wheels. The simple truth is men need male networks, and we shouldn't be jealous or derisory of them. Women, too, need their friendship/interest groups. The one thing I have realised is that no matter what man comes into my life, I will never give up friends and family or my interests while making room for Mr Right; I am sure of that and hope he does the same for me.

JACQUELINE T. **MAY**

CHAPTER 15
NORTON ROB
THE SEX TEXTER

From the last chapter, this leads me nicely to the 69-year-old man who, for the last 10 years, organised motorbike tours around Asia and the Himalayas on equally elderly Norton Classic machines. He had twelve bikes based in Nepal. He also organised large motorcycle charity rallies. I was fascinated by his energy. He had a small carpentry trade, and I loved his Irish accent. His name was Rob. We met at the at a Yorkshire Dales Hotel. Medium height, casually dressed in jeans, quite fashionable with his neat goatee beard. He had a sparkle in his eye that made him look young and cheeky.

We chatted for a couple of hours, me mainly listening to his motorbike adventures. I had to interrupt at one point to say that it was very unlikely I would be seen on one of his machines. He laughed and said, "I haven't met a woman I've fancied that would; besides, I have a car too." He winked to check my reaction.

I gave a nervous giggle in response. Partly because I homed in on the word "fancied" and the wink. Then the uncontrolled blush took over as I felt ridiculous. A woman in her late 60s flirting with a motorbike enthusiast who clearly wanted a woman, not to enrich his already amazing life, but maybe possibly for intimacy.

We finished the meeting, and I knew tons about him, but he knew very little about me, which is not untypical. The following morning, he texted me on WhatsApp. We had a few pleasant chats, and then he said he was flying to India in three days' time. Surprisingly, I wasn't disappointed; I took it as another "too-busy-for-a-relationship" message. However, he continued to text throughout his travels, and when I set off to South America for a trip I had planned a long time ago, he showed genuine interest in my plans. This was beginning to feel like we had something worth pursuing and we discussed meeting up as soon as I returned.

We did meet for a couple of hours in a nearby town and had lunch and a stroll. He had to leave early to be at the soup kitchen where he volunteered. He promised we would meet again very soon as he felt really good about us. But the meeting didn't take place as soon as I hoped. He declared that his ex-wife was an alcoholic and had started causing him grief, he hoped I would understand that she needed him just now, not in a relationship sense but for practical support. I agreed to keep in touch until he could free himself from this unwanted responsibility. He also said the soup kitchen was struggling for volunteers because of viruses. I didn't know what to make of all this.

Then, out of the blue, our messages went from sexual innuendo to sex texting.

`"Good morning sexy, lying on my bed in my boxers looking at your bikini photo."` It was probably one of my less sensible decisions, posting a photo of me on a beach on my dating profile. I did get a few unwanted sex pest comments. What wasn't evident in this photo was my cellulite and bingo wing arms. It was probably one of the most flattering beach photos I had. Therefore, I was proud of it, if not delusional; come on, we all like to think we are better looking than we are.

Body shaming often comes from within, and my sixty-eight-year-old body was what you would expect, I imagine, but in my head, I was 40. Although do say so myself, at 10.8 stone, I didn't carry too much fat. Three years earlier I was 13 stone, the heaviest I have ever been; after comfort eating over a three-year period during my grieving process, I steadily put on over three stone. Thankfully, I decided that if I was to embark on searching for a new soul mate, I needed to lose weight and get fit. I dieted for the first time in my life, which wasn't easy as I had never dieted before. My secret was cutting out or reducing carbohydrates (sugar, bread, pasta and alcohol) on weekdays and partying at weekends, plus exercise, walking two-three miles a day.

Rob: "Tell me about your naked body"

Rob: "I want to know every inch of you"

Rob: "How do you feel about being intimate over text? Not the real thing, I know, but could be fun, no pressure."

I didn't answer immediately, I had been here before with a younger FWB (friend with benefits) who will feature in a later chapter. It was exciting and a totally new experience then, but the truth is now I'm not sure I want to do it with someone I barely know.

Rob: "Are you still there? I haven't offended you, have I?"

After a few minutes, I decided to give him a brief description of my body.

Me: "10.8 stone, size 38b bra, firm breasts with pert nipples (one slightly larger than the other), I have very little blonde pubic hair. Phew."

Rob: "Oh Girl, that is so enticing. Shall I reciprocate?"

Me: "Yes, but don't make it sleazy lol."

Rob: "I shall be respectful; you are a lady and I love that."

It wasn't unpleasant at first telling each other what turned us on. Moving on to almost live texting intercourse, it surprised me how horny one could become after imagining ourselves in bed together, touching and pleasuring each other. He encouraged me to masturbate at the same time as he did and to explain my emotions and whether I was having an orgasm (which I pretended, of course); I could hardly keep up with the texting and actions simultaneously; I needed three hands and dyslexia is not a friend in these situations. Invariably, he would start the process by dominating the instructions and telling me to go crazy. On one occasion he started to use aggressive language and made me feel vulnerable. I went silent.

He realised he had gone too far and sent me an apology. I forgave him but warned him that the phrases he used were a turn-off. We continued sex texting most weeks, but after a while, I noticed he was getting more out of our sex texting than I was; very little dialogue about other things. Once he was satisfied, the conversation would end and he would say he had a busy day ahead. It was all beginning to feel artificial, I wanted to experience the real thing. Even the conversations felt hurried. My gut feeling was there was something else stopping our relationship from progressing.

Feeling a sense of déjà vu and being used made me decide that it was time to confront. "What is keeping you from seeing me?"

He kept waffling on about his work, the soup kitchen and his ex. Repeating a few times, he would definitely see me soon. Three months went by, and I began to avoid his "good morning" messages, thinking this might be the trigger for him to change his approach. It did; he rang and said he was booking himself a day off to see me. Could he visit and should we eat out somewhere? Like a fool, I said eat at mine. Besides, we hadn't seen each other's homes, which would be a nice way to start.

It was a beautiful sunny day, I was looking forward to seeing him. I changed my bedding, I wore my best M&S underwear; I didn't think it was appropriate to wear the black lacy Teddy I bought when dating Peter. I prepared a light salmon salad lunch and sat and waited with excited anticipation, reliving some of our sex text in my head, smiling to myself that I hadn't even had a proper kiss from this man. What if it is all a big mistake and I don't like his kiss, as with the vicar?

He arrived an hour late; something had cropped up with his business, he could only stay an hour; he hoped I would understand. It was then I realised I was wasting my time. Several months and only meeting three times; what a mug I was. The following day, I told him that in my search for a future partner, I wasn't looking for a rich man but a man who was rich in time and commitment to a relationship. He was not rich in either. I never heard from him again.

On reflection, I think there were more personal reasons behind Rob not wanting to commit to our relationship. Was it possible that he talked the talk sexually but couldn't walk the talk? Maybe my self-assuredness was intimidating for him and he could not see things through from the sex texting promise we both demonstrated. It was beginning to be my understanding that many men of a certain age were experiencing prostate problems and erectile dysfunction. Maybe Rob could only deliver in text form?

TWILIGHT

She holds her breasts at night
Reliving the moments in twilight
Finding her warm soft stickiness
Scent lingering of her willingness
As she probes to capture a high
Wet between her smooth thighs
An empty void crumpled in her bed
Voices relived in her aching head
Music and stories in soft tones
Hear the pleasure and the moans
Darkness brushes her final ecstasy
Taking her dreams into a fantasy
Wanting his strong embrace
Lips between stockings and lace.

As I progress through my writing, I reflect on revelations about past encounters with elderly men. When we are in our 20/30s we assume that sex is a normal part of a relationship. During marriage, this assumption can be challenged at various stages. For example, women can lose their libido when rearing very young children; energy loss with disturbed sleep is not untypical. Men, too, can struggle during this time with heavy responsibilities. They feel rejected by their wives, who give more attention to their babies. Women also struggle with hormonal changes in their 50s; menopausal mood changes often affect men's patience. Some men say that their wives are never the same afterwards. Hence, many divorces are undertaken around this age range.

Maybe I am the exception, but I doubt it. I have found that post-menopause has improved my libido. I believe this phenomenon is called "Widows fire"; I can still become moist (too much information for some, yet true), almost too late for men of my age, who will struggle to perform. So why does society approve of men having younger women when biologically women are capable of having sex much later than men and live longer? The problem for women to partake in sex is their libido is driven by emotions. Men have sex to release their sperm. A basic analogy I know, yet I feel it's as simple as that. I have heard from men that they often have to deal with the consequences of one-night stands, etc, where women become obsessed emotionally with them. As for a woman giving her body to a man/woman she fancies is a symbol of love and trust. Why wouldn't he/she want her again?

We women feel confused by this, and rejection is hard to deal with, whereas most men can move on quickly without a second glance, ego undamaged.

However, mature men over 60 have a whole bunch of ego issues to deal with. They might have been the 'love them and leave them' type in their younger years, or they may have been happily married. But in old age, all that changes, and things go wrong; many who were the breadwinners and protectors of the family now find themselves retired and redundant in various ways. Children no longer need them, and their partner has other interests and distractions. They are terrified of being ridiculed.

The big one is admitting they 'cannot get it up'; they are not as fit as they used to be and dealing with health issues. It is natural to feel for them, and no amount of empathy and saying it doesn't matter is unhelpful because it does matter. Many will avoid the subject and not continue their pursuit of happiness rather than admit their fears. Viagra should be their saviour, but accepting this groundbreaking drug means admitting they have a problem in the first place. I have a few enlightening experiences on that subject later.

JACQUELINE T. **MAY**

CHAPTER 16
THE BORING LOVE LOST ENGINEER

Stan arrived at our meeting point after a couple of days of texting. I am starting to get impatient about meeting men; I just want to get it over quickly without months of texting, a lesson I learned from Rob, who strung me along for several months.

Meet the prospect, see if there is potential, and if not, move on. At my age, I do not have time to waste. I hope to find a man who is not afraid of commitments, adventurous and prepared to take small risks. A man with the finances to enable budget travel is respectful, exciting and has no dependants. Sounds simple, but many mature single men have commitments or struggle to move on to a new relationship. Some like the idea of a woman in their lives, only on their terms, often misogynistic. A generation when male chauvinism was considered the norm is still alive in my age group. It often surprises me that even in the 2020s men struggle with independent, free-thinking women.

It was a beautiful sunny day, and I was happy that my journey was familiar and only 25 minutes from home. I considered any man living over one hour away distant dating and, therefore, required more effort and planning by both parties. I wore my pale blue coat with a belt, which looked good, along with my jeans and ankle boots. I considered my look classically modern.

Stan drove up in his bright red Mazda MX5 sports car, a big smiley face with square-rimmed glasses. He unfolded himself out of his small sports car and stood 6'2" tall. He bounded over to me and immediately gave me a big hug.

'Mmm,' I think, 'this is promising.'

He opened the door of the rustic Barn Café for me and asked me where I wanted to sit. I choose a table away from others. Over our coffee, we make the usual introductions. We are both widows. His wife died of cancer six years previously. He talks about his grown-up son and daughter and their assistance in enabling him to retire from his small engineering company, mainly managed by his son, who is the father of Stan's first grandson.

We then move on to revealing other relationships. His tone becomes soft as he describes his five-year relationship with Sue. How sad it was that they couldn't agree on how to move on with the relationship and how to move in with each other; she wanted to be near her daughter so she could help with grandchildren; he resented the expectations of her family, which on reflection he regrets now, admitting he wanted more time than she could give, but he conceded he was fighting a losing battle. He tells me about his road trip to Italy with Sue. I try to join in the conversation with my experiences of a similar road trip with a caravan, but I don't want to interrupt; he is so animated and keeps touching my shoulder whenever he tries to emphasise a point.

His face beaming, he asked, "So, what are you looking for in a man, Jay?"

Here we go again. I wish I had £10 for every time I was asked that question. I gave my standard answer: "I don't try to set my expectations. That way, I might be pleasantly surprised, as everyone is different and may have something special to offer.

Whilst there are a lot of potential frogs to kiss, I'm sure there is a prince out there. Who knows, it could be you."

He laughed, then told me everything that was good about Sue (that name will come to haunt me) and how disappointed he was that she couldn't be more accommodating. He said that they were still in contact but not in a relationship.

I started to have doubts about where this date was going. He eventually listened to my life and interests, which lasted about 10 minutes. Then he launched into his engineering feats, his love of motorcross bikes (not again!) and how he built his own motorbike. About being technical support for his grandson's motor cross competitions. At first, his enthusiasm was endearing; I couldn't help but observe he needed to tell me as much as he could about his life in our first meeting.

We didn't discuss much outside his life and little about mine. However, he quickly moved on to planning our next meeting. I was unsure, but that phrase didn't come out of my mouth. I agreed to talk on the phone the following day, and we could decide then.

We did meet at the coast a few days later as I had a touring caravan stored there and needed to pay the farmer cash.

Stan was happy to drive out with his MX5, its top down. The East Coast beaches are spectacular in the sunshine, and at this time of year, the purple heather carpets the moors for as far as the eye can see are beautiful. Sandsend is a fabulous example of a wild North Yorkshire coast, with its vast sweeping gold sand beach, the village nestled by a small stream which meanders down to the sands. Children make sandcastles and try to catch minnows as they paddle in the stream, giggling and screaming with delight. I have taken my own grandchildren there – creating special memories.

Over a fish and chip lunch in Whitby, he never stopped talking about his collection of motorbikes and engineering achievements, including Sue's attitude to his sport. As we were parked outside the farm, he lunged forward to kiss me. Or, should I say, he grabbed me by my shoulders and tried to devour my face. I did reciprocate initially but struggled leaning over the gear stick. Besides, I didn't feel a spark. I made excuses that his car wasn't the right place to be intimate and he agreed. Phew!!!

Stan told me he had built a large extension on his home to display his collection of motorbikes and went on to explain the makes, their rarity and potential value. Would I like to see them?

Yes, I did follow him to his home. The bike museum was on the top floor of his large house. It was then I told him that it was unlikely I would be a pillion. He laughed and said they were too valuable to have pillion passengers. That told me. Ha ha!

He started to giggle, and without warning or hinting at the change of subject, he asked. "Have you ever tried anal? I love a woman with a nice round bottom."

I turned on him, stuttering. "What the fuck Stan!! That's a crazy thing to say; I hardly know you," and quickly walked downstairs. I knew he was following me and my car keys were in the kitchen.

He shouted after me, "I was only joking, just making fun to see if you had a sense of humour. Sorry if I went too far; no harm meant."

He tried to move in close to me a couple of times, but I managed to sidestep him.

"Do you have coffee?" I asked in an effort to distract him. Desperately looking for my keys, I was starting to feel vulnerable. This could turn into some unwanted attention.

He quickly changed the subject, talking at full speed about the influence Sue had on the design of his new kitchen and saying, "Every home needs a woman's touch". He added, "Let's face it, women are much better at organising and cleaning than men. I miss having a woman to sort me out". As he stroked the granite worktop, it is evident that this woman still had a place in his world. No wonder she left. I don't know which was worse, his neediness, the anal comment or the boring conversations.

Keys found, I made excuses and left as quickly as possible.

I sent him a message the following day saying I thought he needed more time to get over Sue. It was nice meeting him, and I wished him all the best. No mention of the anal comment. He wrote back and agreed with my suggestion as he was still getting over the hurt and only started dating because he had hoped a new girlfriend would distract him from his feelings for Sue. He thanked me for being honest with him.

I have to admit I found him very creepy and boring; he talked at me and had very little interest in me and my life or welfare. The name Sue will continue to haunt me. Another car crash was avoided.

NEXT!!

JACQUELINE T. **MAY**

CHAPTER 17
DADDY DAY CARE
- DRINKER

I met Rick in Costa Coffee in a nearby town. Again, I instigated the meeting rather than going through weeks of correspondence. We were local to one another after all.

He was about 5'8", not quite white thinning hair and casually dressed, wearing khaki shorts and a long-sleeved white shirt with a gilet over. Immediately, he asked what I wanted to drink; I waited at our chosen table while he ordered; it gave me a chance to study him at a distance. I once read that we should always view potential partners that way as it can often indicate whether you are likely to fancy them or not. He had a nice smile and a soft voice. I couldn't detect an accent.

He apologised that he only had an hour as he had to pick up his kids from school. Their mum had called him.

Rick was a 69-year-old man trying to juggle earning money and looking after his five children's needs. He had two grown-up children and three under 10 with 7-year-old twins. His much younger ex-wife still lived in their five bedroomed house with their children and her lover. Rick rented a property half a mile from them. There was cheeriness, positivity, and charm about him; he was likeable in many ways.

He said in his profile that he was no longer a rich man but much more prosperous in other ways. His children and friends meant everything. He also was the owner of a villa rental business in Spain. I could empathise.

His profile didn't say he spent most weekends ferrying his three younger children from one sports hobby to another. He was also a cricket captain for his local team, spending most evenings in the sports bar.

The twins were a boy and a girl. The 10-year-old was the apple of his eye, a daddy's girl. He had much more to say about her than the others. He showed me photographs he kept in his wallet, one of the twins and two of her, proudly showing me her confirmation dress. It didn't feel like the natural order of things as he was 69; I had five grandchildren of a similar age. Obviously, his wife was much younger than he, by 25 years.

Nevertheless, I was attracted to him, for he looked fit for his age, and his charisma was young in spirit, which is why his wife may originally have made allowances for the age difference. I understand he was wealthy then and provided her with a large family home in an upmarket suburb of Leeds, overlooking his favourite social haunt, the cricket ground. They were both well-travelled before having the children, and he purchased a property in Turkey. But all was lost when, during a large building project on the family home, his wife had an affair with the builder. Whilst devastated at the time, Rick was now very philosophical about it, saying...

"It was only a matter of time. I was a fool to think it would last, but every cloud has a silver lining, and I have my beautiful children. I'm a much better father this time; my first two children didn't see much of me during my first marriage. Hence, my son doesn't have much to do with me now; he has addiction problems and has been in and out of rehab. I feel a sense of guilt over him." He looked into his drink.

"After the divorce, my ex did her best to make sure the children were estranged from me. They were tough years. But I built up my business, and, I'll not lie, I played the field with women in my 50s. Yes, I had many women, loved them and left them. I was ready to settle down when I met my second wife, but I didn't expect to attract someone so young. She chased me, actually. Of course, I was flattered. What man wouldn't be? I didn't want to marry again, but she hadn't been married before or had children, and I didn't want to deprive her of either. I was totally in love – hey ho."

His tone changed as he continued. "He's moved in, the builder, made himself comfortable in my house. It hurts, to be honest, particularly when she keeps asking for more money from me." Then he grins. "Anyway, she's high maintenance. He'll find that out soon."

I smiled and congratulated him on his magnanimous and positive attitude. So, what made him start talking to a 68-year-old? I suppose I was part of his breakup recovery, needing a mature woman's shoulder to cry on.

We agreed to meet again at his beloved Cricket Social Club in a few days. I dressed pretty modern, with black skinny jeans, boots, and a smart collarless leather and fabric jacket. My recent weight loss allowed me to wear things I would have never considered once. I walked up the stairs to the club. The bar was situated in the centre, with a few men of various ages standing propping up the bar or sitting on bar stools. There was one woman, the barmaid. All looked in my direction as I approached. I was beginning to feel like a fish out of water. This was a mistake.

"Can I help you, love?" the girl smiled. "What would you like to drink?" she asked while pulling the next pint for one of the grinning guys staring at me.

"It's okay; I'll get this one." A commanding voice came from behind me. It was Rick. I was relieved, although he wore the same shorts and gilet he had on our first date. I thought, "You could have made more effort, Rick." It was another "take me as you find me" moment from a man. It makes you feel you are not very high value to them. I put the momentary thought behind me and concentrated on the introductions.

"Guys, this is Jay, a friend of mine." Most nodded, some raised a hand, and others said, "Hi." However, an older gentleman, whom I guessed was older than us, walked over to me.

"Welcome, lovely lady. What are you doing being a friend with this old rogue?" The rest laughed in the background. Rick hurriedly guided me away to a table at the side of large patio doors overlooking the cricket green, then returned from the bar with a ¾ bottle of white wine. He had already started without me, I could see.

"Is Pino Grigio okay?" He started pouring into both glasses. "They keep a bottle behind the bar for me." He pointed past the cricket green and remarked, "See that house with two gables in the corner?" I nodded "That's my house. Great position. I used to love walking to the bottom of the garden and across the green to get here." I could see the loss of his home in his eyes.

We were there an hour when he invited me back for coffee, which I declined. I still felt there were things I needed to know about this man. His old mate might have been joking, but I didn't want to be seen as easy.

The following day, he texted me in a very friendly way, saying how much he appreciated my coming to the club. Would I like to join him for Sunday lunch this coming weekend? His Yorkshires were legendary, and the beef was not bad either; just bring a bottle. I accepted.

He had rented a three bedroomed 1980s, white, mock Tudor semi-detached house on a lovely leafy road. The garden was well tended, with freshly planted geraniums in the borders. A fluffy tabby cat followed me up the garden path. Rick opened the door wearing an apron with the words 'Dad is the best' and a big, smiley yellow emoji.

"See Pickles has introduced herself. Come in, make yourself at home." He started to walk to the kitchen, then turned on his heels and gave me a big bear hug and kiss on the lips with a little groan.

"Been wanting to do that for a long time."

I smiled and responded, "Cheeky." We both giggled.

And yes, he was a good cook. Dinner was excellent, although his serving on my plate was large enough for two. I had to leave some and apologise that, since losing weight, I thought my stomach had shrunk. He laughed.

I didn't keep an eye on how much wine I had drunk that lunchtime, but I knew I was well over the legal limit. He offered coffee in his lounge, and before I knew it, he was kissing and fondling me. I was wearing a V-neck dress, so as you can imagine, there was plenty of opportunity for wandering hands to find their way to my breasts and thighs. I was ready, if honest, but not sure if that was the drink influencing me or this horny-60-something-me excited at the prospect of a new lover.

After a few moments of him fumbling to undo his belt and me desperately needing a wee, we decided to go upstairs. He showed me the bathroom and his bedroom door where he would be waiting.

In the bedroom was a naked man with the biggest grin I had seen in a long time. Oh, the other part of his anatomy was standing proud too. He then sat on the edge of the bed and patted the duvet beside him, beckoning me to sit next to him. I did, and he removed my dress, then knelt before me to remove my tights. I sat in my M&S underwear shaking.

"Gosh, are you cold?" he said with deep concern in his voice. I didn't want to tell him I might be quivering with excitement and adrenaline, so I nodded.

"Come, get inside the duvet, I will warm you."

I giggled. "I bet you will".

He disappeared under the duvet, and I could feel his warm cheeks against my thighs; his tongue was even warmer.

He asked, "Is this okay?"

I responded each time with "Mmm". When I saw his penis, I wasn't overly excited to give him oral. Thankfully, he didn't seem to expect it. His age did show in his performance, but I was at least pleased with the fellatio; that was the was the best bit. Clearly well-practised, he made me orgasm.

Orgasms

This might be a good time to talk about orgasms. For men, as far as I can tell, it's an overwhelming physical thing; ejaculation is all-consuming for them, and some have the desire to thank God. I've found that they react in many different ways.

Ejaculation reaction	Translation:
The screamer	(it worked!!!)
Oh God, oh God!	(thanking God that it worked!)
Crying/ laughing	(happy it worked, no joke!)
Expletives	(F*#* F*#*, at last, it worked!)
Grunting	(keep going a little bit longer)
Body spasm	(body in shock, it worked!)
Dead weight	(I'm fucked, but it worked!)

I can guarantee most men shoot (forgive the pun) the usual question, "Did you come?" or is it cum? I say "Of course" or "mmm mm" or nod. Male ego needs the reassurance that he has performed his best for you. I cannot speak for other women, but the whole orgasm topic feels like a big hype created by men to make them feel better. I know I will get lambasted by some women for saying this, I can only go on personal experience.

For me, an orgasm is not a guaranteed event; it is often foreplay or erotic games (i.e. Frank) that arouse me the most. Oral in particular (including "69"), penetration of the penis rarely, although some larger ones do. I do know if I am in love with someone it certainly heightens my experience and chance of an orgasm.

So, which reaction was Rick's? Well, he collapsed on me like a dead weight with the occasional exhausted grunt. Eventually, rolling over onto his back with that 'question' again. I grunted back with a nod; it felt appropriate. Although inwardly, I'm ashamed of my insincerity

He responded, "Good, good, it has been a while for me. You?"

"Yes, me too. Shall we have a cuppa? Not sure I am in a fit state to drive now."

I stayed the night, he snored; it wasn't the best of nights for me. He was cuddly, though, and I enjoyed that part of his attention. I rarely sleep well in another man's bed or after the first night of intimacy; my adrenaline is usually running too high. We slept together several times over two months - much the same experience.

One day. He invited me to a barbecue for his soon-to-be-11-year-old daughter's birthday. I was flattered that he wanted me to meet his children. It was a beautiful day, and I helped him prepare the salads, etc. He chatted constantly about the new app he had discovered that monitored foreign exchange rates, and he explained that if he got it right, he would make considerable money out of the various fluctuations in foreign currency.

He admitted that he was struggling to make ends meet and was also considering taking in a lodger to help him with the rental cost of his house. I had not appreciated how financially insecure this man was. Later, I learned that he delivered parcels for Evri from 6 -12 a.m., four days a week.

I also started to notice he had a dependency on drink to relax and thought nothing of driving ¾ of a mile to his house with a skinful of wine and spirits. I couldn't understand why he didn't walk. I did tell him on a few occasions he was over the limit, but he brushed it off, one of the reasons our relationship didn't blossom. However, he was the one who stated that maybe it was best we remain friends. I walked away that afternoon, not even to partake in the barbecue, as I couldn't see the point of carrying on with the charade. I felt I was adding to his financial burden. He clearly wanted to live the life he had before the divorce but struggled to fund it. I admired his work ethic all the same.

A few days later, he sent me a nice note saying I deserved someone better. He hoped to get back with his wife, and he was concerned that his children might return to her with news he had a girlfriend. Crazy, I know. Why invite me to the BBQ? Oh well, I was relieved if honest.

NEXT!!

IN THE SAME CHAIR

Are we just lonely souls in the night,
Waiting for a message, a soft tone
Tripping from the lips of another,
Filling the quiet voids of our time
And moments of solitary existence?
Opening our vulnerable hearts
To a perfect stranger seems fair
For another in the same chair.

69@69: A NAIVE WIDOW SWIPES RIGHT INTO THE WORLD OF ONLINE DATING

You might be my perfect lover,
A soul mate who whisks me away
To a world of tender holds.
If so, let me gently into your world;
I've little pride in my loneliness.
I'm here now, nowhere to go.
Take my wanting body and heart
Exchanged for yours. I willingly part.

JACQUELINE T. **MAY**

CHAPTER 18
THE UNCOMMITTED CHARMER

I had celebrated my 69th birthday the day before when a message arrived in my Plenty of Fish dating app mailbox.

"You sound interesting. Fancy a chat?"

After checking his beautifully written profile, I decided to answer, although I was in no mood for hours of text messaging.

I responded, "I would rather we have a telephone conversation first if that's okay with you. I'm free at 7 p.m. if that works for you."

He responded immediately, "Wow! You know what you want. Of course, it will be my pleasure. My telephone number is … I look forward to it. Speak at 7pm."

I had a good feeling about this one.

Our telephone conversation was varied; I loved the sound of his voice. He was in the middle of writing a book, which interested me. I kept our chat short because I knew I wanted to meet him, and we agreed to meet the following day in a town near me.

"I don't have a car," he said, "but that's okay. I will take the bus. I'm used to public transport. I have decided that now that I am embarking on dating ladies, I hope to have a car by the end of the month."

That took me back a little so I offered to drive a little closer to him, but he insisted on sticking to the initial plan.

I met Dennis in an out-of-town hotel; he was waiting in the restaurant. A tall, well-dressed man stood before me. He had thick white hair swept back, a pleasant smile, a strong jaw line and blue eyes. For 70, he was still a very handsome man with manners. He offered me a chair opposite him and pulled out the chair for me to sit on. Then he caught the attention of a waitress and asked me what I would like to drink. He was in command of the situation and clearly had the confidence to match.

When he smiled, I was mesmerised and fascinated that this good-looking man had travelled 15 miles on public transport to see me. I asked about his journey. He was very relaxed about it and said he had arrived early to wander around the town and river. I could have listened to his voice all day.

He was well educated, I could tell, and he told me he went to public school from age five, admitting it wasn't a happy time for him. His parents were employed by the foreign office and travelled worldwide; therefore, he and his brother were boarders at a very early age. He quickly changed the subject and asked if I had always lived there. It was such a refreshing change that a man wanted to know about me early in our conversation. Instead of the usual, "So what are you looking for in a man?"

I gave him a brief background of my life. "I am the eldest of seven children, always lived in Yorkshire, widowed after 42 years of marriage, met my husband when I was 16 years old, have two daughters and five grandchildren, and was a stay-at-home mum for the first 10 years. After a few years of part-time work, I decided to start a career in a computer company with no qualifications other than experience as a Personal Assistant for a company director (I was the worst PA he had ever had, but he liked my tea). This was before I had children; therefore, starting as an administrator in my new job made sense. I worked for the first company for five years, progressing to selling computer services. An ex-colleague asked if I knew the "information super highway". I had heard of it and was used to using an internal email system, but otherwise, not much. "

"Great," my ex-colleague Simon said. "Do you fancy learning more and seeing if you want to work with us?" I continued as Dennis seemed really interested in what I had to say.

"I met Simon the following day. I agreed to join his company, seeing it as something that could take off."

I was on a roll recounting my past to Dennis. He was a good listener; it was one of those rare dates where I could talk about myself.

I told him, "In 1995, it was the very early days of commercially viable internet provision. The company had invested in its own network and web server farm (data centre), and my job was to help this small start-up company develop its telesales and marketing. For the first few months, I spent most of my days ringing companies (cold calling) and working through Yellow Pages phonebooks. There was minimal budget for advertising. It wasn't long before I realised that the "prospects"I was talking to knew nothing about the Internet, and it was clear that we needed to educate companies before selling to them. We changed our approach and ran several seminars to educate businesses on the commercial potential of having a website and email. Word travelled fast in the business community, and our seminars were over-subscribed. We ran them weekly. They were a great success. The national newspapers featured us as an exciting new enterprise and one to watch."

Dennis called the waiter over, and we ordered more coffee, "do continue; this is fascinating."

"Are you sure, I'm not boring you, am I?"

"No, not at all. I'm a dinosaur regarding IT but still fascinated with its history."

Smiling back at him. "I continued to work in the internet industry for eight years; my last role was head of an international division. Hence, I travelled throughout Europe, often flying alone and working 14-hour days. When a larger corporation bought us out, it didn't suit me, and I was asked to join another small start-up company. For the last two years, I worked for an online Data Storage company, creating a new division called Advanced Internet Provision. It provided internet infrastructure for online applications and the start of the "Cloud" as we know it today. I had no idea how big this new technology would affect our lives in the future, for I was busy doing something I loved."

I was wondering how to end my career biography. "That's it, really. Here I am, retired and talking to you." I said with an embarrassed laugh in my voice.

"This is a brief overview of my life and career; I was very privileged to be in the right place at the right time during an amazing period in the early Dotcom industry. For, at that time, I was a woman in her mid-40s who never succeeded in academia and was partially dyslexic, with no qualifications."

I giggled nervously again after that sentence and added, "I doubt I could do the same today. I admit that I suffered from terrible imposter syndrome, asking myself how I got here?" Feeling I needed to make excuses for showing off.

Our second coffee arrived, and for a minute, there was a pause in our conversation. He stirred his cup and smiled while looking into it.

"I love that you took on these challenges thinking you were not qualified, yet persevered and succeeded. And, as you said, you had to educate others, for there were no courses or qualifications for the Internet then. I think what you did is something to be proud of."

He coughed into his hand. "Besides, I'm in awe that you have worked in such a technical industry. As I said, I'm a technology dinosaur."

I respond with yet another nervous giggle; the fact that this man has listened and understood what I have achieved is something special. So why do I still need to apologise for my lack of academic achievements? And what's with my nervous giggling all about?

I look out of the window, watching a woman attempting to reverse park her 4x4 car into a tight parking spot. I relate to her problem. At that moment, a guilty cloud overwhelms me. Will he perceive me as bragging? I'm not used to having the space to talk about myself in detail. This made me feel a little exposed. Most men dominate the bragging space on our first meeting. Why is it acceptable for men to brag about their achievements but less so for women? It seems most men don't have a problem with bigging themselves up; however, for many women, this isn't a comfortable place for them.

I was still watching the female driver and hearing two men behind me laughing at her attempts to reverse into a small parking space. She mirrors my experiences and those of other women I know struggling to be accepted by their male peers in new roles. Not all men can reverse park perfectly the first time, but they still think it's okay to mock and be superior in their attitude towards women.

I have often heard that women struggle to negotiate a pay rise or promotion because they cannot articulate their value to their bosses; they would instead prefer to be recognised organically and not have to go through the process of perceived bragging or justification, the glass ceiling forever present in their own mind. I managed to negotiate my position in the main because I was one of the original employees; the start-up internet company I worked for grew from 15 when I started to 300 employees in three years.

I stopped there because I thought I had disclosed far too much. Had I bored him, was I overbearing? Because of this self-conscience moment, sitting opposite a charming man who put me in the limelight, I decided to focus on him and ask what he did for a living before retiring.

His whole language and phrases came across as humble, telling me he qualified as a "simple" quantity surveyor. Eventually, after a few years with the same property developer, he became a director. He got bored and decided he wanted to be his own boss, so for 15 years, he owned his own business manufacturing timber components and accessories for internal finishings for housing developments. It wasn't a roaring success, but it paid the bills and gave him a decent standard of living.

Prior to selling the business and planning his retirement, his younger wife decided she wanted a divorce. The settlement meant he had to buy her out from half of the company and their family home.

Sadly, a year later, there was a slump in the building industry, and Dennis found himself bankrupt. His wife did well. He decided to cut his losses and retired with his small pension, then moved into a one-bedroomed flat in the city centre, close to a supermarket.

"So, no need for a car, until now, although I have to tell you that I had a four-year relationship with a lady from York who was quite willing to do most of the driving. I'm not the male chauvinistic type and am quite happy to be chauffeured around by a lady. No pride in that quarter." He belly-laughed at his own comment, and I reciprocated.

"Sue (omg, not Sue again!) was a very nice lady, but she wanted more than I could give. I've decided I don't want to marry again; I know this was important to her. I would have been number three for her. But no, that's not for me. I realised I didn't love her enough; the pressure was too great. I wasn't keen on moving to York. She fell out with me over it. We've agreed to remain in the friend zone though."

I loved his candidness. He became more attractive as he looked straight into my eyes when talking. No red flags appeared at this stage, and his emotional intelligence was right up there for me.

Yes, it sounded like money was a challenge, but he seemed to enjoy his retirement despite having less money than he used to. He had also embarked on writing a book about his life. I told him I was a poet and that I wrote short stories. That impressed him; he said he liked poetry, particularly one of my favourites, Leonard Cohen. These things made me think we would have lots to talk about in the future.

After our meeting, I drove him to the bus station and he gave me a big hug and kiss on both cheeks.

"Well, I can honestly say the bus journey here was well worth it. Glad I got a chance to see your town." He winked and gave me a broad smile. "Company wasn't bad either. I would love to see you again. And guess what? I might have my own wheels by next week. What do you say?"

How could I refuse his boyish charm? I watched him walk to his bus stop thinking that he was much too smartly dressed to be going home on a bus.

After a few good morning chats, we decided to meet again. He suggested a walk by the river in Richmond and a picnic.

The weather looked promising. He suggested I bring some favourite poetry and a bottle of wine. I loved the idea. It felt like a touch of D H Lawrence, imagining me in a flowing chiffon floral long dress and big straw hat, sitting with him on a gingham cloth with a traditional wicker picnic basket, complete with a bottle of sparkling wine, the river flowing gently near our feet as we shaded under a silver birch tree, listening to his beautiful voice reciting my favourite poems. This was the stuff of romantic dreams; a man had evoked such imagination in me for the first time. I couldn't wait.

Firstly, he was disappointed. He couldn't make the picnic that day. He had to go into Harrogate to pick up a pair of glasses from the optician.

"Do you mind awfully if we meet outside Betty's and we can walk down Valley Gardens, maybe coffee in the café there?"

My dream partially shattered and soon passed. I agreed to the change of plan.

I sat on a wall near Betty's café; it was a hot day, and I needed to sit in the shade. I ditched the idea of the long flowing chiffon dress and large straw hat and opted for a short, colourful skirt and loose white blouse with a V-neck. I'm fussy about necklines and hate T-shirts for that. Vee and boatneck tops are so much more feminine than high necks. I have to say I felt good about myself that day. Not often, I do, again suffering from imposter syndrome. I worry about looking inappropriately addressed for the occasion, so I decided simple is best, and my freckled legs look tanned enough to forego tights.

I watched a couple with their arms around each other walking up the hill before me, not noticing the smartly dressed man behind them. OMG, there he was, striding up the hill in a pale blue linen suit, a big smile, looking straight at me.

"Wow! You look good," were his first words. He kissed me on both cheeks. He smelled good too.

"Nice suit," I said, trying not to sound too blown away by this romantic DH Lawrence character.

"I don't have many occasions to wear it," he said in a humble way. "Thought today would be of those occasions." Oh my, what a contrast to Rick and his khaki shorts.

He grabbed my hand. "Shall we go my lovely lady?"

His hands were large but soft and gentle. Mine were lost in his hold. Gosh, I could feel the sparks flying everywhere in my body. We walked and talked for a good hour. Pointing out the flowers on the borders of Valley Gardens. Nothing fazed either of us, we were in tune, both in the arts and our family values. We were both well-travelled and had similar taste in the kind of experiences we valued. Eventually, we stopped for coffee and agreed that it was too hot to continue with the walk. He suggested we return to the main entrance by walking under the covered walkway. I loved that he had such a considered command of most situations, almost as if he had studied what makes a woman feel safe and comfortable in male company.

We strolled under the canopy, and within a few minutes, he stopped. Turning around, he held my shoulders and asked if he could kiss me. Most men I dated seemed to lunge into the first kiss, but he was polite and asked. Oh boy, I thought he would never ask. I think my knickers had been damp for hours just watching his lips as he was talking intently to me, trying to imagine the effect they would have on me orally. Yet I desperately tried to delete those thoughts because they were so distracting. I wanted to concentrate on every word he said. Still thinking about his effect on me and the shame of my wet knickers when he said, "Well, is it okay? I'll understand if not; it is a public place."

"Yes, of course," I said as I moved closer to his face. He bent over, held my chin gently, and planted a warm, soft pair of lips on mine; I quivered. We then kissed deeply, touching the tip of each other's tongues as he held me in a closer embrace. We were both oblivious to our surroundings when a woman shouted, "Jimmy." And Dennis turned. A large golden Labrador ran towards us and jumped up, putting his big paws in Dennis's groin. He doubled up and cried out in pain. What an end to a beautiful kiss. I made him sit down on the nearest bench to recover while the woman chastised her dog and shouted apologies. He put up his hand and reassured her no permanent damage had been done while he had a little groan under his breath.

"Are you okay? I'm sure that really hurt," I said, trying to have some empathy without laughing at the situation. He laughed and was glad he had put his padded underpants on that day. We both stood up and hugged one another while giggling. Two elderly people were snogging in a public place. What were we thinking of?

We eventually organised a picnic by the river, I arranged to meet at his flat. He had a private parking place in an underground car park.

"Park next to the cheap green Fiat," laughing down the phone. "Don't worry about scratching it, it's mine."

I wore a mid-length summer floaty skirt, walking sandals, a vest top with an open blouse over the top. It allowed me to cover up from the sun or cool down if I removed it, which was more practical than the flowing chiffon dress.

He showed me around his small but tidy apartment, which was modern and had an assortment of antique and modern furniture, purposeful but not coordinated in any way. A bachelor pad it was, with French windows overlooking the city. The picnic was prepared and put in a rucksack, my bottle of wine in a wine cooler was added and I was given the blanket to carry. It was a beautiful walk by the river and he took me to one of his favourite spots to sit, on a bend of the river, overlooking willow trees stroking the water's surface on the opposite bank. He found a spot with partial dappled shade and laid out the blanket. We must have been there an hour talking, then decided we were actually hungry; the tin-foiled parcels were revealed from the rucksack, and he poured two glasses of wine and agreed this was the perfect day for a picnic.

Our idyllic moment was broken by two large Springer Spaniels running between us, one picking up a half-sandwich, the other trying to, both en route to jumping into the river, after which they promptly headed in our direction on the way out as Dennis did his best to protect the remainder of the picnic when a young couple appeared on the bank beside us, shouting at "Ben and Jerry" to leave us alone, but the badly behaved wet pups were having nothing of it. They bounded on and off our blanket, wagging their wet tails on us for what seemed an age, their wet paws leaving their prints on everything. Finally, their male owner grabbed both dogs and apologised, at the same time lecturing us that having food by a path where there were dog walkers wasn't a good idea.

The two of us were fated. I laughed and said it was all Dennis's fault, he was a magnet for dogs. We returned to his apartment, laughing at our disastrous picnic while he was hugging me around my waist. I loved the electricity of his touch on my body.

"Are you busy tomorrow?" he asked while putting the paw-trodden remains of our picnic in the bin. "Because if you are not, you could stay the night, and we could finish off the wine," smiling towards me with a wink. "I don't want to be presumptuous. I'm happy to sleep on the sofa."

I had a little think, knowing I had packed a spare pair of knickers, a mascara and tooth brush in a Morrison's carrier bag in my car. I didn't tell him though.

"It would be nice to share a drink with you now, without worrying about driving home."

Of course, we shared his bed. He admitted that maybe a cuddle would be all we should do initially as after a drink his performance was likely to be disappointing and he would hate that if so, particularly for the first time. Again, I was overwhelmed by this man's considerate nature. His long arms enveloped me, and he soon started to snooze. Even though he snored, it was a gentle rhythm, and I, too, fell asleep.

Dawn arrived with the sound of Rooks squawking in the tree outside his apartment, probably 5 a.m. when I felt his hands exploring me.

His large hands almost hovered over my breasts and worked their way down to my stomach.

"Morning, lovely lady". I put my arm around his neck as he leaned over and kissed me. We gently and unhurriedly made love as if we were savouring every moment. He was virile enough to satisfy me even if I didn't experience an orgasm. His was an "Oh God, Oh God". It is not often I use the phrase 'making love'; I usually say sex because there is often no emotional driver behind it, just lust, whereas I was beginning to have feelings for this man already.

For the rest of the morning, we sat in bed drinking tea and reading from the book of Leonard Cohen's poetry and lyrics I had brought with me. He was much more well-read than I and would recite and compare other writers and their impact on his own writing.

His own novel was all but finished, bar the cover design and getting it printed. He had already approached some publishers and either didn't get a response or were uninterested. I told him not to give up, as many best-selling authors had to initially trawl through several publishers before finding the one who would take a chance on them.

It was a few days before we met again. Another meet in Millenium Gardens and lunch. We kissed a lot, but no dog interrupted us. I invited him for dinner at mine. He stayed the night and we made love. He admitted to taking Viagra in a way that sounded like he was cheating. I told him not to worry as I was the beneficiary of his drug taking. He loved my response and things only got better, even 69.

During our first two months together, we did various things: visited a writer's talk, attended one of my daughter's band performances, and took him to see my friends in the Dales. They all said how much they liked him and were pleased I had found someone,

We went to London to meet his son and girlfriend, took them for lunch and had a walk in St James Park. We held hands all the way around, then stayed in a simple but comfy bed at a Premier Inn hotel. He said his son and girlfriend liked me and were happy for him. I was so happy. I also arranged to visit a friend of mine in the West End, had lunch with her, then headed for the station. We were both quiet on the train. I wasn't feeling too well, but I had a headache and slept on his shoulder for half the journey. I thought we were both exhausted from 48 hours of non-stop tube rides and visiting.

A few days passed after our trip with the occasional good morning; the tone seemed to change to being more formal. I don't know why, but I started to feel nervous about contacting him. My gut instinct told me there was something wrong. It was a Monday morning when Dennis came through with a message.

```
Hello J,

Please forgive me, I'm not good at saying this stuff
face to face; you could call me a coward and I
would not blame you. I have been thinking a lot
about us over the last few days and the conclusion
I have reached is, I can no longer continue with
our relationship. I cannot give a lovely woman like
you the relationship I would wish to give and you
deserve. There is not enough 'spark' there for me
to commit myself emotionally. Since reaching the
grand old age of 71, I have started to appreciate
the advantages of a quiet life. You, however, are
looking for the opposite; you want to travel and
experience as much as you can while you can and
that I totally respect. I would only be a burden
to you in the end. I have loved our intimacy but,
realistically, I cannot see me keeping up the pace
you need in the long run. You need a younger man than
I. Also, I have also decided to give up on the dating
sites and maybe while I'm not looking, I will find
the 'one' naturally. On that note, I will not make
any more excuses, just to say I will never regret
```

```
meeting you and the happy time we have had together.
Wishing you all the best lovely lady, and be happy.

With much love D xx
```

I was gutted and sat crying, mystified as to what had caused the change of heart. What had I missed? I replied that maybe we needed to talk face-to-face and see if we could salvage things. He said he couldn't in the short term as he knew he had made the right decision and felt there was no need for a post-mortem, but he would be happy to meet for a catch-up sometime in the future because he enjoyed my company. Again, he said I deserved better and not to settle for second best. I was devastated, yet I totally respected this man who clearly had issues I was unaware of. Plus, I didn't want to press him further because I thought the lack of money was one of them. Little did I know. I felt so sad at losing him, for he was the only man I found closest to being a soul mate. He was a rare find, but he didn't have courage in his convictions or was too scared to commit. "Oh, Dennis, why did you spoil our future? It was going so well?"

The catfish

After a few days of feeling sorry for myself and sending him messages stating how he had made me feel, why was I doubting his intentions? He said all the right things, honourable as always, but I couldn't change his mind.

A week later, I decided to move on and return to the dating scene to help me get over Dennis. And to my utter shock, Dennis was listed under my potential suitors on Plenty of Fish. I knew he had cancelled his account when he was dating me, so he must have opened this new one within the week. I felt sick and betrayed. He lied to me about going back on dating sites, saying everything to make him look considerate.

He once gave me a video called 'Catfish', featuring people who create fake dating profiles on dating apps such as Tinder and Plenty of Fish. These people pretend to be someone they are not, usually using complete strangers or a fashion model's photos to attract unsuspecting victims, either for attention and hopefully love or to scam them out of money. Some do it for revenge after being dumped by a previous partner to hurt them. After seeing Dennis's photo and profile, I was incensed and decided to set up a fake profile to see how he would respond to a new lady, particularly so soon after dumping me.

I found a suitable photo of a sophisticated-looking lady wearing glasses, and I wrote a profile of Carol, which I knew would attract him. I wrote, "I am a retired 68-year-old widowed teacher with various interests. I am interested in historic places, European holidays, and enjoying quiet evenings with a nice glass of wine, classical music, or a good book. I am not looking for marriage but a gentleman who would hopefully be a soul mate and partner in crime, sharing good times together."

He messaged my fake profile within a day, "You sound like my perfect match. I would be honoured if you were interested in chatting with me."

My fake profile responded. "Hello Dennis, how nice of you to write. I have only been on this dating website for a few days, and I have to say your profile description sounds attractive. My last relationship didn't blossom; he became very needy and jealous and made it difficult for me to keep the flame burning, so to speak. I have been single for 2 years now, not looking for a wealthy man, just one who is rich in time and intelligence and looks after himself. And here I am looking for the right fit, navigating this online dating process. Have you been on it long?"

Dennis responded immediately, "I am humbled that you responded so soon. Yes, I have been here a little while and had a few dates but not found the "one" yet. Do you have any thoughts on what you are looking for? I see you like books and wine; I tick those two boxes."

My fake profile answered, "You are a few dates ahead of me then. Perhaps you could tell me a bit more about you and your experiences, likes and dislikes in a prospective partner."

This bit gets interesting. He obviously wanted to impress my fake profile with some facts and went into full Dennis mode:

"Hi Carol, So, what don't I like? Well, yes liars, that's a given. And women who have too high an opinion of themselves. I just ended with one like that! And women who are opinionated had that recently, too. Good, you mentioned wealth; I don't have any! My newish city centre flat is rented, and the landlord is a housing association, but they are great landlords, very efficient; keep everywhere clean, whole outside repainted this year. No neighbour issues, just no complaints whatsoever. My state and few private pensions enable me to run a car, have a modest annual hol. in the sun (but don't want to go on my own!) and have a nice life. I have simple tastes, I guess, like reading, writing, walking, driving, and music (not really a live band fan, though, I prefer listening at home - thank you, Spotify!) So, you might say I need to be cautious with money even though not my natural instinct! Sharing costs, of course, though am inclined to say, 'I'll get this!' every time. Habit, I guess! Don't like cheapskates, had one of those too! Don't think she could help it! Jealousy, yes like you I can't abide it. Maybe a natural instinct within us, but I don't recall last time I felt it, so must be hidden deep! I also don't care for insincerity, but do like banter and fun; don't take myself too seriously. World affairs? We could soon sort those out, I'm sure. And don't get me going on the price of apples! How am I doing? Hope you didn't get bored reading all this and lost the will to live?!!! Dx"

I read the reply several times before running to the toilet to be sick. How could he be so insincere, so nasty, so arrogant? I suppose I asked for it; I should have left things as they were. Was it the truth or was it him trying to impress? Whatever, a part of me felt a stab in the heart. I had totally misread this man. I closed the app, went straight into my email account, and started writing to him. The title I gave was "High Opinions."

"Just as I was getting over you, I found you on Plenty of Fish. I also happen to have a copy of your messages to a retired teacher named Carol. So, there was I thinking all the time you respected me and found me sexy, interesting, amusing, honest and open - your words! I fell in love with a charmer, that was all. And you came out with that shit about, "Women who have too high an opinion of themselves"(which is supposed to be me) to a stranger. You stabbed me in the back!! I once called you weak. Say no more! The word "shallow"for you is too kind. Yes, and the truth about you had to surface. I've been truly honest with you, telling you my emotions, and have said nothing but positive feelings about you, blaming my immaturity for the break. I always gave unconditionally. How blind was I? All this crap about wanting more and no ties. You never had that from me. Your maturity and integrity that you try to convey couldn't be further from the truth. You stabbed me in the back within days to a stranger, after saying to me you wouldn't go on the dating sites, you'd just let things happen (insincere and a liar). Your last words leaving your apartment were, "I have many dislikes,"now I can see. I think you should take a look at yourself D. "High opinions"are

> far more honest than insincere, disloyal, hurtful, lying arseholes who have disingenuous opinions of their own. The above info was given to me freely. Be careful who you write to D. I'm lucky I have friends and I'm happy now I've seen who you really are. Finally, I pity your next relationship. I hope she doesn't keep her honest opinions to herself. Also, I suggest you don't take too long over your quest for a 'spark' as your next blow job, if you are lucky, is likely to be a toothless one in a nursing home!
>
> Jay"

My mailbox was quiet for a few weeks. I thought he might have blocked me in disgust; however, I received an unexpected response from him. I think he had been stewing on my Catfish for some time.

> "Dear Jay,
>
> Please know, re. an earlier message you sent, that I have no intention whatsoever of hurting you in any way. Always found you interesting, attractive, and fun. What you did to me, now I look back on it, was actually flattering in a way. And if a part of me was upset and I felt silly or hurt by it, well, probably I deserved! The Catfish film, I went back to buy, in the hope it was still there. It was. It's so interesting, truly. Anyway, you may not want to pursue meeting up which I shall understand. Let me know? Dx"

We had a couple of chatty messages about the COVID-19 pandemic beforehand. I told him I was in Richmond for a meeting with a friend. He wanted to meet for old time's sake. I suppose I still had a little piece of fondness for him. He also told me he had been bitten by a dog when he was at the cash machine and had to go to hospital for a dressing and tetanus jab. I laughed as dogs and Dennis were a disaster. And guess what? Sue was back in his life soon after we broke up, then six months later he broke it off because the relationship was going nowhere. The man is destined to be single.

Bloody exes named Sue are the bane of my life. Think I will change my name to Sue!

After I acknowledged his last message, he wrote again.

"Hey Jay, There's something about me I haven't told you. Though if I did tell you, you might well say 'too much information'! Also, that it's not important. Sadly, to me right now it IS important! Sorry to be so mysterious! I will tell you if you really want to know! It's a bit personal!

Dennis"

I couldn't help but feel that there might be a hint of karma in his message; I had a feeling it had to do with his prostate. He did get up for the loo a few times in the night. I responded.

"Dear Dennis, if it's personal, then I think it best if you leave me out of it. I believe you decided our relationship was over; therefore, there is no need to share personal info. Do you agree?

I'm a realist, and I believe in our 70s, our options in life become more limited. Trying to find the "The One" is becoming a mountain most of us are not fit enough to climb and if we do with someone younger, the chances are we will find it hard to keep up the pretence that we are still youthful. But who knows, never say never. Happy to meet for a coffee if I am in your area."

We met again at his favourite café and that coffee meeting did me the world of good. He tried his charm on me, with over-the-top compliments. I told him to cut out the crap, it didn't work on me anymore and I couldn't trust his sincerity. I prepared myself to leave, and he rose from his chair and tried to kiss me, but I leaned away and gave him a shoulder hug.

"Good luck with your search for "the One,"Dennis, and thanks for the coffee."

I walked briskly to my car, leaving him to pay the bill. I had nothing more to say to him; feelings of loss and grieving for the opportunity we both missed faded away that day.

NEXT!!!!

CHAPTER 19
CATFISH REFLECTION AND SUPPORT

I kicked myself for a few days after the Catfish "experiment", not sleeping, my appetite gone, struggling with my shame and disappointment. Had I really stooped that low to get my own back? It backfired on me for sure. Even as I write, the phrase, "a woman who has too high an opinion of herself" hurts my head. Did he hit a nerve? He did; our conversations were constantly in my thoughts. Perhaps I did mention too often things I was capable of and didn't show enough humility. I don't know. Being on the receiving end of someone who is judgemental is something most of us have experienced; it makes us question how we are seen by others. Maybe I should take on board his description of me, show more humility or admit I need other's opinions and perspectives. I know I came out of the Dennis situation the better person but doubt kept picking away at my thoughts.

I shouldn't keep beating myself up. Depression isn't something I generally suffer from. However, the way I was going, I was close to suffering one, relating my current state of mind to grieving over my late husband, which took three years of my life. This wasn't worth that kind of grief, I knew.

It was time to ask my girlfriends and Kitty to come over; I needed to find some perspective. They arrived armed with two bottles of wine and a bunch of yellow roses, chatting and laughing as they walked through the door. Once Penny had unwrapped the roses and filled the vase, she and Ann came to join me at the kitchen table.

"Is Maria and Kitty coming?" Ann reached for the crisps I had put out earlier in a glass bowl, taking a few and eating them out of her hand.

"Yes, I hope so."

"It has been too long since we were together, and I apologised for letting a man have priority over our friendship. It will never happen again." Ann poured the wine and gave me a head-and-shoulder hug.

As you can imagine, when I told them of my Catfish experiment, they were aghast!

Penny was the first to comment. "You did what! You catfished him? Oh my God, how?"

I explained that he had dumped me because he needed more spark, and a quieter life and couldn't see our relationship developing into love. He was still on a mission to find "The One."

"What? What does, 'The One' look like? And why did he take you to London to meet his family? Dick!" said Ann, who had started opening the second bottle of wine and then putting it in the wine cooler. I loved her angst; sometimes wish I could be as expressive as her.

"Anyway, tell more, how you go about catfishing someone," as she took two large gulps from her wine glass.

Maria arrived late, as usual, that girl would be late for her own funeral. Wearing her latest charity shop bargain, this Oxfam queen always looked a million dollars for less than ten. She had an eye for hanger appeal and coordinating accessories. Helped by her slim body and long wavy dark hair, she was a head turner. Tonight, she arrived in an abstract patterned dress with a crossover bodice, showing off her breasts. Earrings, necklaces, handbag, and shoes were all coordinated, picking out the orange in her dress. Her olive skin carries the colours I could never wear. We all admired her outfit as she gave us a catwalk twirl in my kitchen.

"French Connection £8 for the dress," she says, running the backs of her hands down the fabric. "£5 Russell & Bromley for the shoes. I already had the earrings, etcetera."

We all applauded her, trying not to feel too envious. If I managed to find something in a charity shop that appealed to me, you can guarantee it would be the wrong size or have some damage on it, certainly not a designer label. I'm too impatient to keep looking. Maria makes time to check out the eight charity shops in our nearest town, spotting the really good bargains.

Penny passed her a glass of wine. "We are here to talk about Jay's relationship breakup and her catfish experience. She needs us to help her make some sense of it all." Looking at me "Am I right?"

Maria looked puzzled. "Oh Honey, sorry to hear about the breakup. Dennis sounded like your perfect man. Who catfished you?"

The others were shaking their heads.

"What? Did he do it?" Looking puzzled again.

I sat next to her at the kitchen table. "Maria, no, he didn't; I did. I was so incensed about how he dumped me and his excuses. Plus, he said he wanted a quiet life and that he wouldn't be going on dating sites anymore. But he did!! I spotted him within three weeks on Plenty of Fish."

She looked shocked.

"So, I decided to set up a fake profile and see if I could hook him, and he responded within hours." I was holding a copy of his responses to my fake profile Carol's question, complete with his hurtful phrases.

"He lied to me Maria," as tears welled up in my eyes. "This is what he wrote when my catfish asked him what he did and did not like in a woman. I feel such a fool for doing it."

Ann passed me a tissue. While Maria hugged me. "You deserve better my lovely," then stroked my back.

"He's a Dick!" said Ann with venom in her voice.

Penny read the response and passed it to Ann. Penny looked at Ann as she read it. "I'm not saying you were wrong to catfish him, Jay; he deserved it; his comments are so out of order and arrogant. You are not someone who has too high an opinion of herself," she continued. "Out of interest, does he have many friends?"

I shook my head.

"Figures."

Kitty arrived. "Sorry, I had to take the dogs out; they had been shut in for most of the day. Have I missed anything?"

I had already shared my catfish story with my sister Kitty when I first received a response from Dennis. I needed to tell someone. She understood, but I got the usual lecture, telling me she didn't know why I kept putting myself through these disastrous relationships. Her view was that most men on dating sites were losers. Going from her own experience, which wasn't much, she couldn't cope with the games, ghosting and 'only wanting one thing,' as she would say. Kitty did suffer from depression and anxiety, and I could understand that the whole process was not easy for her. Until now, I had managed to bounce back from each setback, but Dennis was different. He well and truly got under my skin.

"Ah, you've told them?" The girls nodded. "Awful, isn't it?" She starts to go on about online dating sites.

"Kitty, don't," putting my hand up to stop her. She went quiet, but I could see she wanted to say more.

Ann throws the paper on the table while Penny continues, "He sounds very insincere, and all I can say is, it's a car crash avoided" (that phrase again). "And well done you for exposing him," before clinking my glass.

Ann is suppressing her anger, I can tell. "It's Dicks like him that makes us girls so nervous about dating, and men wonder why we have trust issues. Grrrr!" she growls.

"Well, good for you. He certainly underestimated your intelligence, Girl. What a twat!!" Kitty nodded with each phrase.

"The trouble is, Jay, you give men the benefit of the doubt too easily. You are too nice. Men prefer bitches. It's all about the chase." Ann finished pouring four glasses.

Penny empathised, "I know what it's like to throw yourself into a relationship that ticks many boxes for you. You end up giving of yourself too much, and if it is not reciprocated, you make allowances and ignore the signs, thinking that they feel the same when they don't. Sadly, when we get attached all the red flags are ignored and we think we can change them, we can't."

She hugged my shoulders and passed over my glass of wine. "There's a desire for them to please sometimes because you massage their ego, and they enjoy the attention without ever intending to be serious. They often know you have stronger feelings. And, sadly, they cannot keep up the pretence. It's natural to think they have used you when it is over. They haven't had the guts, to be honest, and you, maybe, missed the signs."

She added, "I truly think that many men don't mean to hurt and anyway a good relationship shouldn't feel difficult."

Penny always had a way of seeing things from both sides, and I needed her perspective.

We finished the second bottle and started laughing at my catfish experiment and the process I went through. I was taking jibes from the girls, who were comparing me with the film Catfish. My Girl Tribe was just the tonic I needed, and we promised each other to organise another evening together soon. It was long overdue.

"So, who's got some other news? I'm done with moaning; time to move on." I lifted my glass to the others. Only I noticed Ann staring into her glass as if she had shut herself off. I could see her steaming, but I totally misread her mood.

She looked up with a half-smile. "Well, it's my time to moan if that's okay?"

We all nodded politely, keeping silent to enable her to speak. After another swig of wine, she coughed. "I've got breast cancer." She sat in our silent void, looking for a reaction.

I spoke first. "I'm so sorry, Ann, sorry you had to hear all my crap when you have this to deal with." I walked around the table to her to hug her but she shied away.

"Don't make me cry; I've done enough crying," rubbing her forehead with both hands. "Hopefully, the mammary scan has discovered it early. I have an appointment for a pre-op discussion on options and procedures available to me with a specialist tomorrow and then he will operate, all being well, on Friday."

Penny, in shock, like the rest of us, stuttered, "That's so quick, Ann. I'm glad they are taking it seriously. I don't know what to say other than I think I speak for us all; we all love you, and we're shocked at this news. Please let us know how we can help you."

Ann half-smiled back. Penny continued, "Oh, do you want any of us to take you to your appointments tomorrow and Friday? I'm free."

"Its fine," looking more relaxed now. "My daughter knows everything and will be coming with me to all my appointments, but thank you."

Ann went on to explain that she might need distractions and the support of her friends during recovery. She didn't know yet if she would need Chemo or Radiotherapy. All would become clearer tomorrow, and she insisted that she didn't need loads of sympathy, to treat her as usual, like the crazy friend she is sometimes. She didn't want to say much more or make any assumptions. "I need to take each day at a time." Looking at me, "You can give me that hug now." I couldn't get around the table fast enough, and the others joined in too.

We all try to laugh, but deep down, we are so upset for her. I try desperately to put my self-pity of the last hour behind me. Ann's news is life-changing for her, and we have to support her. I vow to myself to recount only my funny dating episodes in the future when she is around.

I drank a lot that night, and I'm glad I did, as I slept better than I had for a long time, despite Ann's news. What is more, the following morning, I was hungry, a sign I had my appetite back. Rightly, I felt less hurt about my own situation and more for Ann's. A reminder, we never know what is around the corner for any of us. Health is everything and I must keep reminding myself. I needed perspective, and boy, did I get it last night.

THE HANGOVER

Incessant blind thumping in my head
Keeping me awake. Yeah, I should have
Drunk a gallon of water before bed,
That last tequila slammer was so bad.

Stupid arse, I call myself, you see
why the hammer won't decease. Doh!
"Dehydration" my mother's tone hits me
Hand on hips, sour face, you know.

Commitment was made to fall in the bed
But the room now spins like a top on its axis.
An immense effort to rise from near dead
Then to find my bloody sister is in the khazi.

Tripping obstacles of abandoned clothes
Mirror, distorted pictures, old hanging coat.
My bedrooms dim light makes it all worse.
Monday morning looming, time for sick note.

CHAPTER 20
FRIEND WITH BENEFITS
– PART 1

It was early December, and I was 68. I had nothing planned for Christmas except the usual family gatherings. It is this time of year when I miss having a partner the most, someone to join me, a social single man I can flirt with or start a friendship with. But alas, no events.

I was getting tired of being the single one at my married friends' gatherings, accepting every invitation in the hope I would meet someone interesting—no such luck. Parties are usually made up of couples who have been together for over 30 years and think they know all the answers to finding me the right man.

1. *"Have you joined any clubs where there are more men than women, golf maybe, camera club?"*
2. *"We know people who met on a holiday cruise, solo holiday, trekking."*
3. *"We've heard online dating is the best way to meet people."*
4. *"Do you do any sport? gym, tennis, table tennis, cycling, running, etcetera?"*
5. *"What about ballroom dancing?"*
6. *"Have you asked all your friends if they know anyone single?"*

7. *"We have a friend of a friend who is single, although he might be too old, too young, too shy, too poor, too grief-stricken, too drunk, too involved in the family, too into his golf and so on."*

I know they mean well, and I try to thank them for their advice, knowing I've heard it all before. Or I answer, "Been there, done that, worn the tee shirt." I ask myself, "Why don't you introduce me to one of your "TOOs" and let us see how it goes?"

I often leave early from these events, deciding it is too painful to mix with people who knew my husband well, speak fondly of him, and, at the same time, try to find solutions for my single status. Often, the women are more enthusiastic than the men. This makes me wonder if their menfolk are concerned that I might influence their wives to leave them. To be honest, some of them deserve it.

Today, I decided to give online dating another chance and to pay again on Match.com. I needed to feel more secure with my options. Certainly, ask more questions before meeting and understand aspirations and personal circumstances. After rejecting many of the likes from an assortment of men on my profile, I came across a 59-year-old from York. He had the one photo showing him propped up in a hospital bed with his arm heavily bandaged, raised in a hoist. Lovely smile and eyes. His profile description read, `"Hands up if you are disillusioned?"`

I laughed, as this was not your usual, `"… nice, honest guy looking for someone to spend time with, hopefully leading to a long-term relationship…"`

I responded to his question, `"That would be me then."`

An hour later, a message arrived in my inbox. `"Hi. Have you anything nice planned today?"`

I thought for a minute. `"Are you still in hospital? I don't have much on today. What time is visiting` only I cannot promise grapes; I hardly know you?" He replied with three laughing emojis.

"No, I am all fixed now. That photo was taken a few months ago. But thanks for the offer; it's the best one I have had all day☺." Next message:

What are you doing now?"

"I am actually in the kitchen, emptying my cupboard under the sink (it was smelly under there), trying to find the source."

He replied, "I can smell it from here, and you've missed a bit. Shall I rinse the cloth for you?"

I laughed to myself. This guy was fun, and I needed a bit of light relief in my life just now. He told me he was doing his annual tax return and was bored, needing a distraction, and my kitchen cupboard challenge was what he needed. We chatted for at least 30 minutes, and I eventually closed the chat as I was getting nowhere with my task. He said that was okay, and he enjoyed the banter.

I have not given much thought to Alan (that was his name) or our conversation yesterday. I have lots of little jobs I have set myself, including putting everything back in the cupboard after it dried out. The drain pipe was dripping slightly, and it just needed the connection screwing tight. Must admit I am pretty chuffed with myself for getting to the bottom of the problem without a man to help me.

"Good morning, how's the leak in the cupboard?" "I hope we haven't fallen out already.

We haven't had one of those kitchen dramas, have we, before we've met ☺?"

It was not until the afternoon that I found two texts from him in my inbox.

`"No, I'm just a busy girl, what you up to?"`

He responded immediately. `"Not much, do you fancy a chat on the phone, that's if you are not too busy?"`

I took a little while to respond as I didn't want to appear too eager. `"Okay, once I've finished my ironing."`

He sent another emoji `"☺,4 p.m. okay?"`

`"Perfect."`

I am trying desperately to keep my responses short as I believe one of my past mistakes is giving away too much about myself too soon. According to Kitty, I should leave a little bit of mystery, as men love the chase. But I'm not good at mind games and unsure if I can keep them up. I'm a mature woman with lots to say, and it is hard not to engage in meaningful conversations. Clipped sentences are not me.

He gave me his telephone number and I phoned after 4 p.m.

"Nice to put a voice to the photos."

I start to update him on my successful leak cure. We are both laughing at the absurdity of our first conversation. He sounds soft and interested in what I have to say, telling me that he owns an Electrical and Aircon maintenance company and is used to women not fixing simple things for themselves. He congratulated me but advised me it wasn't a good idea to tackle electrical problems. I notice the chuckle in his voice; he doesn't sound patronising; he seems to want to make light of everything. It is refreshing.

"Do you have family?" I ask.

"Son and Daughter; both have partners and my daughter plans to marry in May. I'm cooking Sunday lunch for them all this weekend; pray for me. I'm not used to cooking roast dinners, and I might cheat with the Yorkshires." He chuckles. "Roasties should be good though."

I try reassuring him: "I'm sure they will all muck in and appreciate anything you do. Besides, there is always M&S; you can prepare everything from there."

"Wow, I knew there would be a good reason to contact you. Great idea—take the pressure off." He then changes the subject and apologises for having to leave the call as he has a client to go to at 5 p.m.

I am so relaxed and happy I have had such a friendly encounter with someone who sounds genuine and hasn't asked what I'm looking for in a man, and there is no mention of future aspirations or past relationships. I vow I will keep things simple and enjoy the attention and fun elements. After all, Alan is nine years younger than I am; our liaison is not likely to progress to anything meaningful. Besides, he is still working, and I doubt he will retire soon.

But why shouldn't I consider a much younger man? Nine years is only a number. Society and some religions have considered it the norm for men to date or marry younger women, but not the other way around. Men will often lie about their age to achieve their desires. However, the irony here is that men my age are often too old for me in looks, attitude, dress, and energy. Women live longer and are often healthier and more adventurous.

When my friend, who is 48, was being chased by a 35-year-old man on the Hinge dating app (not one I have tried yet), she confided in me. And to my surprise, she didn't consider the age gap a problem, nor the prospect of casual relationships. So why should it be a problem for me? Maybe I should follow what men do, lie about my age, and move the age preference slider left. Anyway, in the meantime, I will enjoy my Match.com liaison.

Thursday, Friday and the weekend passed. It was Monday morning.

`"Happy Monday 😊!"`

Again, it was the afternoon before I logged on to the dating app inbox.

`"Hi, did you survive the roast dinner?"`

The text came back, `"Yes, I LOVE M&S!! Sorry, I cannot text more. I am on my way to a job."` Five minutes later, `"I am outside the customer's house. Are you free for a coffee tomorrow at 3 p.m.? If so, you name where."`

In the evening, I texted him to arrange to meet at a Costa café halfway between us. We didn't continue texting.

When I arrived at the venue, he was standing by the counter. His smile immediately attracted me as he looked over his shoulder at me. He initially seemed a little nervous, putting his hand on my shoulder and asking what drink I would like. Once served, he carried a tray with our drinks to the first floor. It was quieter there, away from the noise of the coffee machine and more private.

"Well, here we are after our crazy few text messages," I started the conversation.

"You can say that again." He smiled and passed me my coffee. I was so surprised at how attractive he was. He was six feet tall, had wavy, mid-brown hair, and had signs of grey, green eyes and clean hair. His shoulders are not too broad but manly. No sign of a beer belly… and that smile! Perfect, I thought. But why was he here?

He initially asked what I did during retirement, as he wasn't quite sure what he would do with his time; work kept him busy and left him little time for hobbies. He enjoyed cycling but not in groups or racing. Rugby on TV mainly, although his son would occasionally join him on both. He was now a grandad of an 18-month-old little girl; it was evident that this little person was a delight for him. His daughter was planning her wedding in May. It was refreshing to hear from a man who viewed his life so positively, even though he was a little frustrated with dating sites.

We both recounted some of our funny stories and agreed that online dating was difficult to navigate, time-consuming, and sometimes addictive, with very little success. I told him I had dated many men, mainly coffee dates, and was getting to the point of giving up my search that way. I noted how philosophical he was, always turning a negative into a positive.

"Well, we wouldn't be having a nice chat now if we hadn't gone on Match.com." He smiled looking into his cup, stirring his coffee. "I've had a relationship which lasted four years. We met through Match.com. Unfortunately, we drifted apart; she was from Belarus, and it's possible there was a cultural reason we couldn't agree on a future."

He gazed out of the window almost wistfully, his green eyes highlighted by the sun streaming through the window. "She didn't want to live with me in York, preferred Leeds where her work and friends were, and didn't have a car, which meant me going to hers all the time. I couldn't persuade her she would be better off living with me. I understood, but our conversations were frustrating." He continued after a sip of his coffee.

"Prior to her, I had a couple of short flings with French girls. I know," he laughed. "Before you ask, yes, I did go over to France for dates. I have a thing about foreign ladies: I love getting to know different cultures. One of them was crazy but taught me a few things in bed. And even in my 50s, I still had a few things to learn."

As he winked across the table at me, I could feel a twitch in my knickers, saying to myself, for goodness sake girl, keep your composure. The more he spoke, the more I was attracted, but the age difference kept picking at my brain. Why is he here? Maybe I am a distraction, amusement, an ego boost. Then again, he could be genuinely attracted to me. I tried to ignore the nagger in my head and concentrate on the moment, be wrapped up in his experiences and learn from them.

I told him about my travels and how I wanted to visit more exotic and challenging places, such as Eastern Bloc countries and South Africa. He listened with interest and admitted he wanted to do more, but other things, work, and his aging father had priority now.

We talked about our music taste, and I was pleasantly surprised to find he had very similar taste, almost as eclectic as mine. We both loved Pink Floyd; his favourite track was 'Wish You Were Here.' What a coincidence, I was only playing that track recently, so I suggested we exchange some music on WhatsApp for a little light entertainment.

After nearly two hours of chatting non-stop, he said he had to visit a Fire Stove shop across the road before it closed, explaining to me he was in the middle of refurbishing his 1970s house. He admitted he was finding it hard to be motivated to decorate. "I'm usually shattered by the time I get home."

We said our goodbyes in the car park, and I leaned forward to hug him. To my surprise, he held my shoulders and pecked me on the lips.

"Shall we do this again?" he said almost shyly.

"Yes, that would be nice. Let me know when, I have a more flexible diary."

I then gave him a little hug before returning to my car. I nearly floated back to my car which was parked around the corner, while he walked across the road to the Fire Stove shop. I looked back to see how he walked and was pleased to say I fancied him even more.

While driving home, I called Kitty. "You will never guess what? I've just left a coffee date with a gorgeous man who lives in York, and he wants to see me again!!" The teenager in me came out again.

This is another example of my lack of confidence. Why should I feel surprised a man is interested in me? He should go home and say to himself, "I've met this incredible woman who wants to see me again." Why don't I appreciate my own value? Nor should the age difference matter. We both exchanged messages to say we were home and had agreed it was an excellent way to spend a Tuesday afternoon.

Over the next week, we chatted most mornings. I noted that the conversations became flirty as time went on, with sexual innuendo and banter. On one occasion, I described the view outside my kitchen window as I sat at the table.

He replied, `"What a lovely view you describe, made all the more lovely when I come up behind you to kiss your neck."` This sentence excited every bone in my body. I loved that he had a romantic, sensitive side.

He suggested we meet for coffee or a drink again and would be in touch once his Aircon Services business had been inspected. Apparently, this was something which put him under a bit of strain. His biggest clients insisted on him being safety checked every year.

It was mid-December, and I wandered around the city's annual German Christmas Market on a cold, dull day. I decided that a warm mulled wine would be a tonic as I tried to get inspiration for my family's Christmas presents. I sat looking at my phone as the intoxicating atmosphere of Christmas music, lights and smells surrounded me.

I remembered Alan's last message and the kissing on my neck. I knew deep down that there was no future in a serious relationship (our age gap bugging me again), but I would love to explore the idea of having a short-term intimate fling with him. I started to write to him. Probably my first big mistake. Why, oh why, didn't I let things take their natural course and not chase?

I texted him, "Hey, I've been thinking. I know, dangerous, lol. It makes sense to me that there is no long-term future for us. However, I'm alone, as are you. We don't need too much extra in our lives, that is until either of us finds "The One". While we continue our search (I cannot believe I'm writing this.) I am happy that we make each other smile - nothing heavy. And I'm really cool with that.

Proposition: You don't have to read further if you dare not. I wanted to suggest this ages ago.

I could do with "rewiring" occasionally, and I'm sure you could do with keeping your hand in, too. No bills, no contracts/ties lol no families or friends involved. Just us with our FWB. Short-term is fine. Or just see. I've been told I'm good at what I do, too. I need a lovely, honourable man occasionally. I'm hiding now behind my keyboard, blushing. Never done anything like this before.

Block me if this is outrageous.

J 😗"

That evening, my mobile phone pinged, a note on WhatsApp.

Alan: "Just got back home."

"Wow, that's some message J!

I don't feel uncomfortable with it. I'd say that at our stages in life, whatever works is good. And I must admit I'm perked up 😊 x"

We texted briefly on WhatsApp. He went on to say,

"I just want you to know that what you have written was flattering, but I will not put you under any pressure if you decide to change your mind." Again, he showed signs of consideration. I was a bit nervous, struggling to speak.

"Okay, thanks for saying that; I will contact you tomorrow."

The following morning, I sent him a description of my body. Oh, I cringe now in some ways, yet I am confident enough to include it in my book. I suppose there is a hint of vanity in this 68-year-old woman, the confidence that comes from snaring a Toy Boy lover. From this point, I started to refer to him as 'my Toy Boy'.

MY BODY

"Hi, it's lovely hearing your voice today. Just a little 😺 amusement: to be read in private and for your eyes only, a glass of wine is essential.

I started writing this earlier. Thought it might be amusing to describe my body so you can imagine me in my bath. I know it takes the mystery away, but it's worth saying it's not perfect in an erotic way, with no illusions. It does have its plus points though. Let's face it, none of us are perfect. Yet, I know I'm sensual with it and women of our age can wear better than you think. Have to say it makes me horny even now just to know you are reading this and can imagine me lying here naked in bubbles as I smile and stroke myself.

Skin: As you know, I have fair skin, lots of freckles, and no body hair, lol. I am slightly creased in places. My stomach is almost flat and smooth, with no stretch marks or other anomalies. I'm not muscular, just soft and womanly, or maybe girly, to look at.

Breasts: Are round. I have one breast slightly smaller than the other and one nipple slightly larger (that one likes attention). I'm fairly pert and a size 36c (a mouthful/handful). I used to dream of having larger ones, but I am so pleased they are not now. Some ladies do suffer from gravity. I know I'm lucky.

Legs: go all the way up to where they should be, smooth with slight cellulite. I can still wear holdup stockings. Have a couple of scars around my ankles. I bruise easily because of the tabs I take. But still capable of wrapping themselves around.

Bum: round not yet sagging. Lol enjoys spooning, something about that after intimacy moments, being cuddled.

Arms: Yes, they have bingo wings, but they're not bad for my age. Still capable of a big hug.

Important bit: The perfect part of me ☺, cute, snug fit, very neat with the right amount of tidy blonde fluff:-) Moist! Likes oral, too. (Sometimes it makes me giggle).

Lips: Soft with a warm mouth and exploring tongue.

Hands: I love to stroke and softly caress all body parts.

Other: All my own teeth and hair. I have been known to fart occasionally during intercourse, lol. (All that squeezing!). Passion killer for some lol. Plus side, I multi orgasm.

Me: I don't care anymore what people think about my body or my enjoyment of physical affection. I'm open about who I am and what I want, and that's what counts. If you ever have to apologise for who you are at our age, it's a recipe for unhappiness. I will admit teasing a little turns me on. Imagine it might bring a smile to your face, too.

Maybe you think this is plain wacky. It's no matter, I had fun doing it. It reminds me I'm alive and a lucky girl. I'm a realist, emphatic, and very aware that there are lots of ways to give each other satisfying pleasure. It's the intimacy that matters to me.

There is no need to respond. I've had my orgasm knowing you have read it. 😃

J xx"

On reflection, what was I doing? Maybe experimenting, living a fantasy, trying to prove something to myself; was it sheer vanity or a horny old lady hitting on a younger man because she thinks she has a chance of winning him over? I feel so embarrassed writing this part of my story. However, it is essential to highlight my hopeless narrative and determination to grab this man's attention.

Alan:"I am at home, and I am reading it, I'll keep you posted 😊😉"

Alan: "Wow, that's a lovely message. You painted a picture of a very sensual woman. Maturity becomes you and is very attractive to me. X"

Alan: "Play for me! xx"

Jay: "Play or pray? 😂"

Alan: "Ha-ha, too late for that one 😊 Imagine my hand gently running over you, feeling your underwear, going around your curves, teasing. xx"

Jay: "Yes, I can but I've no underwear on at the mo. Just out of shower 😜"

Alan: "Oh, I can adapt 😜"

Jay: 😈 Devil!

Alan: "You're soft and very clean"

Jay: "Of course, and a little damp. Lol"

Alan: "Mmm, I can feel."

Alan: "Kissing your warm mouth."

Alan: "Hand softly touching you, feeling you stir."

Jay: "As much as I'm enjoying this virtual seduction and don't want it to end, I've gotta get stuff done. 🙀🙈🙃"

Geeze, I was steaming after this first experience of sex-texting with him; I could hear his soft voice in my head and imagined his hands on me. Wandering around my bedroom, rereading his messages, I doubted myself. What was I thinking? What had I started? How ridiculously forward and maybe immature I was. Would I be seen as cheap? What if I turn out to be a disappointment? Will I get hurt again? Talk about setting yourself up for a fall, you stupid woman. Who am I kidding?!

But out of all the dates I had so far, he was by far the most appealing: nice-natured, good-looking, nicely dressed, self-sufficient, owned a business, no baggage and sensual. The whole package, except he was nine years younger!

I tried to compose myself in preparation for going to work. I had started a part-time job with a friend of my daughters. She needed help with her sales and marketing strategy. Sounds posh, doesn't it? The reality is she needed someone to talk to potential clients about her consultancy business. She was a lovely lady, but she didn't have much experience in selling, but however, was brilliant at what she did. I had a lot of respect for her.

When I returned home, I received a WhatsApp message from Alan, suggesting we meet for a drink and a chat wherever suited me.

We agreed to meet the following day; I suggested a pub halfway, but then somehow we ended up deciding I meet at his house. I felt better with that suggestion as I could always leave if I felt uncomfortable as I had made a mistake in the past of inviting men to mine first and having difficulty in turfing them out. Yes, you can say how fool hardy of me to trust men early in a relationship, but I always felt I could get myself out of most tricky situations with my gift of making them think they decided to leave.

I felt we had already set ourselves up with the expectation of being intimate (that would be my doing I suppose). I asked him what I should bring. He told me he had a bottle of wine and to bring myself. I even asked him if he liked nice underwear! What the 'effing was I doing? I think I must have lost all sense of fear or what my mother would have called, "gay abandonment". I was going for it!! My first Friend with Benefits. However, if I am honest with myself, some of the relationships in the previous chapters could have been described similarly as more lovers with little friendship.

He texted me his address and said he would confirm a time once he had finished work. At about 4 p.m. I received a message from Alan.

"Hi J 😊 Can we postpone tonight?"

"I'm not sure it is the right thing for us to do. It might be that I'm just feeling worn out due to work being relentless and I've got a busy day ahead, I'm not sure.

Let's keep in touch, though, and maybe I'll feel different soon.

Xx"

I would be lying if I said I wasn't gutted. I had prepared myself all day mentally and relived his hands touching me and the feel of his soft mouth on mine. How should I respond to this? I told him I understood and was sure we would sort something out in the future when things settled down for him. But I was still interested in pursuing what we had started.

A few days later, I dropped him a note to see if he was okay and his workload had improved. I tried not to sound desperate, but I wanted to know if he was still interested, as I had the offer of another date coming up. I pondered at the idea that he must have got cold feet.

"Morning J.

Sorry I haven't been in touch. I enjoyed our chats and banter too. 😊

I'm just not in the right place for a relationship at the moment and feel that maybe you were thinking we could move ahead with this. A chat and a cuppa is good though.

Hope you can understand that.

A xx"

What a turnaround. I was so confused. Maybe Mr Perfect was not as adventurous as I thought. I answered.

"It's okay Alan. I liked you and thought your raison d'etre was a relationship or Friend with Benefits and you needed more from your last one. Flirting was nice, I could easily sleep with you. Maybe wise, as you know, we girls get attached when we are intimate. Lol. Thought you and I might have a spark. I'm such a loon.

You have my number. We can go somewhere fun for coffee another time. I'm considering a request from another potential date on Match.com. Let's see how I go.

Have a great day XX"

He immediately responds. One thing I have learned about Alan is that he always has the last word in text, yet in face-to-face conversation, he is the opposite. I'm not sure why.

Alan: "Just looking up raison d'etre 😊 We did hit it off, and I do realise that women become more involved once things become intimate, which is why I need to be responsible when it comes to that. Away to friends for the weekend too (hopefully for a chill out after a hectic two weeks).

Let me know when / where to meet for another catch up, maybe you can de-brief me on this new guy. Or I can give you my man's viewpoint on him. 😊

You have a great one too; looks like mine will be a wet one (got to clip big cables 25 metres up a hill in Grassington).

Xx"

Oh boy, another slap in the face. Yet I was not ready to give up. He had already given me a reason to hope: *"... we did hit off."* I decided to give myself a break from pursuing him for now and concentrate on Christmas.

I could not resist contacting him a week before Christmas to ask how his Christmas shopping went. To my surprise, he responded immediately. He said he wasn't looking forward to it and wanted to cancel Christmas. It would just be him and his dad. Dad played a big part in his world and I had the impression he felt he'd had to please him most of his life. Alan's mum left him, his dad and his brother when they were 10 and 12.

His Dad had custody and struggled to be affectionate with his boys; he fulfilled the parental practical care side of their lives and made sure the boys shared the household chores. There were no extra-curricular activities like football or rugby unless it was through school.

Alan remarked that his dad was more preoccupied with working and always seemed tired and grumpy. Not until his sons left home did his dad embark on a relationship with another woman; even then they didn't live together. His mother had a soft nature, more adventurous. His dad ignored her needs most of the time, which made Alan more empathic towards his mother, leaving them for he was a difficult man to live with.

Some of this family history and experiences explain many of Alan's traits, such as leaving his wife when the children had left school, not committing to a replacement partner, and drifting from one temporary relationship to another.

The Belarus girlfriend was the nearest to a permanent relationship, but he didn't consider compromises to make it work. Her life needs were not as important as his business, and he felt he had more to offer in the relationship than she did. The fact that she was an intelligent woman and a talented musician made me not surprised that she wanted to be close to her circle of friends, her students, and the music circuit. Alan had very little to offer on that score; like his dad, he considered his practical breadwinner side to be enough. The old saying "all work and no play makes Alan a dull boy" fits. Yet I felt I wanted to know him more on a deeper level and physically. My late husband was an engineer, I could see the similarities. I have always loved the strong, quiet types, and he fits that description in my mind.

I told Alan not to give up on Christmas, make it low-key, take his dad out, and do something different. He agreed he needed to think outside the box.

He then inquired about my Christmas plans, which I kept brief. Then he started flirting with me, sending cheeky emojis.

Alan: "So sexy lady, what have you got planned for this weekend?"

Jay: "Nothing much, catching up on Christmas shopping mainly."

Alan: "Are you around this evening?"

Jay: "Yes."

Alan: "Fancy getting together for a catchup? Up to you, no pressure."

Jay: "Why don't you come round here, I bought a couple of nice steaks this morning; I'll make us a meal. Nice to have the company on a dreary Friday night."

Alan: "Great idea, thanks, that would be nice. What time? I'll bring a bottle."

To say I was excited would have been an understatement. I suddenly started rushing around the house like a woman possessed, tidying away the clothes drying on the radiators and clothes airer, emptying out the rubbish, clearing the coffee table of crisp packets, mugs and tissues, disinfecting the sink, putting a toilet roll on its holder rather than it sat on the floor, replacing the mascara-stained towels in the bathroom for clean ones.

Then planning what to wear. I didn't want to be too obvious with a come-hither look. Red stripes could have been considered a warning, like the red-backed spider, do not touch for some, so I opted for a black woven fabric dress with a few red and white stripes above the hem and on the sleeves. It clung to my body in all the right places. However, I decided my hidden 'come on' was the stockings and suspenders I secreted beneath. The hem was at knee length, showing off my legs when I crossed them. The high heels were the maximum I could wear, otherwise I was in danger of breaking an ankle before we got to the meal.

He arrived at 5 p.m., casually smart, wearing a light khaki-green jumper that matched his eyes. He was smiling and handing me his bottle at the same time. "My favourite, Malbec. I hope you like it?" He kissed me on the cheek.

We were both a little nervous. I tried not to stare at him too much and looked in the cupboard for two wine glasses. I could barely reach the top shelf. He leaned over my head and took them easily from their position in the middle. His aftershave was almost intoxicating. His height was clearly way above my 5'5" plus 4" heels.

I suggested it was a bit early to eat, and we went into the sitting room to relax and chat with our wine. We sat next to each other without any thought. It seemed the right thing to do. It was easy talking with him and he gave me an update on his Christmas dinner plans, taking his dad to a favourite pub.

I was smiling at him, agreeing it was a good thing for both of them. Then, out of the blue, he asked if he kissed me. A sort of choking grunting sound came out of my mouth. He didn't try to translate, held my chin and gave me another tender kiss, then held me in his arms and kissed deeply, his tongue exploring my mouth. I reciprocated. It was amazing, we were so in tune with each other. His hands started to go down my legs, and all of a sudden, he stopped and sat back, chuckling as if mocking me.

"This is a nice surprise. Is this your normal Friday night attire?"

I replied, "Of course it is - makes a change from jeans."

He smiled again, returned to the kissing, and continued to move his hand down my leg. I cannot remember who suggested the bedroom; all I remember is that my shoes had been kicked off in the sitting room, and his jumper was on the sofa.

Once in the bedroom, he slowly removed my clothes, kissing me on parts of my skin as they became available then on the neck. He removed my bra and started kissing my breasts and sucking each nipple in turn. I could feel my wet vagina twitching and my body aching for a long overdue, satisfying fuck. He sat on the edge of the bed as I knelt down and started to undo his belt and trousers. While he removed his own shirt, I fondled his penis and was pleased he was already erect. It was very warm and felt lovely. With my other hand, I leaned over and searched for a condom in my bedside cabinet drawer.

Our lovemaking (sex) was as synergetic as our kissing; we both instinctively knew what the other wanted. We moved to various positions and gave oral; it seemed so natural. I actually reached an orgasm when his hot tongue flicked my clitoris, trembling and calling out, "That's amazing, do not stop."

He groaned occasionally but wasn't vocal. I knew from his sounds that either he was happy with what I was doing or he was happy doing things to me. After a while, he seemed to be getting more and more near climaxing, then he spoke.

"Squeeze my nipples as hard as you can, don't hold back, really hard; it raises my excitement."

I did as he said and he made a few noises as if he was hurting and then sped up his movements to a crescendo and ejaculated. Accompanied by heavy breathing he murmured, "Oh yes!" before rolling over onto his back. I rolled into his side with one leg over his and my head and shoulder cradled into one of his arms. We lay there for some time, stroking each other without a word. The silence was broken by the dishwasher pinging in the kitchen, warning me the washing cycle had ended. We both laughed.

Alan moved over to look at his watch.

"Hey, did you stay there was steak, or was that it?" he laughed, as I did in return,

I took my clothes and went into the bathroom and left him to dress in the bedroom as I needed to clean up, then realised we hadn't used the condom! "Not again," I said to myself, hoping he'd not got any diseases. I could not bear visiting that STI clinic again. When I looked in the mirror, my face was bright pink and my eye makeup was smudged, looking like a pink panda. I didn't bother to do a full restoration; wiping away the smudges was enough.

I found him in the kitchen pouring another two glasses of wine. We chatted about my house, family and neighbours, why I moved into the area, and why I do not have any regrets about moving.

The meal was a simple grilled steak with oven chips and a side salad. I cheated with the ready-made pepper sauce. He seemed to appreciate it but I struggled a bit, unable to eat it all. I think my adrenaline was still running at full power. He was happy to finish my steak.

We retired to the sitting room and discussed his ex, who worked for a nursing home. He told me about how they met and how he now felt that he went along with everyone's expectations that they would get married. He admitted he experienced cold feet and contemplated cancelling the wedding. The pleaser in him took over, and he fulfilled his promise. His two children were a bonus. She took responsibility for the primary parental duties. He worked really hard, building a business and renovating and modernising their family home in his spare time; he had eight vans and 16 employees and decided that this was enough growth for him. However, he claimed that his wife thought he lacked ambition and could have expanded and diversified. I had the feeling she felt disappointed in his laid-back nature.

He drank most of the wine in his glass and sat closer to me. "Shall we do it again?" His green eyes darted towards my legs, which he then pulled both over his knees with his big hands.

"What now?" thinking I hadn't understood what he was asking.

"Yes, now, I think I can do it again. That's if you want to."

It must have been the wine making me so brazen, as I stood up and grabbed him by the hand and dragged him upstairs, sitting on the edge of the bed and waiting to see what his next move would be. He removed his watch again and slowly undid his shirt while I watched. I hadn't studied his body the first time; it was good to have the time to take in his muscles and almost hairless chest. I loved what I saw. He was probably the manliest man I had ever had sex with. Slowly, he undid his belt and removed his trousers. All six feet of him stood before me in his boxers and socks.

"Very nice but you haven't finished," I look at his socks, laughing. He quickly whips them off, including boxers. He looks amazing and very erect.

"Now your turn," as he sits beside me on the bed, his penis already excited and twitching. I feel under pressure now, sitting next to this beautiful man; my 68-year-old body can't compete. Thankfully, the light is dim from the one table lamp. He might not notice my bingo wing arms and the cellulite peeking through the tops of my stockings. I've set myself up now. What if he asks me to remove my stockings? I am so overcome with nerves now. My mouth feels as dry as dust.

Struggling at first to pull off my dress over my head, my necklace caught on a button. I must have looked really awkward, like the Hunchback of Notre Dame, not exactly making this moment look sensual. Eventually, he came to my aid, and there I stood in my stockings, suspenders, panties, and bra (all matching, of course), trying to look confident and disguise my trembling.

I remembered to put my panties over the suspenders, a trick a friend told me: the panties will save the day if the fastener breaks; also if you want to keep the stockings on during sex, it's easier. I stood before him for a while; all these things were going through my head, trying not to grimace simultaneously. Please don't study me too much, I pleaded in my head as he sat there quietly stroking himself.

"Really nice," he said in a soft tone. "Now come here."

I sat next to him, and he kissed my neck and, put one of his hands inside my bra and, revealed my nipple, then circled his tongue around it. I was quivering with excitement for the slower pace was almost driving me mad. Automatically, I traced his thigh with my hand and stroked him between his legs.

He returned my hand to the bed and said, "It's my time. You will have yours soon."

This second session was on a whole different level to the first, which I suppose was pure lust then. On this occasion, he slowly explored my body both with his hands and his hot tongue. Overcome with erotic images, I didn't feel embarrassed anymore, totally ecstatic. I groaned a lot and giggled when he licked my vagina. I was running like a river, telling him I was cuming at one point, and he groaned, too. He was considerate and gentle, seeming to know what would please me. I loved his attention to my breasts, too.

Once I had reached a high, he turned over onto his back and placed my hand on his balls; obviously, this was my cue to give him attention. And I certainly did my best, for his body was more delightful to explore than any other man's. Thankfully, he doesn't have a hairy back; I struggle with those, not exactly an attractive feature for me, but Alan had very little hair, and what he did have in the pubic area was soft and silky to the touch, not hard, like wire wool. And yes, I did give him a blow job and can honestly report it was as much a pleasure for me as for him.

He stopped me from getting him to ejaculate too soon. "I want this to last; don't rush."

We then both moved to a 69 position and pleasured each other. Eventually, after the amazing reciprocal touching, licking and sucking, I sat on top of him. I felt it was my turn to take the lead, and he seemed pleased.

At this point in my writing, I question myself as to how much graphic description I should write. Is it not better to use your own imagination? Or am I assuming my readers and Girl Tribe will know what the next stage would be? I sometimes struggle at the thought of people I know reading this; maybe, to them, it is a horror movie in my mind. Yet I know deep down that what I experienced was a beautiful thing, and it would be a shame to ridicule it or consider it as pornographic.

While striding him, I repeated the hard squeezing of his nipples, and he ejaculated with a more triumphant groan than before. Again, we both fell into the same position as before, my leg over his and him cradling my head on his shoulder. We dozed and then chatted for a short while until he leaned over and retrieved his watch.

"Sorry, I have to go. I have an early appointment with a client tomorrow. He is only free Saturday morning, and we keep missing each other."

He quickly got dressed. I didn't dress; I grabbed a towel. He gave me a kiss and smiled, "Happy Christmas."

I could kick myself sometimes, for I replied. "Thanks for the early Christmas present."

He laughs and leaves. Closing the door behind him, I lean my back on it.

"Why am I thanking him?" I shout at myself, standing against the door for ages, thinking about what has happened that night, how two sessions of sex in the same evening could be so different and exciting. I also feel there are other things we could have done but held back. Nevertheless, the synergy between us was an absolute delight. Everything felt normal, not forced.

I slept like a baby for the first five hours and then couldn't stop thinking of him. What did he think of me? Was this a spontaneous one-off? What next? He would be a hard act to follow, would I be too? All I knew was I wanted more. Besides, I enjoyed his company too, his smile and his voice. The whole package. Except his age! There I go again.

GREEN EYES

I met a tall man of a gentle kind.
His head filled with future dreams,
Came to me with green eyes.
What may these eyes want of me?
His years and looks mystifying,
For I'm not the woman in his dreams,
I'm sure of this, as he awaits a kiss.

I'm impatient for his touching,
For my tremble is hard to disguise.
"Take my hand," he whispers softly.
"We have no reason to fear,
We are both here for a reason.
I'll be gentle with you, trust me.
Come the revolution, everything will be fine."

"I'm good at what I do," I tell him
Drowning in those green pools,
Abiding by my reckless instincts.
A mouth and lips dry as dust
Yet I'm as moist as a river below.
He strokes my hot thigh in recognition,
My inhibitions smiling back at him,

Mesmerised by reflection in his eyes.
He holds my shoulders in his hands,
Assisting me in my willingness
As my wild thoughts prepare for his hard form.
My neck, hot lips, his kisses mmmm!
Our bodies hungry for the tasting.
Yes, we came here for a reason.

Alan and I exchanged a few messages, but nothing that represented reminiscing over our night of passionate sex. It was starting to feel as I suspected, just a one off and no encouragement to repeat. I hoped the memory wouldn't fade too fast

I met my Girl Tribe on a Saturday evening at a local wine bar. I was dying to tell them what had happened but a part of me felt ashamed and protective of the experience. I could not chance to spoil the memory with their 'dishing the advice of selling myself too cheap' and how could I break my quest for "The One" and settle for a "Friend With Benefits" comment? I decided today was not the day. I would savour this one for a while. Maybe there would be another meeting.

Leading up to Christmas, his messages became short and unengaging. I felt hurt and kept thinking he might have found someone else. I kept my messages light and asked how he was doing with his Christmas shopping. No reply. Therefore, I assumed he was busy or didn't want to engage in conversation. I decided to back off. We exchanged Christmas greetings, and that was it.

Christmas came and went. All the time, I couldn't stop thinking of him. Not knowing the reason for his ghosting me was driving me mad. I checked in again.

Jay: "Morning 😊 How was Christmas? Did you and Dad have a lovely meal at the pub?"

Alan: "Yes, thanks, but it was a bit cold when it arrived - think they were short-staffed. Dad doesn't mind; he is so slow, and most of his meals are cold by the time he finishes. Lol. Otherwise, yes all went well. Saw the kids on Boxing Day and went for a walk. Son has bought a crazy pup which entertained us most of the day."

We chatted for most of the morning, agreeing on many of the crazy Christmas traditions most of us put up with. There was no mention of why he was absent over the last two weeks. He then started to flirt, first with an aubergine emoji and then with a peach. I responded with a devil emoji.

Alan: "Where are you? I'm still in bed."

Jay: "I had a rough night, so I'm having a lay-in."

Alan: "That's nice. Fancy a play? Are you on Facetime? We could video chat."

Jay: "We could, but I'm a mess 😌"

Alan: "Don't worry about that; I've already seen you in a mess, don't forget, and I wasn't petrified. Lol"

Jay: "Okay, give me 5 minutes."

I jumped out of bed and rushed to the bathroom, cleaning remnants of yesterday's makeup and panda eyes, putting a little slip-type nightie on. As I was finishing brushing my teeth, the ringing tone was coming through my phone. My heart raced and my mouth went dry. Pushing my hair behind one ear, I answered. There he was, bare-chested, smiling and wearing glasses. I wasn't used to seeing him in glasses. He still looked good.

Alan: "You are dressed?"

Jay: "No, it's a nightie. Are you naked?"

From there, he asked me to be naked, too, and to describe how I felt stroking my breasts. My body was still partially covered by the duvet, yet somehow, I felt more exposed than when I was standing in front of him in the dim light of the table lamp. I decided to close the blackout blind and put the bedside table lamp on.

Jay: "Just a minute. I'm closing my blinds. I don't want the neighbours to see. I will put a lamp on instead."

I felt much better in this light. I know, crazy that I should feel so bashful about my appearance, but I did.

Alan: "Now, where were we? Well, I am excited just to see you, are you okay with this?"

He pointed his phone to his penis, which was erect. I nodded and pushed the duvet down so he could see my breasts.

We continued with our virtual arousal actions for about half an hour, describing how our bodies felt, him masturbating and me probing my vagina for him to see. It wasn't long before he wanted to know if I was orgasming and he sped up his own actions until he ejaculated onto his stomach. It all felt a bit surreal and I couldn't help but feel he got more out of it than I did. However, I was just glad we were back on speaking terms and I recognised that my offer of Friends with Benefits was all part of his expectation.

He asked me if I had done anything like this before. I said I hadn't; that it was an interesting experience, but I preferred the real thing. He laughed out loud. We told each other what we had planned that day. He was working. For over a month, we chatted most days, some sex text and banter. We used the video a few times, but it never felt satisfying for me, although I was always glad to hear his voice and see his body.

One morning he asked me if I was still on the dating site. I told him I was, but not very proactive, more reactive, I had a couple of chats with men, and that was all. I had noticed he was still on the dating site and every time I looked, he was "live", possibly searching or chatting with other women, which I suppose riled me a bit. Who am I joking? It made me physically sick, because I knew I felt a connection with him. I felt jealous.

I had to accept that I had no hold over him, and I knew it wouldn't be long before he met someone more his age or younger. He was a catch in my eyes, but to him, I was a Friend with Benefits.

I kept up the pretence of friendship for most of the time; however, one Friday, I told him I was at home and would like his company, suggesting he come over for a meal, etcetera. He didn't reply straight away and I started to experience an overwhelming feeling of rejection. For some reason, I wrote to him again and said I was really looking forward to him coming over, and I was beginning to regret saying I would be happy with Friends with Benefits when, really, I would like to see more of him.

He replied, `"Just thinking Jay, we need to have more self-discipline if we are not to leave you feeling unhappy. Best I don't come over."`

My stomach churned that evening, as I had moved the goalposts, so to speak, and he got cold feet again. I was demeaning myself by chasing him.

Later, I texted him and said I understood. He had more discipline than me, and I was happy to keep in touch occasionally. I appreciated that he was a considerate man, sparing my feelings, and that said, it made him all the more appealing to me.

He contacted me one morning a few weeks later; he had met someone and was trying to concentrate on seeing where the relationship would take them. I felt he was tormenting me, but rather than show it, I told him I, too, was seeing someone, Norton Rob, the motorbike Indian tour guide. Alan was fascinated to know more about him, but I kept the conversation short, happy that he had been in touch, and wished him all the best.

A few months later, I received a, "Hello and good morning. How are you?"

I didn't answer straight away. I was writing a goodbye note to Rob.

Alan: "Have you fallen out with me? "

Jay: "No, just busy, I'm still working. How's life? Are you still dating?"

Alan: "My last relationship, from Newcastle, has been called off by me; she mixed in posh circles, and I just didn't gel with her lifestyle. Not her fault, not my scene. You know me. I don't do pressure very well. Need to chill for a while, I think. How's the motorbike man, working for you?"

Jay: "Yes and no, it didn't quite blossom, few meetings, he ventured on to sex-texting and never progressed from there. He had an alcoholic ex whom he felt responsible for. It was a waste of time, really; although he had potential, I liked him. It's the story of my life, really. I have sent him a goodbye note today."

We continued to chat about families, holidays, and dating sites, had a bit of banter, and left it at that. I couldn't help but wonder why he kept in touch; in my heart, I hoped it wasn't only the physical he wanted from me. I assumed he wanted friendship. Oh, here I go again, living in a fantasy.

From that day on, I decided that as much as I loved our interaction, I would not proactively contact him. My heart was aching too much for him. He would affect my mental health, and that would be a barrier to finding "The One".

CHAPTER 21
"BIG FOOT" – THE 6'5" MAN CHILD

After that day, Alan contacted me a few more times, enquiring about my dating escapades. I told him I was seeing a 6'5" chemical engineer from Thirsk, 60 years old, called Calum; he had not long left his second wife, who was nine years older than him. Hoping that the same age difference would hit a chord with him, he didn't bite.

Callum's first wife died when the children were quite small, and he admitted he relied heavily on his parents to support him in raising them. Whilst I was doubtful at first, he gave me every reason to be hopeful. Gail (his second wife) left him for another man younger than him. I had to laugh. What had this woman, who was the same age as me, got that could form relationships with much younger men—money and influence, maybe? Or she has the confidence and attitude that age is just a number.

He was fun to be with at first and we met a few times for drinks and a couple of walks. He loved the same music and travel and had very similar life values. I could hardly keep up with his enormous stride and he gave me a crick in my neck when I was talking to him. However, he was very boyish in his attitude and humour, the kind that liked to play practical jokes. It wasn't long before I realised, he preferred older women because he needed a mother figure. I had endless text messages, day and night, describing the issues he was dealing with, including his work and his kids, his mother, his ex-late wife, his ex-second wife and his past mental breakdowns. There was a lot going on.

Out of the blue, he sent me a message.

```
"I've booked a holiday in Lanzarote, needed to get away on my own and sort my head out."
```

Well, part of me wasn't surprised; he was all over the place mentally. He sent me photos every day of isolated places he had walked to. It looked so barren and soulless.

One of his messages seemed to be addressed to another woman; I think he sent it to me by mistake. Her name was Jane.

He had cut and pasted much of what he had said to me previously in his last message, only there were a few answers to questions she had clearly asked him specifically. He even remarked about the time they had first met which was a different venue to our first meeting. My gut instinct told me he was still talking to many women from the dating sites and I let him know I suspected this. Telling him that I didn't feel he was ready for an exclusive relationship; he needed the attention of many women to distract him from his other problems.

He responded and said I was very intuitive (pretty obvious to me), and he hadn't met anyone like me who understood him so easily; he felt he was punching above his weight with me. He asked if I minded him keeping in touch as he felt he could be completely honest with me and loved the banter we had.

I couldn't help myself and replied, `"Maybe you should let Jane know too."`

He sent a shocked emoji with the words, `"I'm a fool, sorry."`

On his return from Lanzarote, he moved to a small rental cottage and it wasn't long before he asked me if I would like to visit; he was in a much better place now and would like to treat me to a meal out as friends.

I set off that early evening, thinking this relationship had no future, but I liked him as a friend. I'm not cut out to be a therapist for a man-child anyway; see how it goes.

He sent me a message that he was in his local pub and had been there since 3 p.m., and they had good food. Predictably, after four hours of drinking red wine, he was drunk. There was I, a 5'5" woman, trying to help a legless man a foot taller than me to get home. We eventually arrived at his cottage after he fell a couple of times, grazing his elbow against a wall and nearly taking me with him. How I managed to drag him up the high street I will never know.

Whilst I was dressing his wounds, he lunged at me, saying he had wanted to kiss me for a long time. I backed away immediately. This wasn't my idea of a first romantic kiss from a 6'5" drunk. I made him a coffee instead, gave him a cuddle, said, "There, there," and told him he ought to go to bed. His eyes already heavy and ready to close, I left him slouched on his settee, picked up my coat and bag and closed his cottage door behind me

Partly bemused and partly annoyed for I hadn't eaten and I was starving as the promise of food never came.

The following day, I received an apology.

```
"Hiya Jay.

So upset with myself about yesterday evening and
sorry if I was completely out of order. I really
hope I didn't do or say anything that has spoilt
things between us. The only sensible thing I did was
to warn you that I was drunk before you actually
```

arrived. Actually, I was pretty hammered!! I had a fairly difficult afternoon with Gail (his ex), but that's no excuse to get like that. It was the first time since our split up that I've properly let it get to me and let rip. I can't have made a very good impression on you. You are such a lovely person and so caring, and to come over to see me was so kind, especially in the knowledge I wasn't exactly myself. I really hope I've not put you off through anything I said or did. I'm much more sober now. The comment I made about you being out of my league, although written when I was drunk, just after you left, does have some truth in it as it is the main thing that has been causing me problems and holding me back from making any romantic moves with you. I'm a bit of a bad lad and have shown myself in a bad light. I hope you can forgive me.

Love,

Big Foot" (My nickname for him when we were walking)

There was no point doing a post-mortem on myself over this very short fling with a man-child. Had I been fooling myself from the beginning that a man nine years younger would want a future with me? That question again!

I did discuss the episode with my Girl Tribe when we met for coffee at the café.

"What a dick!" shouted Kitty. That description has been used for a few of my dates now. I was beginning to think I had no ability to recognise these "dicks" before I embarked on a liaison.

Maria was more inquisitive. "Love the name Big Foot. Did he have other large parts of his anatomy? Just asking for a friend."

We all fell about laughing. I had to admire Ann, laughing with the rest of us, sitting there, losing her hair through chemo and still the funniest in the group.

I told them how I had to manhandle him up the high street and how he lunged at me, the age difference, the message mistake, all his woes, and his last apology.

Suddenly, Penny jumped to her feet and shouted. "NEXT!!! Anybody for a sausage sandwich?"

STREET FOOD

The street reeked, smell of onions,
An aroma that assaults the nose,
pervading, invisible, yet has a union
with a baker's vessel carrying a cargo
of rusk and ham, smoky and smooth,
A famed label with no reason that I know.

The image appeals to our primal senses,
complimented by a swirl of mustard,
or a favoured partner tomato relish,
All loosely wrapped in paper, mastered
by the street vendor, not embellished.
Waiting queue all agog for a simple... Hot Dog

JACQUELINE T. **MAY**

CHAPTER 22
FRIEND WITH BENEFITS
– PART 2

Yet another *"Happy Monday"* message arrived in my WhatsApp messages. I responded with a good morning and carried on with my day. By the evening, three more messages were waiting.

Alan: "How's the dating going"

"Are you still seeing the big Guy?"

"I take it you are busy today"

Once I had updated Alan on my "Big Foot" experience, he started flirting with me and saying he missed our banter. Then, he wanted to know how I was; his questions were random as if trying to pick up on the past, testing the water with me. His absence from my life recently had been a mystery, but I wasn't going to pry. I hated the feeling of wanting and then disappointment, so ignorance was a blessing.

I was bored with the dating scene and wanted to concentrate on my other interests. Returning to occasional sex texting and video sex was an early morning and evening familiar distraction for me.

He was single (I believed), and so was I; therefore, there was no harm in it.

As time went on, though, I desperately tried not to look as though I wanted to win his affection. I stopped sending him poetry. Although he said he enjoyed them, I was not sure now if he was being kind and humouring me so he could get what he wanted from me. All I wanted was to be in his arms again, but that was a silly fantasy I know now.

We discussed the subject of holidays and I told him that, as I wasn't in a relationship at that moment, it was probably a good time for me to plan a big holiday. Another year had passed and I was ready to embark on an adventure. I had a few holiday brochures and hadn't yet decided on which one to choose. He said he was free for a coffee if I fancied meeting him at Costa and he could help me choose. Oh, how my heart fluttered. Wouldn't it be wonderful if he was in a position to join me? Stop it, Jay!

When we met that afternoon, he was very attentive and listened to my options. I decided on a three-week South American tour finishing at Brazil and the Rio Carnival. It was so lovely to see him and we had no difficulty in sharing our travel aspirations, but he always made the excuse he couldn't take time away from his business for more than a week. I started to realise Alan presented many negative obstacles for not doing things. He lacked adventure and risk taking, the opposite to me.

We said our goodbyes and agreed it was nice to see one another again. But no plans were made to be physically intimate. Nevertheless, I felt we had opened the door to some kind of friendship, albeit mainly online.

He did take me out for a meal once as he was in the area and asked if I had eaten. We had a giggle, and he took me home, and at last, we ended up in my bed. I thought I was cool with it all. But was I?

A week later, he texted me to say he was having a drink in Leeds with a girl he had known for four years, just to catch up. He didn't have to say anything; I knew it was the girl from Belarus.

My heart sank again. Only this time, I decided to keep calm. We talked on and off, and he never mentioned her name or what had happened at the meeting until a few weeks later, when he announced that he and Laura were going on a long weekend to London. She had asked him to accompany her to a concert. That was it for me, the end of my crazy 'Friend with Benefits', and YES I was hurt. I thanked him for telling me, wished him a happy Christmas, and told him to be careful in London as there was a nasty virus expected in the UK from China called COVID-19.

Despite the COVID warnings, I booked a last-minute South America trip, leaving the UK in mid-January; the virus was not a major threat at that time. I dropped him a note.

Jay: "South America booked whoop whoop! xx"

Alan: "You did it! Go careful and enjoy… more adventurous and warmer than London. I'm always glad to get away from that city. Nearly missed the train back!!"

He didn't say anything else about his trip and I didn't ask. I was now looking forward to my new adventure.

South America was amazing, and while we did hear about COVID-19, the countries we were travelling through were not announcing any significant case numbers. Sadly, the Rio Carnival was struck by the worst rainstorm they had in years, but nevertheless, it was still spectacular. The other highlight of the trip was the 'Iguazu Falls' on the Argentina/Brazil border; the weather was perfect, and the scenery was spectacular.

It was a solo trip, and as usual, the majority of my travel buddies were female. I made some wonderful memories and friends.

I sent Alan a couple of photos; secretly I felt he should see what he is missing. That was my fleeting moment of peevishness. I tried desperately to exclude him from my thoughts, but he would turn up in my dreams and mess with my head. Somehow, I must find a way of ridding him from my life; I know I am weak and can understand perfectly why abusive relationships perpetuate. We women don't let go of our fantasies easily, and hope the bad things about our subject of desire will change. They don't.

My Girl Tribe wanted to know all about my travels, so I arranged for them all to come to my house. I told them how my solo trip was 90% women, one gay guy and the other taken. It was then I decided it was time I told them about Toy Boy too.

"I've been seeing a younger 59-year-old guy on and off for the past nearly two years, or more. Sorry I haven't confided in you all, but this one was special, so I thought, fancied the pants off him. I've never been so attracted to anyone. It was obvious from the start that he fancied me too, however, our nine-year age difference became a commitment hurdle. Rather than walk away, I suggested we become 'friends with benefits.' There were no commitments, just fun, and we could carry on dating others until we found 'the one'; then, we would end our arrangement. No surprise, he accepted."

"What!!! You sly old horny thing, fancy keeping that to yourself. Photos please." Penny sounded almost envious when I showed a photo of him on my phone; her mouth dropped, and I passed my phone on to the others.

Ann said "hot" and Maria couldn't wait to start asking loads of questions.

"Well, where does he live? What's his background and why hasn't he found anyone yet? Not that you aren't a catch, but there has to be a red flag somewhere; besides, if you don't mind me saying, you throw yourself into friends with benefits, which, must be difficult as you said; he must have had a big impact on you."

I tried to answer her questions honestly, telling her about his background, business, and family life. My sister Kitty kept quiet and looked at me with concern. She was the only one I had confided in, and regularly, she would voice her opinion of the situation, particularly when I was upset over his hesitance and rejections. Today, I think she was waiting to hear what the others had to say.

Penny closed her jaw. "Well, it's a brave thing to do, but I am sure I couldn't do it; I would get too attached, and by the sounds of it, you have been too." She looked again at the photo. "He is certainly attractive. I see why you wouldn't want to let go. What is his personality like?"

I told them about the early days and how considerate he was and that he didn't want to hurt me. How he never put me under pressure, we had fun banter and sex texting. Our physical sex was mutually respectful and exciting. But most of all, there was a lot of synergy between us, and we were both Geminis, too. I thought I could manage to deal with this modern approach to an independent life with sexual benefits, no exclusivity and keep on dating. It seemed straightforward.

"Oh well, the same star sign should make all the difference," Penny said with a light sarcasm in her voice. "Really, Jay, after nearly two years, what has made you share this with us now and not before?"

I was beginning to feel judged, but I think that was because she was confused by it all.

"Penny, I suppose I was embarrassed, felt people would judge me, consider me cheap and desperate throwing myself at a younger man who has no intentions of committing to me. At this moment, I will admit I am now struggling." My eyes started to well up. Kitty reached out to stroke my shoulder. "He has just informed me he is going back to a previous girlfriend with whom he had a relationship for four years. The impact of this news has affected me more than I expected. I am not eating and feeling closer to depression than I ever have." I examined their faces to glean some kind of reaction.

"Lovesickness, I suppose. How stupid, I am nearly 70 and cannot come to terms with what was always inevitable."

Maria also sounded confused. "Well, 59 is hardly a Toy Boy, is it? He's not a kid! I am sure you were blown away by him, but honestly, you should keep away now. He has clearly made his choice. I feel for you, Jay. It's tough being rejected; we've all been there."

"Here, here, but hey, what an experience and one for a chapter in your book," said Penny, who raised her glass.

She then lightened the mood. "These days I would consider myself lucky if a man I was dating was breathing."

She continued, "It's not my niche area of interest, but I remember watching a documentary about a woman who worked in a morgue to get access to the stiffs. She had a saying, "If the hearse is rocking, don't come knocking." As someone who has terrible memory loss, that is etched on my frontal lobes forever! "We all laughed and cackled out loud with some disgusted groans.

Maria piped up, "I think you may have issues Penny. And how the fuck a woman gets a dead man hard will probably be etched in my mind for tonight, thanks for that." My kitchen was electric with dirty laughs and describing the horror of it all.

Penny, clearly wanting to continue on the subject, added, "It's beyond anything I even want to imagine in a TV programme; it was mind-boggling that she didn't seem to have any shame about it. Think she did jail time though."

I felt so much better for confiding in them and, as expected, behind a little judgement and concern, they were secretly impressed that I had the guts to pursue such an arrangement as Friends with Benefits. I couldn't resist writing a poem about the obsessed necrophile female in the mortuary. I'm sure some will consider this tasteless, or is it just titillation?

As the girls left, they all gave me a big hug and made me promise to contact them anytime if I was feeling low.

MADGE AND THE MORTUARY

The thing about simple Madge,
She might as well wear a badge
"Hello desperate here for a shag."
Someone spare this sorry nag
As she drags, drags n drags
On her papery rolled up fag.
Or is it a spliff? Who knows if
There is an odour, there is a whiff
maybe her breath or smelly pits,
Her sweaty crotch or sagging bits?

No, she's on the medicinal weed
To hide all her memories indeed
The night she worked in the mortuary,
Giving a stiff oral and debauchery.
The moon shone between her legs
It was her norm to get the dregs
Madge, an eerie unpleasant sight
She even gave the corps a fright.
Yet despite her unhealthy addiction
She mastered an almighty suction
And whilst her want was satiated
The poor departed was left deflated.

CHAPTER 23
SOLDIER AND TEDDY BEARS

I was determined to distract myself from texting Toy Boy, and the way I could control my urge was to carry on dating.

A very attractive 65-year-old widow started writing to me, Trev. He lived 50 miles away, which was really my maximum distance for any potential relationship. Stupidly, I was attracted to his looks, and clearly, he kept himself very fit; photos of gorgeous scenery behind him, wearing his walking clothes and boots. I was subconsciously, looking for another lover, but I wouldn't admit that to myself or others.

He didn't have a car as he had given it to his son who needed it more for his job, though he could always ask to use it if necessary. He felt he was lucky, as he had everything that he needed within walking distance from his apartment (sounded familiar). We agreed to meet anyway and I offered to drive over to his town, the other side of the Pennines, on the M62. I hated that road, particularly in bad weather.

I arrived at the agreed meeting point, a café in the middle of a large housing estate. The urbanisation had the feel of a new town built in the 1970s: light-coloured brick and three-story apartment blocks, townhouses and a flat-roofed shopping complex, a post office, surgery and other services, very little greenery or trees.

The uneasy feeling about the place, which could have been the dark skies and sea fret, gave the streets that doomed look. Parking my car, I felt conspicuous as there were mainly vans outside the cafe. I wish I had worn jeans instead of a dress. He was sitting by the window of what I can only describe as more like a works canteen than a cosy café.

Was I being snobbish? Maybe I was initially, but did my best to see past the austere appearance of this environment and concentrate on Trev. After this experience, I learned to use Google Maps and Street View to check on where potential dates were being planned so I was prepared or rejected where I was meeting. I also checked out their homes if they gave me their address. I know it sounds as though I should not be so suspicious, but there are stories, and we women are vulnerable when it comes to sexual predators.

He complimented me on my appearance and said I looked like my photos. I also said the same about his. The conversation was a bit hard going; I quickly realised that we didn't have a lot in common. He talked about his days in the forces in Ireland, Libya and Afghanistan, his injuries and how he had retired from the Army on ill health. He had several jobs after that, but his injuries had limited his choice of career. Like me, he was dyslexic and found it hard to work where there was admin involved. "I'm good with my hands," he said with a wink. "Became a carpenter, loved working with wood and was lucky enough to work with a company who were understanding. I needed weeks off work for the several operations."

Explaining that he had the last operation five years ago and had embarked on a rigorous training programme to get himself fit again.

"I am probably fitter now than before the explosion". He told me that his army vehicle ran over a land mine; he lost two of his friends and another was an amputee. He felt he was the lucky one, with a badly broken leg and ankle, plus, ruptured spleen and lower back injuries. I must admit, his graphic descriptions I struggled with. I have a vivid imagination and it was difficult for me to block out the images. I admired his determination to be fit again, though, and I have to admit he did look good.

He then went on to praise the quality and quantity of the English breakfasts at the café and suggested I should try one sometime. I looked around the room and felt the various white van man occupants and café staff were listening to us and staring at me.

"Do you like black pudding?" his face beaming.

I nodded with a quizzical look.

"You should see the size of it, the best ever," then paused, "the pudding I mean!" He laughed. The first sexual innuendo, I had to admit, was a bit of an icebreaker.

Still feeling uncomfortable, I was concerned this conversation would not progress beyond the breakfast menu and was aimed at the mature lady at the nearby counter, she seemed to be constantly cleaning the same area of surface nearest to us. "Is there somewhere else we could go to talk, or walk even?" I ask.

"We can go back to mine if you are okay with that. It's around the corner and, don't worry, I will understand if you are not comfortable when you get there. No pressure from me."

I know, I can hear you all saying, what is she doing? I had driven a long way and needed the toilet, so it made sense to go to his. Well, that was my excuse, pathetic, I know. We walked around the corner as he said, to a two-story block of apartments.

His was on the first floor. I have to say his home was very neat and tidy. The sitting room was tastefully decorated and furnished, with some lovely artwork on the walls and a green tropical palm in the corner of the room. There was a modern wooden feature, which incorporated the TV a living flame fire and shelves with teddy bears!! Several of them, wearing clothes, looked like collectable Steiff bears. I didn't know how to react.

The last thing I wanted to do was offend him. So, I paid my attention to a beautiful mock Tudor doll house, sitting on a nest of tables. This was beginning to feel even more freaky.

"What a lovely doll's house." My voice went up an octave.

"I've nearly finished it for my granddaughter. There's the fence and wiring for lights inside to do; hopefully, it's ready for Christmas." I walked over to the doll's house to admire it. There was a small front garden with a picket fence still under construction.

There wasn't an ounce of sawdust or tools around. This clearly was a man who liked order and was incredibly creative. He showed me the photo he had used as the basis for the design.

"I built the shelf unit, too," he pointed at it. I love working with wood. Unfortunately, this place is too small to do much; my dream is to have my own workshop."

"Teddy bears," I said, again with a high-pitched voice. "I love teddy bears."

He smiled and picked one up from the sofa, gesturing to me to sit on it. "As you can see, so do I. The collection snowballed; I have been given many presents from family and friends. My nickname is Teddy, too. Long story."

I was feeling a little uneasy at first, but he didn't come across as a psychopath or someone with a deviant obsession. He seemed a gentle man, who wasn't embarrassed about his collection of Teddies.

He made me a cup of tea and told me about his son, whom he was very close to and considered his best friend. He was an excellent photographer, which explains the model-like photos he took of his Dad for dating sites. I, too, talked about my girls and my grandchildren.

I finished my tea and was about to end our date when he told me he found me very attractive and that he could kiss me. We did. I know. What was I doing?

We ended up in his bedroom where there were even more teddy bears, some lined along the wall on the edge of his king-sized bed. To my surprise, he had grey satin sheets on the bed. I sat on the edge, to begin with, while he stood over me and stroked my hair. I think I have blocked out a lot of what happened next. What I do remember was how strong he was and how he manhandled me into position. It was when he was at full penetration and he did a large thrust that I heard my back crack, literally, and cried out, "My back, my back, I think it's broken."

He stopped immediately and tried to help me sit up. I was in agony and the bloody scattered bears were staring at me, like Valley of the Dolls. I could imagine them becoming animated and telling me I was a stupid old fool. He helped me dress and took me into the sitting room, apologising all the time. The other bears looked at me accusingly, mocking me. Yes, I was getting paranoid now, deciding this was really freaky, being surrounded by dressed-up bears. He went into another room and brought back some Ibuprofen cream and a glass of water.

"This should do the trick; lift up your dress, and I will apply it for you. Some paracetamol should take the pain away too. I'm an expert at pain control," he added with another wink, handing me the glass and the pills.

How on earth was I going to drive home? He massaged my back with the cream, and within half an hour, I could feel some relief, but every time I moved, I could feel some pain. He gave me a carrier bag with two tubes of cream, telling me he had a large supply from when he had his back operation. I thanked him and gingerly took the stairs to the front door; he helped me all the way, opened my car door and expressed concern I was driving a long way in such a condition.

I found myself looking at a man who had suffered physically through horrific injuries and emotionally from losing the love of his life, being tortured for years and finding some comfort in Teddy bears, a man who showed a softness not many men willingly show. There was no arrogance in him, just a handsome man who was capable of love. I reassured him I was much better and the massage did the job.

I was glad of my automatic transmission car, as I drove at 40 miles an hour along the inside lane of the motorway all the way home. I was in agony and cried some of the way, cursing myself constantly. "Vanity Jay, you responded to compliments like a teenager and look at you now!"

He must have messaged me when I was on my way home, apologising for what happened. It wasn't his fault I knew. I said not to worry, I was home safe and sound. And no, I did not see him again. I had back pain for several weeks and had to use a physiotherapist, too, telling people, including Toy Boy, that I had done it lifting a concrete plant pot in the garden. Well, if they read this, they will know now what a liar I was.

The following day my sister Kitty asked where I had been the day before when she noticed I was holding my back. Part of me wished I hadn't confided in her. Not my finest few hours I know.

Kitty gave me the kind of lecture only a sister could give, as Penny and Maria sat with us in the local pub beer garden. Ignoring my pleading face not to say anything.

"I cannot believe you drove all the way to Liverpool to meet a strange man, to have sex and be thrown around like a rag doll, hurt your back, and then drive back on the M62 motorway!" in an exasperated tone, "You are unbelievable and mad."

My Girl Tribe looked over their wine glasses at each other, waiting for one to react, and then Penny broke the silence.

"Ragdoll!!! Liverpool!!!" they all simultaneously broke down in hysterics, Maria had tears running down her face and couldn't control her giggles as she pointed at Kitty's disapproving face.

Kitty admitted she was a prude, then broke into a smile and added, "But my sister is as mad as a hatter; he could have been an axe murderer."

"It's okay, Kitty. He was more into collecting Teddy bears." Then all hell broke loose. They all started laughing and lecturing me at the same time, about how desperate I must have been and irresponsible.

Penny continued, "How dare you deprive us of future stories if you end up axed."

I did reflect on my rash decision to meet a man I did not know and had sex with. Did I actually regret it, probably? But then I survived to tell the tale.

NEXT!!!

JACQUELINE T. **MAY**

CHAPTER 24
A MAN WHO NEARLY DIED IN MY BED

My back almost back to normal, I embarked on finding a man who had the ambition and the money to travel with me. Not a rich man, but self-sufficient with enough savings to achieve a few adventures.

It was difficult to ignore the physical and mental ache that felt like a vacuum after Alan (Toy Boy) moved on again. He still sent the odd, `"Good morning, how's things?"` message on WhatsApp. I tried to ignore them but couldn't and there was no way I could consider blocking him. I usually update him on my latest news, including dates. He would offer a few words of wisdom and banter. `"You went where? That's a long way. Teddy bears? Jay, you don't want to be travelling over the M62 this time of year; it's a road to hell."`

Says a man who used to date women in France… I didn't divulge the sex or broken back though.

—

My new interest, Sam lives in Pickering. We talked on email (he didn't like WhatsApp) and then on the phone. His voice sounded warm, and he had a dry wit; I liked that.

The only downside is that he didn't have a car (a pattern repeating itself again). He had moved back to the UK from Spain after leaving his wife, who had an affair with his business partner. She was living in their villa with her lover, and they continued to run the business but told him if he didn't return, then they would fold the business, and he would have to fight for the proceeds. It all seemed very unfair and challenging. I really felt for him when, in reality, alarm bells should have been ringing. I don't know why I didn't run a mile; he was another case of not learning from past red flags.

We met at the York railway station. He passed me twice before realising who I was. I can still visualise his big smile today as he stopped dead in his tracks on recognising me. There was almost a little amusement in his voice. "You came! I passed you earlier, but I thought you looked too young for my date. And do you know there are four clocks in this station?"

I laughed. "Yes, I'm here and no, I didn't know there were four clocks, but I do now. Thanks for the compliment too, but maybe you need to go to Specsavers."

He described his journey by bus and how good the Coastliner number 840 was. He had a boyish charm and banter which instantly created rapport. With silver, well-groomed hair, clean-shaven, nicely dressed, modern rimless glasses and slim, he carried himself well. He instantly gave me a kiss on both cheeks. Obviously, Spain was not far from his thoughts; they always kissed on both cheeks there.

We chatted all the way to the city centre. It was spring, and the city walls were fringed by swaying carpets of yellow and white daffodils. It was a beautiful day, York looked ready to burst into blossom. There was a cold wind, which didn't help my breathing that day.

To escape the wind, we quickly found a table at the nearest café to the bridge. My cough and wheeze were getting worse, so I apologised and said I couldn't stay long, then disappeared to the bathroom, I was coughing constantly. My asthma was bad, and the inhaler was hardly a relief. I could see the disappointment in his face when I told him I had to go home.

"Hey, don't apologise, I am glad I found you under the right clock. Let me walk you back to your car." He helped me with my coat. "Are you sure you are okay to drive? I could drive you home if you want me to, then catch the bus home." He was so gentle and concerned for me.

"I will be okay. It's only a fifteen-minute drive." I was coughing between every word now.

I stopped off at my friend Maria's on my way home, needing to take my inhaler again. When she saw me on her doorstep, she was shocked at the state I was in gasping and shivering, lips blue. Without me asking, she had phoned for an ambulance. "You've been on a date in this state? What are you like, Jay?"

The paramedics arrived quickly, a male and a female. They checked all my vital signs and agreed my oxygen levels were too low, and the temperature was too high. A ride to the hospital was essential. The usual questions were fired at me. "Date of birth, address, do you take other medication?" I answered all their questions between gasps behind the plastic oxygen mask.

I couldn't remember the name of one of my meds and asked Maria to get my handbag. As she passed the bag over, it fell on the floor, emptying the contents. There in the middle of tissues, my purse, glasses, pen and pill box, was a shiny blue condom packet. Maria spotted it immediately and tried to scramble to the floor to hide it. However, the female paramedic got to it first. "Now, this doesn't look like medication, but good on you." They all started laughing; the male paramedic kept winking at me, telling me to breathe slowly and try not to laugh. I was mortified, but a little piece of me was proud that they all respected me for having such a thing in my handbag.

The following day, I sent Sam and Toy Boy a photo of me in the hospital, all wired up with intravenous drips and an oxygen mask. Sam immediately volunteered to visit me. I declined his offer, as family were visiting, but that once I was better, he could treat me to that coffee we missed. Every morning, I would receive a message from him and Toy Boy, checking to see if I had a good night's sleep, but no offer from Toy Boy to visit me.

Recovered, Sam and I eventually met up in York again and visited the same café I hastily left the first time. The daffodils were fading, and the blossoms from the trees were scattered onto the ground like confetti. There is no wind today. We must have been there for two hours and decided to eat there too. He was so easy to talk to, listened and laughed in all the right places. We both knew the same area of Spain he had lived in for 10 years, as I have friends there, whom I visit every other year. The two hours flew by, and we agreed that I would visit Pickering next weekend; he would show me the sites and make lunch for me. I blocked out of my mind all the potential issues with this relationship because I loved his company.

I visited Pickering, a modern terraced house he rented by the river. The willow trees were brushing the water with their new leaves, creating a beautiful and peaceful scene; he loved it there.

He made a salad for lunch, and we took a walk along the river. Not once did he try to get physical with me; he chatted and laughed all the time I was there, occasionally putting my arm through his. We said our goodbyes, and I offered to reciprocate with a walk and lunch, too.

It was a 40-minute drive home. All the way, I was thinking, "Can I do this on a regular basis? " I told myself he was good for me and distracted me from Toy Boy. I needed that distraction more than ever.

I met Sam at the bus stop; he was standing there with a bouquet of mixed flowers. I could probably count on one hand the number of bouquets I have been given from my dates. I've concluded that Yorkshire men don't do flowers, almost as if it's a sign of weakness. My late husband was the same.

We did kiss on the 3rd date, but nothing heavy, no petting. On the 4th date, it was my turn to entertain him, and I suggested I book a local Italian restaurant, and he stayed over so we both could have a drink. We were both too drunk to even consider sex, we cuddled, and he fell asleep very quickly. We did share my bed for part of that night, but I removed myself to the other bedroom because I couldn't sleep. Come the morning, I crawled back into the bed he was in, and he started talking about the last time he had sex. We agreed that we would take things slowly. I suggested he stay another night, and we keep the wine to a minimum. That afternoon we went for a long walk and bought fish and chips for tea.

In bed later...

After a few minutes of exploring each other's bodies, and our first missionary position, I moved to be on top of him; Sam strangely stared past me and at the ceiling, his face contorted as if in pain. Initially, I thought I had hurt him. Prior to that, our lovemaking had been very tender and he was undoubtedly aroused. I loved his kissing and could have kissed all day, but at this moment I knew something wasn't the norm.

"Sam, Sam, are you okay?"

He seemed to grunt. Scared, I immediately jumped off him and shouted again. He eventually focused on me and started to shake at the same time, still grimacing.

"Do you need anything?" I shouted at him as if he was deaf. He groaned and told me to wait a minute and he would sort it. Whatever "it" was. I quickly passed him a glass of water; however, he was clutching his chest as if in deep pain. Oh my God, he's not having a heart attack, is he?

I grabbed my phone, wanting to call an ambulance, but he grabbed my hand and told me not to. It was a terrifying fifteen minutes or so sitting on the edge of the bed, not knowing what to do. He eventually settled, sipped the water and started to speak.

"I am foolish, Jay, I so wanted us to have a good time this evening, so I took two Viagra tablets. I do have a mild heart condition and the Viagra has probably put my heart into overdrive. I'm so sorry if I frightened you." As he rubbed his chest in a circular motion, I raised my voice

"Frightened me? I thought you were dying!"

I suggested that I take him to A&E anyway. He refused, saying he was embarrassed and was sure there was no harm done, although he was still feeling the after-effects and his face looked grey. I was terrified he would die on me.

I stayed awake all night next to him; his breathing was very erratic and the slightest noise had me sitting up in bed to check on him.

My anxiety and concern for him reminded me of what happened to my late husband Tony, who died in his sleep next to me. I will never forget being in a small hotel in the middle of rural France, our last overnight stop before driving to our ferry home. At midnight finding myself and two male hotel guests taking turns to do CPR on him, in the hope it was enough to keep him going until the ambulance arrived.

I should have known he had gone as his eyes rolled backwards when I was shaking him moments before I cried for help down the hotel corridor. After 35 minutes of the two guests and I desperately trying to keep up the CPR, a crash team with a doctor came, but despite using the paddles of a defibrillator several times, there was no response. I couldn't go through that again!

I was stranded in France, in a hamlet of a dozen houses and a Marie (Lord Mayor's Office). The two guests, who spoke some English, had to leave that day. I had never felt so desperately alone, stuck in a bare room with a bunk bed at one end and a double at the other. I had no idea where they had taken Tony. My school girl French was very inadequate.

Thankfully, after 14 hours alone and in shock, one of my daughter's old friends, who was fluent in French, drove from Paris to help me. I was high on hydrocortisone to help me cope with the shock.

Tony and I were one minute having a lovely meal in a cute little French restaurant, going to bed early, and then fighting for his life. Tony had a pulmonary embolism, not a heart attack, which was confirmed by the UK autopsy report. All this kept going through my head like a bad dream. Not something you get over quickly.

My daughters joined me in France within 48 hours, and it took six days to complete the red tape and plan Tony's repatriation and our flights home. No, I definitely couldn't go through that again, ever!

It took several weeks for it all to sink in. I was numb and, I suppose, in denial that this was the end of my life as I knew it, having to fend for myself from now on. I certainly empathise with people who suffer from PTSD (post-traumatic stress disorder), waking after two hours of sleep, sitting bolt upright, in cold sweats, looking for him next to me, crying out and constantly trying to figure out why I did not notice any signs of ill health. I was to be reassured later by a UK specialist that no one could have saved him, and that these things can happen without warning.

He was 64, had been retired since he was 50, had a good life and wouldn't have known a thing. Therefore, there were positives, if you could call them that. I was always looking for some kind of consolation to justify it all, and I still do.

While Sam and I waited for the Coastliner coach, I made him promise to talk to his doctor about his reaction. He waved from the bus, looking very fragile and sad. I think he knew he had blown it. I had a sense of guilt about my reaction to his situation as he had been so lovely with me over my pneumonia, but I couldn't help feeling that there were other issues he hadn't shared with me. Moreover, my past experience with Tony would only haunt me if I stayed with him.

On the way home, exhausted, I decided that, as lovely as Sam was, I wasn't cut out to deal with another man's health crisis, well not at that moment, as I had to prioritise myself. Being a carer for someone I hardly know is not the future I envisage. Perhaps 'Friends with Benefits' would suit me better, after all. We will see.

I chatted to Kitty on the phone about Sam.

"He did what? And you stayed up all night watching him?" I was ashamed and my embarrassed laugh showed it. "Jay, you must be more careful; you cannot go through all that again. Besides, how on earth do you explain that one to your girls? Oh! he took two Viagra to satisfy their horny mother." We then giggled at the absurdity of it all and were sad for him at the same time.

"Yeh, you promise to be more careful and then there is another drama. Slow down, crazy woman, I worry about you. Get a dog!"

NEXT!!

—

Toy Boy wrote not long after I finished with Sam. I talked about my Viagra trauma experience and he laughed at first, then empathised when I told him of the flashbacks I had over Tony's death.

```
"I must say you don't need that Jay. You have gone
through a lot over the years and need to look after
yourself. Us men often have a tendency to rely on
their women to care and nurse them, man flu and all
that. It was best avoided… Besides, he had other
```

issues, by the sounds of it. A car crash avoided." That phrase again!

I agreed with his comments, but all I wanted was to see him and have one of his manly hugs, for him to take some of the past memories away. Instead, I asked him how life was treating him, secretly wanting to know if he was still with Laura.

"Not bad, same old same old, just plodding away. Laura has gone to Slovenia to see a friend, no invite for me. Think she is getting bored. We will probably drift apart like the last two times."

I couldn't bring myself to answer and just told him to take care and finished with "Bye for now..." my way of leaving the door open for him to chat with me another time. I was torturing myself with the vain hope he would want me and I wished I knew what kept him in touch with me, fooling myself I mattered to him, but then I convinced myself it was more 'Benefits' he wanted than Friendship. I vowed to myself again that I wouldn't be proactive in contacting him; any slight rejection would hurt too much. Chasing is something I have done too much of in the past, at my emotional cost.

PROMISE

I'll weep no more, I promise.
Accept the consequences.
Remember I'm alive. Be honest.
Keep the memories real.
It's easy to bend the image.
I will never forget the feel
I've little left of life's hours.
It's time to see the rainbows
And play among the flowers.
I'll weep no more, I promise.

JACQUELINE T. **MAY**

CHAPTER 25
THE OBSESSIVE ROCK CLIMBER

I was a bit reluctant to continue a conversation with Tony, aged 65, as he had the same name as my late husband. Silly thoughts are going through my head ... will my girls struggle with me seeing a man with the same name as their dad? I checked with my eldest; she was cool about it. His profile clearly said he was retired, loved rock climbing and enjoyed the outdoors. Living close to the countryside in the West Pennines, he was a 35-minute drive away on decent roads.

Tony told me he had been an editor of a farming magazine for many years, and he knew Yorkshire like the back of his hand, most of the farmers, too. I was getting excited about meeting him as he sounded like he would have many interesting tales to tell. He also knew the area of Spain where my friends lived. Again, that was something we had in common. He told me to book a nice lunch venue somewhere near me, as he said his car could do with a good run out too. That amused me. Was he giving his car a trip out or was he really wanting to see me? I booked an Italian restaurant in the next town to my village. I didn't want to be tempted to show him where I lived at this stage ... made that mistake before.

I spotted him in the car park as I drove in. He was casually dressed: smart jeans, a white T-shirt, and a checked blue jacket. I have to say, I like that look on a man. He was completely bald and had a big friendly smile. I also liked the confident way he walked towards my car. Some men do seem very awkward on their first date. I understand that now and try not to stare at them too much.

I had just closed the car door when he said, "It can only be the lovely Jay. You look just like your photos; it makes such a nice change." He kissed me on my right cheek. I didn't bother to return the compliment, as I felt this one was confident enough not to need it.

We had a pleasant lunch and chatted for nearly two hours. Not that I wasn't enjoying our conversation, but I felt two hours on the first date was enough. He was very polite and agreed it was time to take him and his car home.

He wrote to me the following day. Clearly, he was taken aback by my telling him his date was almost over my two-hour limit and made fun of the fact that no woman had ever given him a time limit. But despite this, he loved our date and could he see me again? Soon?

We met halfway this time. My suggestion. I think he liked my forthrightness. It wasn't difficult for me, as from experience I find many men prefer you to tell them what you want, not be ambiguous, and not appear overly grateful if they look to you to lead in decision-making. Trying to please all the time makes communication awkward, and you become indecisive and confusing. Some men lack imagination and understanding of what many women need and therefore, guidance is essential. Just tell them what you want and why, then negotiate from there. However, it sounds simple, but often confidence in taking the lead comes with experience, and for some men, this can be seen as a negative; if they do so, move on. In the end you can only be you.

"Perhaps not the nicest of places to have a first kiss," I said with a slight giggle in my voice.

"Are you teasing me and are my two hours up?" He winked and grinned, his head slightly shaking at the same time. "Or, does a 'first kiss' mean there could be more?" as he imitated stroking my arm with the back of his hand.

"Could be, but I am sure there are much better places."

We chatted for a couple of weeks on WhatsApp while he was on a climbing holiday in France. The banter came thick and fast, as did his descriptions of where he was climbing and his fellow climbing companions. I loved the way he wrote, his education showing through, a much better wordsmith than I. He told me the last time he visited this site was with his last partner, who also climbed, and was better climber than he. They were still friends; she had another partner now.

My heart sank. There was no way I could contemplate climbing; I hate heights! I told him so and he laughed, saying climbing was not a prerequisite for a partner. But still, I was not sure this was going to work. And there was no way I wanted to go down the sex texting route again.

I spent a lovely weekend at his big apartment on the ground floor of an old woollen mill, with a very high ceiling, big metal beams and lots of pine furniture. I brought flowers and a pavlova I had made. He told me he had a sweet tooth so I knew pavlova would be just what his tastebuds would desire. We had already drunk a bottle of wine before it was 2pm in the afternoon. Suddenly, he announced he needed something from the shops for the meal. It felt like not much preparation had gone into my visit, so a feeling of not being high value came across me. Am I selling myself short again?

We walked through the old Yorkshire Industrial Revolution village with its almost black stone walled cottages, cheek by jowl on the high street. The place looked deserted except for a small Spa supermarket, which was much bigger inside than I expected. He got what he wanted and we walked back. Halfway back, the heavens opened, and the rain was almost biblical, so we sheltered under the thickest bush we could find. He kissed me and said he was so glad he found me and he knew we would get on. It was a bizarre moment, really, as I wasn't sure he was sincere, for my trust in men has been severely tested over the last few years.

Soaked to our skins, he offers for me to change out of my wet clothes in his bedroom then comes in with two towels and offers to dry me. We both laugh at the cheekiness of his suggestion and I find myself saying, "Easy tiger, only after I am dressed."

Still looking amused, he asks, "Well, how does that work then?"

Passing back the smaller towel, I tell him, "You can dry my hair."

"Ah, a bald guy with no hair drier, there's a challenge," as he walks out of the room with the small towel and winks as he goes.

When I arrived at the kitchen, my hair almost dry, I noticed a book on the table.

"We are celebrating tonight; my latest climbing book has been published."

I picked it up and flicked through the pages, which contained lots of maps and instructions, much like a walking book. I congratulated him as he passed me a glass of bubbly, and we clinked our glasses.

"I've never published a book," I told him. I've written a few short stories and started a book I didn't finish."

"It's my third one," he responded as he moved over to a bookshelf to show me the others. I should have known he would have no difficulty publishing because he was an editor after all. We went to bed not long after we had eaten. There was no romantic slow undressing, it was more frantic kissing and stripping each other at the same time. We both fell on the bed naked; I was glad of the low lights. He was very muscular but not in a bodybuilder kind of way, with some hair on his chest. He had been circumcised too.

I'm not saying sex with him was boring, but I kept wishing Toy Boy was in this bed. I've never felt the same or as aroused with any other man. Tony did all the usual, stroking, fondling my breasts, licking, kissing and a brief moment of 69, but I felt uncomfortable and moved back to the missionary position. He was gentle and asked me many times, "Is this okay? Tell me if I'm hurting you," and "Is that nice?"

We actually slept well together; although I woke at 4.30 a.m., I was determined to keep my head in the now and not on Toy Boy and fell back into deep sleep.

Tony arrived in the bedroom with a tray of freshly squeezed orange juice, croissants and buttered toast with marmalade on the side.

"You slept well," he said as he crawled back into bed, putting the tray on my lap.

"Yes, your bed is really comfy." We sat for most of the morning in his bed talking about his climbing achievements and ambitions, how he was never bored with planning his next conquest. I was fascinated at first, but this wouldn't last. There is only so much a girl can be wowed by ropes and harnesses. Unless, of course, he was going to use them on me at our next intimate session!

Only joking, but it might have spiced things up. He was very serious about his hobby. I was also getting a little tired of his constant reference to his ex-partner, Val this and Val that. I was grateful for our walk that afternoon, to a little-known Pennine valley. What a wonderful place, I thought I knew most of Yorkshire's beauty spots, but this one escaped me and his knowledge of its history only added to the awe of it.

"Well, this is a part of Yorkshire I haven't experienced before. Thank you for taking me here. I love it, just love it." Maybe I was a little too exuberant about my gratitude.

"Of course it's beautiful," he smirked. "It's in Lancashire," he said, nudging my shoulder like a teasing schoolboy. Yes, I felt stupid, but the irony was not lost on me. Yorkshire and Lancashire are neighbours and share the Pennines, England's longest mountain range, often known as the Back Bone of England.

Half way around the walk, he took me to a wonderful café by a stream that sold the best and deepest scones ever, with clotted cream and homemade jam. We held hands all the way round. At one point he put his hand around my waist when directing me through a kissing gate, then stopped abruptly.

"Well?" I looked quizzically at him.

"Well, what?"

He put his hand on the gate, the penny dropped and I puckered my lips. He gave me a quick peck on my lips, and subsequently let the gate go, which hit my leg.

"Oh, love, I'm sorry. What a clumsy idiot. Are you okay?" I hopped around for a bit and told him not to worry; I bruised easily, but it would soon mend.

After our day out, we took turns to visit our homes and each time we planned a walk and a meal. The sex was predictable, as was the conversation. I decided that I would change things. I suggested he arrive at mine with a playlist of his favourite music. We would spend the evening listening to them and talking about what memory each song provoked. He said he was not really into music that much; if he played anything, it was usually jazz or some country music. He liked Snake Davis, the saxophonist, best. I tried to understand but inside I was exasperated.

"Bring some of that, then. We can use Amazon Music and download the songs you like. I can help you tomorrow."

After our walk and meal, I connected my laptop computer to a wireless speaker and opened the Amazon Music app. He looked at me with a look of 'do we have to do this now?' He closed my laptop, his pale blue eyes almost pleading with me."

"I don't know about you, but I'm really tired after that walk. Besides, I have a heavy day's training planned for my level 7a climbing."

Disappointment must have shown in my face, as I stared at the closed laptop.

"No worries. We can try again another time," I said as I turned the speaker off. We went to bed and spooned as we slept.

He left early that morning, and there was no mention of planning another meeting. My gut instinct kept nagging me: I am not for him, nor is he nor me. There was something about him I was attracted to, but I could not figure it out. I texted him a few times that week, and he only answered in general terms. I even mentioned meeting again.

"Let me get back to you; I've a few things to sort out this week."

Another two days passed. I kept telling myself not to be impatient, but I still had my doubts.

I wrote to him to ask if there was something stopping him from planning our next meeting. He phoned me to say that it was a difficult time for him as he had set himself some challenges, many of which were weather-dependent, making it impossible to plan ahead. He was not even sure he should be in a relationship with someone like me. Maybe someone who shared his love of climbing and fell walking would suit him better. He tried flattering me again. But I stayed silent, and he stopped mid-sentence and then wished me all the best. Before he could end the call, I felt I had to agree with him yet tell him how I felt, too.

"I wish you hadn't said all those things about me on Saturday. That was unfair. Maybe a climbing lady would be more suited to you; good luck with finding her. I will leave you be now."

That evening he obviously started to think about what I said.

"Hi Jay, I just want to respond to your comment about Saturday. I never said anything I did not mean. If I was looking for a temporary liaison, we would have been fine, I loved spending time with you. It was always interesting and fun, but my instinct/intuition/whatever we want to call it, tells me that we don't have sufficient in common to cope with my obsession (which let's face it, is what it is). It sometimes sounds unhinged to me – but ever since I set myself this very ambitious goal of leading an outdoor 7a before I die, I have been obsessed by it and will be until I either do it or abandon it. If I do achieve this (only a 20 percent chance) it will be bigger than anything I have done in my live. Just HUGE to me and meaningless to anyone else. Sad, ain't it? Sometimes, I even bore myself. I hope you find someone soon. He will be a lucky man x"

I responded, "Temporary liaison, I see. Maybe you should take time to decide whether a lady is suitable for you before sharing your bed and flattering her. Good luck with your big ambition Tony. And take care."

I was seething, shouting out loud to myself, "Temporary." This search for the right man was getting tedious now. So many obstacles and so very little time. Here we have a 69-year-old man wanting to climb a particular cliff which might kill him, willing to sacrifice his future for it. I am sure there will not be many single 60-something ladies out there who fancy climbing up cliffs with him. Yet a part of me envies his ambition and determination, his fitness and intelligence. If only he was not so boring.

NEXT!!

OUR WALKING DATE

Hand in hand we took a path
Along the water's edge,
Sharing our love of life stories
No sign of committed pledge.

Summer air and wild flowers,
The warmth of our smiles,
As time reflected the clouds,
We disregarded the miles.

Our aim to see the valley,
Became lost in our distraction.
We held our eyes in the moment,
Testing for mutual attraction.

'Twas quizzical minds in doubt
Seeking the glints and wishes?
Yet the fun won throughout
Finished with a lingering kiss.

JACQUELINE T. **MAY**

CHAPTER 26
THE PANDEMIC AND UNREQUITED LOVE

The COVID-19 pandemic did eventually overwhelm Brazil; some newspapers blamed it on the Rio Carnival being a petri dish for spreading it. The tour group which followed ours were stuck in Argentina for several weeks, the borders were closed and many couldn't get home. I was very fortunate in many ways.

According to Government suggestions, I was advised to isolate, also known as "shielding". My doctor's surgery confirmed this in text messages, saying I was regarded as vulnerable because of my asthma.

The first week was a bit of a fog if honest. Still not entirely sure what COVID-19 was and thought it was a seasonal flu; it would disappear as the weather improved. However, after week two and hearing our Prime Minister Boris Johnson and his 'experts' showing charts and the number of deaths, I realised this was a worldwide pandemic and could go on for months. I became anxious, realising that I could be housebound for almost a year or more. I wasn't getting any younger and my future was looking bleak. Finding a partner in this climate would be impossible. I started to realise that all that was left for me was surviving as a lonely old widow. Toy Boy was my only true love and would be forever unrequited.

He wasn't interested in me and I had to face up to some kind of reality that I could control.

Not to be beaten mentally by the isolation, I put an action plan together; write a to-do list; I had lots of jobs I could tackle in the house; write that book I had always promised myself; ask my fit neighbours to do my shopping for me; spend as much time as I could in the garden and arrange Skype, Facetime and Zoom meetups with friends and family. My 10-year-old grandson Harry, offered to read me a story every Thursday; I cannot tell you how much that meant to me. He started with David Walliams 'Gangster Grandma', so fitting.

The epidemic caused much anxiety for many; one thing I could do was ring those whom I knew were isolated too, to chat and let them know someone was thinking of them.

I also tackled my own isolation by putting a sign on my gate saying "Shielding – Isolating? Please wave or chat if you see us in the garden." I put "us" as a precaution because I didn't want strangers knowing I lived alone. And people walking by did stop and wave and some passed the time of day. I put teddy bears in the window for children to see and painted a rainbow for the NHS and put it in my kitchen window. Somehow, I felt a great sense of pride; I was taking care of myself so my children didn't have to worry about me. It wasn't long before I started to receive COVID testing kits. The number of deaths, particularly in the care homes, was extremely high and our government declared it as a major pandemic.

I don't know what I would have done without Netflix during the long days when the weather wasn't so good. It was obvious the internet was busy at certain times of day when my TV would spool and the signal become slow. The internet came into its own during that period. For entertainment, communication, working from home, homeschooling, home shopping, etc. The country carried on operating in a digital world and those of us who were isolated were dependent on it. In the first few weeks, a nearby motorway was empty; I took a walk and photographed it; transport and cars had come to a standstill, giving the Government time to put population movement controls in place. This is my abridged version of what happened in the first year and how it affected me. I do know everyone has their stories of that time and could probably fathom the Government's safety strategies better than I. All I knew was I had to avoid getting COVID-19 (coronavirus) at all costs.

I used to go to bed early and get up late to shorten my days. As time went by, I lost my ability to motivate myself to do anything constructive or creative. I lived from one human contact moment to another. I had plenty of time to write a book, do some painting, or sort out my wardrobe, but a part of me kept saying, "This must end soon; I'll do it later."

My 70th birthday was looming; the weather had been amazing for weeks and I was starting to leave the house for country walks. I only allowed an hour daily, which is crazy when I think of it now.

On my birthday, my daughters decorated my garden early in the morning with balloons and streamers; it was such a surprise. One family arrived with a picnic. The Government rules were that only six people could gather in a garden at the same time. The remainder of my family stood behind the fence. We passed wine and food to everyone, and they all sang Happy Birthday to me. The whole day was bizarre, yet I felt so loved.

70 DOESN'T SEEM RIGHT TO ME

70 doesn't seem right to me
The years crept up like a stalking cat
The careful steps, occasional faults
Planning my path along the way
Yet now I struggle with the time of day

I see the world differently now
Wider than before I grew tall
Smaller now I'm shrinking
As the faults and cracks are growing

It's the blossom that lifts me each spring
Floating petals arrive like tears
Signals the start of another line
And winter winds are left behind

Discontentment isn't me you know
I'll see the seasons travel until I go
Cradled by the certainty we part
Pray I live on in another's heart

70 will never seem right to me
As in my head I'm thirty-three

So, what is all this to do with "69 @ 69," you might ask? Well, I had already had 69 dates and, at 69, started writing about my liaisons and sexual experiences in my diary. I felt the isolation of shielding during the pandemic would be a good time to write a book. Besides I had no chance of dating during this time.

Toy Boy and Laura decided to split; the pandemic had caused too many arguments. He thought it made sense for them to live together, but she didn't want to.

After sending me a happy birthday message, we started having conversations, initially checking to see if each of us was okay and talking about COVID. We did have the odd sex texts and video sex, but I was feeling low due to the lack of human interaction and desperately wanted to see him. The virtual sex was a distraction but no more than that. I felt I was being tormented even more.

There were so many Government rules, 'no go' high COVID case areas, divided into tiers, each tier with its restrictions. For instance, how many people could you have in a family or friend 'bubble', keeping at least a metre away from each other, wearing masks, and only walking outside for no more than an hour? It was like the world had gone nuts. Maps were online showing the number of cases, so you could check if the pandemic was high in your area. I became obsessed by this and all the news broadcasts on the 4 p.m. COVID updates - Boris Johnson (Prime Minister) and his 'COVID experts' giving out daily instructions and updates, promising a vaccine and support for those shielding.

Toy Boy told me that businesses like his, considered as essential services, could carry on as usual. Some of his clients were homes for the elderly, which was worrying as the highest death rates were in those homes. We both did our research about contact, and he suggested that he could bring his ladders over and do a few jobs for me in exchange for a coffee. That way I would have an occasional visitor regarded as legit. He would wear a mask and make sure he changed clothes before coming to my house. He would also make sure he tested for COVID when leaving work.

Well, how could I refuse? Of course, he came over and replaced a couple of light bulbs. After thoroughly washing his hands, we did end up in my bedroom where several bulbs had blown, wink. And made hot, passionate ... most of the time with our masks on!!! Except for 69!! We also experimented unsuccessfully, with Tantric sex (he had to explain that one to me). I know, crazy and a little irresponsible, I hear you say. But that contact was the most exciting thing I had done in months. We did giggle a lot at the absurdity of it all and agreed it was incredibly exciting. We lay in bed with a gap between us as if we needed to at least conform in some way to the rules.

We repeated the same for a few weeks, but only the masks stayed off longer than they were on. Then, the government started to relax the rules, and Toy Boy had more things to busy him: his daughter, announcing she was pregnant, then needing support when she had sadly lost the baby nearly full term. In addition, his son's second baby was on the way. His dad needed more support as his mental health and memory was deteriorating. His workload increased dramatically as people who had started home improvements during the pandemic were now ready for electrical solutions. At the same time, the Government had begun to relax travel both UK and abroad. If you had a vaccine, you could travel to many places. The process was complicated and required proof of having had the "jab", but at least there was some return to normality.

I tried to remain a friend and listened to the various challenges he was facing without putting any emotional pressure on him; I missed his visits terribly. But then, inevitably, our two-person relationship became three again.

Alan: "Laura and I have booked a trip to Majorca in July. Think she's missing our holidays at least, if not so much me."

Almost written in a way you would inform your best friend, not to someone you have been shagging all summer. I know I have given him the impression that all I wanted to have a physical relationship, but that isn't realistic, is it? He should know how I feel and cannot ignore that I have declared feelings for him in the past, or can he? I was so confused and hurt, a gut-wrenching hurt that made my whole body want to scream, "You bastard!!"

I tried to control my feelings and pretend the huge lump in my throat and internal screaming was nothing. He has done it again!! I let him get too close to me and my stupid heart fell for it. I didn't answer straight away, trying to work out my emotions and how I should react.

I recently read David Nicholls's book 'One Day' and couldn't help but feel I was going through a similar scenario. Only mine was a one-sided love affair and less tragic. I cried buckets over that book, but I tried not to do the same today. Anger is an emotion I knew I had to suppress.

"That's great," I wrote, "I love Majorca. My favourite place is Port de Pollença, and you must go on the mini rail journey to Soller," trying to be upbeat and mature.

He replied. "We are staying in Pollença, I've been before with the family."

I remember him telling me that his father struggled with Laura's accent and found her patronising. Toy Boy put it down to his dad being a little racist, based on his grandfather's experiences in WWII in Berlin with the Russians. Belarus was Russia, in his view. Consequently, he didn't take her to see him often over the four years they were dating.

I kept the conversation short and wished him well. I didn't want to know more, and I had a date waiting to distract me ….

WAKE UP!!!!!

Being a good woman
Doesn't make him want you.
Being attractive
Doesn't make him want you.
Making an effort
Doesn't make him want you.
Being loyal
Doesn't make him want you.
Taking care of him
Doesn't make him want you.
Loving him unconditionally
Doesn't make him want you.
Being honest
Doesn't make him want you.
Being there for him
Doesn't make him want you.
You cannot make him want you.

He has to want you enough to fight and keep you, not as a sex toy. You can be the most sincere, sexy, loving and giving woman ever, but if he doesn't want you then none of these wonderful things about you will make him want you. I repeat he has to want you in the first place, warts and all. If not, then bin him. Wake up!! He was never yours to have. Stop wasting your time and live happily knowing you have saved these things for someone who values, respects and wants you.

These were the words that came out of my mouth when talking to Penny, on the phone, who had an equally obsessive, unrequited relationship. We both agreed that some men are never going to commit but are happy to string you along because it either boosts their ego, or they don't have an alternative yet, or else the one they lust after isn't available. Some just need the sex and will pretend they care but don't, or else bachelorhood suits them.

I didn't eat properly for about three weeks; one day, I didn't get out of bed after a fitful night; I was supposed to be on a conference call with work. I had put my phone on silent. At 1 p.m. I was woken by stones hitting my bedroom window, at first I thought it was hail stones. When I pulled up the blind it was Maria, pleading with me to come downstairs. I was so groggy and weak from lack of food and overcome with emotions. My legs felt like lead and my brain seemed in a fog. When I opened the door, Maria, in her strong accent, blurted out.

"Jay, we are supposed to be catching our flight in three hours, and I've been trying to reach you all day. Are you okay? My god, look at the state of you." She rushes over to the kettle and switches it on to make me a cup of tea.

"When did you last eat and drink?" I responded in a croaky voice. I don't know. What time is it? "

"1 p.m. Jay. You look awful, and I'm not sure you are quite with us. You do know we are going to Spain today, don't you?"

My phone starts to vibrate. It's my boss, a message saying, "Are you joining us at this meeting?" I turn my phone off. This was turning into something even I was concerned about, not only Maria.

"Okay, I'm starting to get really worried about you now. You have neglected yourself, Jay, and we have to get you back on track. Men are not worth killing your life and yourself for. This man you have been pining over for the last few weeks isn't going to be your future, you are your future with your family and friends. You will find a man, a good man who loves and wants you. Not one that messes with your head." She passes me a cup of tea and toast. I struggle to swallow both but her motherly finger pointing at my plate was hard to ignore.

She took me upstairs and started putting clothes I had put in neat piles on my floor into my suitcase. "What's this? You packing for winter, it's over 25 degrees there and you are taking a fleece and tracky bottoms?" Her Mediterranean accent and animated personality are taking over.

"Now go and shower", she points me to the bathroom, still packing the case and inspecting every item as she folds them again. When I reappeared from the bathroom, she had already finished packing and was standing by the zipped-up case.

"We are going to enjoy this holiday Jay without men, not think of them, not interact with them and certainly not shagging them – okay?" She made me laugh, and in turn, she opened her arms for a big hug.

I promised her I would be ready in time for the Taxi to take us to the airport. It was so hard to motivate myself, but she was the kick up the arse I needed. This episode in my life was probably the nearest to an emotional breakdown I had ever experienced and I didn't want to go there again. My friends were more important than anything right now. My self-esteem was also at an all-time low, doubting my motivations continuously. Would I be capable of holding any relationship? Was I delusional? I was 70, for fucks sake.

Most days I proactively try to get Toy Boy (Alan) out of my mind, putting his account on my phone into "archive" to make sure I do not see any messages from him and be tempted to answer. I still cannot bring myself to block him though, crazy I know.

THE QUIET MAN

He's gone
The quiet man I was drawn to
With his quiet strength
Shows in the things
He does and doesn't say
eyes reflect in the way
He saw me waiting
For his pleasure words

Body aching for his touch
I've longed way too much
For answers to my dream
No, the quiet man it seems
Locks his words from view
His council remains true

Making him more magnetic
In his quiet, solitary place
Where he knows he has me
In wordless love for eternity
Drowning in unrequited fate
Dying for arms, that hesitate

Alas, he writes soft rejection
Be adult, resist temptation
He cannot taste my tears
The damage of wasted years
A quiet man's sweet caress
Is lost in my cry of weakness

I'll not write again in such a way,
I'll not chase him, I have to say
too degrading, I have my pride.
It's cutting me so much inside
Please know the injury I feel.
Is a wound deep and real

For there is kindness I know
The taste of adversity shows
A way of making us see
The value of what has been
That we don't rely on one soul
Life cannot be swallowed whole

JACQUELINE T. **MAY**

CHAPTER 27
MR TED

It was proving to be a very tedious occupation, trawling through the dating sites. I suppose it was a distraction from my isolation. Having reached my 70th year I have, for some reason, told myself to lower my expectations of men. They all look old because they are and so am I, but do I feel it? No! However, you cannot hide the number and there was no way I was going to lie about my age. Maybe I'd given this search for "The One" my best shot and I needed to face the reality of being single for the rest of my life.

The threats of the pandemic were not over, but access to the vaccine was available to all; normality was beginning to restart and life was beginning to feel less controlled by fear. No more walking alone and people walking across the other side of the road when they meet you coming the opposite way. There were times when I felt invisible. However, there were times when I felt relieved that they were not putting me in danger of catching COVID-19.

My sister Kitty called me most mornings to check I was okay and I would share some of my worries and frustrations. I told her about Toy Boy. She wasn't surprised.

"I don't know how or why you do it, Jay. I would have broken down by now, but you keep going and forgiving. He doesn't deserve you, and you deserve so much better." This was a line she used on me several times, and I would close my ears to it, not wanting to hear anything negative.

"Will you come with me to Harrogate and help me choose a puppy? A friend of mines' spaniel has had a litter of four puppies."

I agreed to go with her mainly for the ride out and a change of scenery. The puppies were gorgeous—only five weeks old, bundles of ginger fluff.

One sat on my feet and fell asleep, while the other three rough and tumbled around the kitchen floor. I picked him up eventually and let him sleep in my lap. I was totally captivated; how could this little puppy affect me so much? Feeling an attachment straight away. This vulnerable puppy will rely on a human to love, protect and feed him for the rest of his life, a commitment I had avoided since losing Tony. Yet there I was, realising that maybe this is what I need, some living being to care for, give and receive love from unconditionally. Did I need a man to do this? I know you are probably thinking this is not an alternative. However, the feeling of affection and responsibility was starting to overwhelm my thoughts. I am ready for this. I love animals, I should do this.

Kitty was speechless. Her friend was surprised she was selling two puppies in one viewing. It would be another three weeks before we could collect them, but in the meantime, we could visit and cuddle. I looked forward to these visits. I named him Ted (also Teddy). I bought all the equipment on the internet to home a puppy, and by the 8th week, I was ready. However, not having owned a dog before, I was unprepared for the work involved.

This bundle of fluff is like having a new baby. Feed every four hours and up at 5 a.m. to have a wee outside, that's if he hasn't already done on the floor. The toddler phase: chewing and eating everything it comes across. Elastic bands, twigs, tissues, my hairbrush, the TV remote control, the tea towels.

Oh yes, the tea towel I didn't see him consume under a chair. He starts being sick, and next, he is at the vet's, having his stomach opened to remove it. He is only 10 weeks old! And I nearly killed him. Little Ted has already affected my emotions. I realised how deep the attachment had become. Little sod will take over my life in so many ways, including drawing on my bank account. No turning back now.

He wasn't a distraction; he was part of my life now, and any relationship I would entertain would have to include Ted. When looking at dating sites, I found myself filtering to find profiles where people listed dogs, either liked them or owned them. This was a whole new approach, and maybe, just maybe, this commonality would be an attraction for both parties.

I began walking three-five miles a day, sometimes twice a day. He kept me fit and occupied, and there was the unforeseen benefit of meeting and talking to other dog owners in the park, on the pavements, and in the cafés. They all admitted that they would remember the dog's name and not their owner's; nevertheless, these brief interactions would make a very positive impact on my life.

I established a new girl tribe, all dog owners, too: sisters Naomi and Keira and their friend June. They were vibrant 60-year-old retired women who had worked hard and were ready for a new chapter in their lives. They were welcomed in by my existing tribe, and we would meet at least once a week in a local café, usually after I had walked Ted along the river first. They all loved him and Kitty's dog Ben.

I missed Ann, who had thankfully been given the 'all clear' from her breast cancer and was living in Essex with her new partner, whom she had met on a U3A (University of the 3rd Age) walking group. I couldn't be happier for her and felt a little bit of envy that she had found her man at 72. I should have been encouraged by this, but I was losing hope. After over 69 dates and no success, I must be doing something wrong.

These ladies keep me focused, always interested in each other, and always supportive when any of them experience life's challenges. The new additions to the girl tribe are included in my discussions regarding my dating stories. Naomi and June are married, and the others are single. The exception is Maria, who struggles with her drinking, gambling, and uncommitted boyfriend. I hear her cry down the phone most weeks over what he did or didn't do to her recently. It's hard to keep up the empathy sometimes.

"He's a loser," I would try not to shout. "How many times have you broken up now? He doesn't make you happy, and he's not going to change, you know that." Then she would tell me she loved him. What more could I say? I'm still hankering after a man I cannot have. And she gave me the same lecture a few months ago.

Ted is now the companion I have been lacking for some time. He sits next to me while I write and occasionally interrupts me for petting, food, drink, toilet or walk, like a needy man really. Occasionally I ask myself, do I need someone else to make demands on me?

TED

He's known as Tea Towel Ted.
He has a reputation for munching
Anything that takes his fancy,
A toy, his ball, my toes and his bed.

One lazy Friday afternoon,
He has secreted a tea towel
Beneath my kitchen chair
With an odd toy and spoon.

Toilet training was my aim.
Every 20 minutes, do a wee,
Every hour, clean the floor
While Tea Towel Ted remained.

Come the morning was a sad little pup
With some whining and a groan,
Not his usual bouncy self.
Phoned the vet to see what's up.

Crying forlorn and off his food,
We could only assume
He had eaten something nasty.
But meds didn't improve his mood.

I took him to the Yorkshire vet;
We are now on first name terms.
Ted not a happy puppy.
Feeling guilty, do I deserve a pet?

Operation in an hour's time,
I thanked and left him there.
As I sat on the chair in shame.
How could this dog be mine?

I nearly killed this happy boy,
Not watching his every move.
Instead of cleaning floors,
I should have monitored his toys.

Telephone call to confirm
He was blocked in three places.
A stone, a cap removed,
The tea towel and a worm.

Although he survived the operation
We have had other visits,
Part tennis ball, cardboard box, a toy
Maybe should call him Dyson.

JACQUELINE T. **MAY**

"Tea Towel Ted", now a celebrity pup
Known fondly for his name
No longer has access to tea towels,
Unless I train him to dry up.

CHAPTER 28
THE LORD OF THE MANOR

I changed my profile on the dating sites to include Ted, who I mentioned as an asset to my life. And it wasn't long before I received an enquiry from Gregory (not Greg). He was my age and wrote lovely things about my profile and dear Ted. He had owned dogs most of his life, but sadly, the last one passed away recently; at least now he had the pleasure of looking after a friend's two dogs from time to time. He would love to meet and see if Ted liked him. It made me smile; looks like I am being upstaged by my pet.

Again, I asked quite early on to talk on the phone. I had lost patience with constant texting; with some men, it felt like I was a pen pal, and they were too afraid to ask to see me. Loneliness and lack of confidence are difficult ingredients for a successful approach to dating.

Anyway, Gregory was far from that description. He had a Scottish accent, from Midlothian he said, but really Edinburgh, a favourite city of mine. The first phone call included memories of both my experiences in Edinburgh and his childhood there. He admitted to being a student of Gordonstoun, a renowned boys' public boarding school, where Prince Charles and Prince Philip attended. He sounded educated and I could tell he had a lot to say. He told me he had sold his business to a famous printing company just before the Stock Market crash.

Maybe a bit too much bragging for me, but I thought he was worth seeing. He lived in the Yorkshire Dales, about 45 minutes from me. A favourite walking area for Tony, we had done most of the public footpaths in that area with lunch in pubs and cafés to finish. I knew the area well. Something else we had in common. I agreed I would travel to him as the weather looked good and it would be nice to see his town again and meet in a little café he recommended, it specialised in chocolate drinks. I was amused as he obviously made an impression on the owners as they greeted him by name when we entered, and in turn, Gregory introduced me to them. Going to great lengths to describe where the individual jars of cocoa came from, Brazil being his favourite, which he ordered for both of us.

After our cocoa, he insisted we pay a visit to his first-floor apartment, which was a quarter share of a small stately home. I couldn't help but imagine him as a laird; all enthusiastic about its history and the views from its hilltop position. I was trying desperately to appreciate the austere splendour and history of this grey stone building, yet all the time thinking I could never live in such a place. Bet it was freezing in winter; it was very exposed on the hill overlooking Nidderdale.

The true opulence of the house interior presented itself with a wide oak staircase, panelled walls and massive varnished doors. Gregory stopped me on the landing, to admire Henry, a full-size porcelain pig with a grin on its face, quite disarming. Ted was not impressed and growled at the pink pot and squirmed around it with his tail between his legs. Behind the pig was a four-foot high wooden butler statue, complete with a tray holding an assortment of things, some AA batteries, a comb, and a used tissue, a hint of the chaotic lifestyle this eccentric man lived in. Again, even in summer, it felt cold to me with its incredibly high ceilings and single-glazed windows.

Gregory progressed to the kitchen, where there stood a beautiful dapple-grey rocking horse with two porcelain dolls in Victorian dresses sitting astride it. He had bought the dolls for his granddaughters, but neither child liked them. I cannot blame them, as even to me, those rosy-cheeked dolls with corkscrew curls and scary eyes felt unnervingly freakish and reminded me of the film, 'The Valley of the Dolls'. As you can tell that film had quite an impact on me.

The kitchen was no normal kitchen, it probably was once, but the working function of it was barely noticeable, with books and paraphernalia cluttering every surface. A huge stripped pine farmhouse table sat in the middle of his untidy kitchen. And under the eight-foot rotting sash window was a rocking chair with a large Steiff Teddy bear (yes, bears again) looking relaxed and almost welcoming. The view from the window was spectacular, with the Nidderdale Valley in view.

This quirky man surely had eclectic taste. When I looked at the ceiling, a shelf the height of a picture rail was also filled with clutter, books, and Teddy bears! I kid you not—what is it with men and Teddy bears?

"Would you like to see the lounge? It's what attracted me to the apartment. I'm very proud of it," he says in a thick Midlothian accent.

At first, I do not notice we are walking on a tartan carpet. The windows are a mixture of ecclesiastical and mullioned. The ceiling is full of beams centring in a half-circled room. I have to say it is magnificent. But would I be happy watching Country Life or Naked Attraction on TV there? Probably not the latter. Anyway, the room, whilst cosy, is crammed with period furniture.

"It was a chapel in its previous life; I couldn't resist it, as I am a lay preacher, you see," he says gleefully, and I smile weakly.

I cannot help saying to my inner self, 'What are you doing here?' I would drive a lay preacher mad. I had already dumped an ex-

Vicar. I remember Gregory sending me an email addressed Lord Dalesman. Pretentious, I thought. I should have guessed this Gregory was going to be an unusual first date.

He took me from one cluttered room to another, telling me the history of the house. I remembered him saying in one of our telephone conversations that his ex-wife never worked and was a stay-at-home mum. She left him because she was sick of being known as Gregory's wife. His son has been pestering him for some time to find a new lady and suggested he try Match.com. Then the penny dropped; this man is possibly looking for a woman to be his housekeeper, skivvy and cook. Although alarm bells rang, I was still intrigued enough to agree to meet again.

I didn't ask Gegory to visit my home on our second date. Instead, we met at the village car park. From the start I had reservations about him, it has to be said. His teeth were brown and clearly not cared for; for a man who smiles a lot, they were difficult to ignore, and his beard seemed more unkempt than I remember. He looked scruffy in general.

We recognise each other across the car park as he strides towards me with military purpose, his brown teeth smiling at me. In his hand, a clear plastic bag containing cooked liver. He gleefully tells me it is for Ted, my 12-month-old spaniel puppy. Must admit I am relieved it isn't for me. This announcement is before greeting each other in the normal manner. I was to learn that Gregory was not your normal 70-year-old. I try not to be judgemental about my dates, however, his superior attitude manages to raise the hairs on the back of my neck. Telling me he has put Ted's name in front of mine on his telephone contact list makes me feel somewhat second best. Not high value again! But I could forgive him for putting sweet Ted first.

He returns to his car and pulls out a walking stick, or should I say a wooden staff, which, at nearly 5'7", is only an inch or two shorter than him. Everything about this man is beginning to feel affected.

"I prefer to walk with a stick, not because I need one you see, but because I like the rhythm when I'm walking."

There he is with liver and staff, fully geared up with over-trousers, a North Face walking coat and hiking boots with ankle gaiters. I have already told him it was a river stroll, no more than four miles, not the Pennines.

We are standing in the Church car park, he with the slimy liver in his hand and Ted jumping like a Jack in a box overwhelmed by the inviting scent.

After our greetings, we set off on our riverside walk. Gregory is clearly used to being in charge and before long he has taken bouncy Ted's lead and marched on ahead trying to tell a 12-month-old puppy to behave, the pup occasionally looking back at me almost pleading with the whites of his eyes showing like they do when he's being defiant with me, only this time it seems like Ted is saying, "Who the hell is this joker?" If that isn't enough, I am lectured on how to train my dog with liver, insisting I take pieces of the slimy stuff to encourage the now giddy animal to come to heel. Eventually, I made an excuse that the liver was too rich for his delicate stomach.

As we approached the end of our walk, two of my female acquaintances, Shirley and Pauline, approached us with their broad smiles and friendly greetings. It was a welcome relief. We chatted, and introductions were made.

He said, "All ladies in this village seem to have lovely hair and hairstyles," as he addressed my puzzled-looking friends. He chuckled, but I could not wait for us to move on. The last part of our walk couldn't end sooner; I felt I was being preached to, and poor Ted, whites of his eyes flashing occasionally, was being drip-fed with liver, which Gregory insisted wouldn't do "the lad" any harm. My patience was tested, and I was relieved when we arrived back at the start of our walk. As we said our farewells, he kissed me on both cheeks, his rough beard scraping my face. Luckily, he didn't attempt my lips.

As I walked away with my faithful pup, I knew I would write that night to say, "It's me, not you," knowing I was content with Ted just now, that I needed more than a dog lover with liver.

He responded to my message that morning.

```
"Good Morning Jay,

Aren't we humans complex creatures? I enjoy your
company and admire your very trim figure. Somewhat
similar to you, I couldn't quite imagine an intimate
relationship with you, which is why I suggested a
theatre visit to see if anything developed further.
However, your note today clarified things, and with
no hard feelings whatsoever, I wish you well for
your future. You will certainly be kept busy with
dear Ted.

Un abrazo fuertísimo!

Gregory"
```

Oh, what a relief that he couldn't imagine an intimate relationship with me. I doubt I would have reached the kissing stage, let alone anything else.

My mobile rings. It's Penny.

"So how did it go with the Laird of the Dales? I didn't know you had another date with him."

It was amusing for her that she found out through Shirley and Pauline that they had met my date in our local beauty spot. I had told her previously about his apartment, its contents, the Teddy bears and my reservations about him. She and the Girl Tribe were fascinated and liked the idea of me being 'Lady of the Dales'.

"I'm not keeping him from you. I was not sure and thought a second date would confirm one way or another."

"Well, did it? Shirley and Pauline thought he was charming. He said nice things about their hair." I could hear her suppressing a laugh.

"Don't Penny, he was a nice man in many ways but definitely not for me. I've already sent him a Dear John email."

"Oh Jay, as usual you try and see the best in these men you date, but they never quite make the grade. Shirley and Pauline were looking forward to meeting him again." This time she was audibly giggling.

I told Penny about the teeth and his cooked liver for Ted; she was almost hysterical at the end of the phone.

"Look, Jay, you could have booked him a dental appointment once you started a relationship and told him liver makes you sick. You are so fussy. He was a Laird, for goodness sake. Not many of those pop up on Match every day!" she is still giggling.

I told her he was looking for a housekeeper, really, and I was definitely not up for that.

"Oh no! You could have insisted on hiring staff for him to do that."

We both laughed together.

"Besides, his response to my "Dear John" email was that he couldn't see himself being intimate with me."

"For fuck's sake, Penny, rather than being insulted, I was so relieved," I said in a high-pitched voice.

I promised I would see her and the girls soon and I would update them all on what I had been up to. Penny laughed.

"That would be great. You are the only one having fun at the moment."

NEXT!!

CHAPTER 29
THE FISHING ROMANTIC

My crazy obsession with Toy Boy Alan was troubling me most days. I would write to him, compose poems without sending them, and listen to music I knew he liked. He would occasionally send me messages.

```
Happy Friday Jay.

Lovely day isn't it?

Hope you are okay?

How are you?

You found Mr Right yet?
```

I would reply briefly to some of his messages and tell him I was fine and getting on with my life. Occasionally, I would inform him of my latest dates. I felt so empty when our chats ended, but I knew I could not let him know how I felt anymore. And even when he started to flirt, I would cut the conversation short. No more sex texting, he had Laura now. Sometimes I would tell him to behave.

Ted the puppy was a big part of my life now, and my yearning for a partner to fill my solitary existence was waning (other than Toy Boy). In the main, I was settled at this time. My 71st birthday was celebrated with Dan, a mechanic from York. I had a couple of meals out with him, but I decided I couldn't live with his high-pitched voice and constant talk of his obsession with refurbishing classic cars and his younger brother being a millionaire.

Then came Ray, with his dimple cheeks and a lovely smile. He stood out on the dating site. With only the one photo seemed to say everything. He looked relaxed in his shorts and T-shirt, obviously on holiday. I looked at it several times before talking to him. We chatted on the phone and laughed for about an hour, talking about his fat fingers and thumbs as he tried to learn how to play the guitar. We both liked the same type of music. He knew my village well and had fished by the river a few years ago. He wanted to come over right there and then, saying he was free that afternoon. I put him off and made up a story. I wasn't ready to meet him yet.

Two days later, I arranged a meeting point nearly halfway between us, a hotel converted from an old mansion house. It had acres of land around it and its own lake. I suggested we meet for a coffee and, if we had time, have a little stroll around the gardens.

I was not disappointed; he was just my type and had the height and look of Toy Boy, only he had large dimples and a bigger grin than him. I loved his curls, too. I dressed casually: light blue jeans rolled up at the ankles, strappy sandals, and a pale pink denim jacket. My daughter said I could carry the look, making me look younger.

He grinned, then leaned over and whispered, "You look lovely. I've ordered a glass of white wine. What would you like?" I nearly went weak at the knees. This was not your usual hug and kiss on the cheek greeting. Or asking about my journey?

We sat on a Chesterfield sofa (chesterfield again) with many cushions in the corner of the room while waiting for the wine to be delivered. The room had panelled walls and a large period portrait painting was in each panel. It was like stepping into Dowton Abbey.

He was easy to talk to and told me he had separated from a long-term partnership. He has one daughter from a previous marriage, and his partner has one daughter, too; both girls grew as sisters. He retired from being a building surveyor only three years ago, and fishing was his hobby.

We discussed our experiences on dating sites, and to my surprise, he had been on only one date, and that went on to a short relationship with a multi-millionaire businesswoman who owned commercial properties throughout the North of England. It wasn't long before he realised she wanted to employ him as her personal surveyor to go around her properties before either buying, selling, or renovating. He said it was like going back to his old job again. When he told her he didn't want to continue, she coldly told him he was of no use to her.

This experience had clearly affected him. He said, "What kind of person goes on a dating site to employ people?"

I responded, "Obviously, a ruthless millionairess."

I was really taken with Ray; I would say far more than any of my recent dates. He had such a lovely way with him, charming, gentlemanly, funny, and I thought he looked sexy, too. Some of you cannot imagine a man or woman in their 70s looking sexy. Well, physical attraction isn't just for the young, you know. We did a little stroll around the grounds, and he immediately held my hand. A warmth and feeling of comfort like a hot water bottle on a cold day, and I didn't want to let go.

Sadly, as the dates progressed, Ray revealed he had many insecurities and baggage you would never have guessed during the first meeting. He was still in a toxic battle with his ex-partner, who was trying to take him for everything - his words. His two girls, as he called them, were at loggerheads, even though his partner's daughter was still talking to him. He claimed his partner, another Sue (I cannot get away from this name), had put on a lot of weight after the menopause. She was insanely jealous, and if there were an attractive woman in the room, she would go out of her way to accuse him of looking or lusting after her, sometimes making a fool of herself and him in the process. She started to alienate their friends because she believed the wives were interested in him.

He insisted he was never unfaithful to her, that he was a big romantic at heart, bought her flowers, and surprised her with treats, meals, and holidays; his gestures were never appreciated. One day, when she was being accusative in front of their daughters, his daughter told her to stop being so vindictive and mean. His partner struck her very hard across the face, knocking her out as her head hit the stair banister. That was the final straw for Ray. She had become impossible and potentially violent. Plus, she was drinking heavily, and her mental health was suffering as a result. He booked counselling for her, but she kept missing appointments.

"The old saying is, you can take a horse to water, but you cannot force it to drink."

He offered his other hand to guide me over a small log on the path. The tree had been blown over in recent storms.

"I feel guilty abandoning her. There was little I could do to improve her life. I suggested we marry at one point. Her response was, "I don't want a pity proposal." He turned around, "What else could I do? She's still drinking heavily, according to my friends."

Part of me felt sorry for her. She was struggling with her weight; her partner, whom she wasn't married to, looked really good in his mature age; let's face it, there are many more single women in their 70s than men. Of course, she would have competition. She did not know how to handle the situation and became angry and resentful. However, I started to get the feeling that Ray was a bit of a man-child. It seemed to me she mothered him, making all the decisions and plans in their relationship. He just went to work, and she did everything for him. Maybe she was frustrated with his lack of input and attention in his retirement.

I learned to my cost that fishing, which I initially thought was an escape from his struggling partnership, was an obsession.

He came to my house for a meal twice. On the second occasion, I suggested we go to his place next. No, that wasn't possible, as he was worried his ex would see my car there; he was convinced she was spying on him. I was not concerned and tried to reassure him, but he was adamant he would not settle if I were there.

On the third occasion, we had a bottle of wine at my house, and I offered him a stay-over. He declined because he had a fishing match the following day and had to be up early—God, where have I heard that before?

After the meal, we sat on the sofa and started kissing and petting. Then, all of a sudden, he jumped to his feet and told me we were going too fast and he had to go. I think he flew out my front door—stupid me.

I remember he said he was having prostate problems and was under a specialist. This hasty departure could also mean he had erectile dysfunction and didn't want to face talking about it. I could have reassured him that we could deal with this together; sex isn't everything. But it's not what men want to talk about, even to their doctor.

I wrote to him several times; he would respond by saying he was fishing, shopping, searching for new locations, planning new competitions or just fishing again. Basically, he ghosted me without explanation. Again! I had met yet another man obsessed with his sport.

Comments from the Girl Tribe were:

Penny: "You've kissed another frog, Jay?"

Ann: "How boring. Who wants to play second fiddle to a fish?"

Kitty: "He obviously prefers pond life…..NEXT!!!"

CHAPTER 30
THE COMPETITIVE CYCLIST

Stan wrote to me whilst I was seeing Ray, and I ignored his first message. A few weeks later, I decided I would respond. He was my age and over six-foot-tall, with thick grey hair, bushy eyebrows and piercing blue eyes. He was very slim, as cyclists generally are. We laughed about men in Lycra as I told him I had an urge to smack cyclists' bottoms as I passed them in my car. All that standing up on their pedals and waving their buttocks about was asking for a quick smack. He said I was a pervert but liked it! I think it broke the ice a bit.

Again, a man obsessed with his sport, he had won several championships and was quite happy to brag about them. I informed him that cycling was not my thing. I was happy to watch cycle races on TV and all that Lycra, but that was it. He wasn't put off by that and insisted we meet soon.

Sometimes, I wish I had cycled. I had a lovely blue one once at 65, but the traffic made me very nervous, and it sat in my shed gathering dust for two years, hoping I would find the courage to try again. I didn't.

We met halfway in Richmond and had a coffee, followed by a stroll. He seemed pretty serious; not a lot of passion or fun in his world other than his cycling. I couldn't see much in common between us. I was getting cynical with my dates now, constantly looking for red flags, yet sometimes I was almost resigned to the fact that if they were decent and self-sufficient then they were worth considering. I had become less fussy in some ways. My main criteria were if they had a pulse, were not in debt, both knees worked, had no dodgy hips and knew what day it was, then there was a chance.

Stan suggested we meet for a meal somewhere next. I agreed. We made it a lunch date, and he recommended a place just off the A1 motorway.

I laughed. "It's not a service station is it?" and he responded with what I considered his first real smile. Other times, his face barely showed amusement. Maybe he is a dour Yorkshireman; banter is not his thing. Nevertheless, I agreed to meet again. He seemed more relaxed this time, although the pub we ate in was a bit austere. Perhaps it fitted his personality. He talked about his training schedule and his up-and-coming competition; he was determined to defend his title. A man of 70 still competing in a fast sport against younger men was to be admired, but he sounded like he might struggle this time.

He asked me about my past and career, my children and my late husband. I must have spent a good hour telling him about my daughters and five grandchildren, telling him I had given them all nicknames. I skirted over my marriage to Tony and how he died but gave him a history of my working life, how I filled my retirement years with travel, volunteering and, more recently, Ted. I was impressed that he listened throughout with attentive interest.

"Gosh, that's a colourful and challenging life you have led, Jay, so much going on. Mine is boring in comparison. Shall we get the bill."

I nodded and almost thought he had decided to end the discussion and the date. I was wrong.

"I want to show you something if you have time?"

I was intrigued. What had he got in mind? He took me to the riverside and to a beautiful tulip garden. The colour and types of tulips were amazing. Some looked more like roses. I had never seen such a display before.

"I like gardening," he said, cupping a black tulip in his two hands, admiring its petals. "There is a small garden centre attached to this park. If it's okay with you, I would like to go there and see if they have any of these."

So, here was another side to him. Being a little creative myself and an admirer of flowers and nature, I was really taken by surprise at Stans's affectionate description of the tulips and his desire to own one of them. We wandered around the rows of wooden raised beds and plastic trays. Some tulips were in flower in pots. He found what he wanted and bought two pots.

"One is for you to remind us of our date?"

This was the passion I was looking for. He was deeper than I thought. I suggested he come to mine next for lunch. I felt now there was much more to this man than I first thought.

He phoned the day before and said he would bring all the ingredients and cook for us both. Was there anything I didn't like? Yet another surprise. He was certainly making an impression now, and what is more, he was making a real effort to woo me.

I was a little nervous before he arrived. I cleaned the kitchen thoroughly, except I was worried about the state of my oven, which was black with ten years of grime. The door was hardly see-through because of the burnt-on streaks of greasy oil. I know I am not alone in having an oven like this, but I am ashamed all the same.

I was relieved when he said that he didn't need the oven, everything would be done on the stove and microwave. We had salmon with lemon rice, a green salad, and a cheesecake he made. He liked to cook and didn't have many opportunities to bake, which he loved to do, too. He told me about his daughter Sally, now single and his granddaughter, how he cooked for them once a week and babysat every other Saturday when his daughter wasn't working, allowing her a night out with friends.

I was starting to think that this man had many qualities that I admired. Besides the cycling, I could imagine he could be a "slow burner," as Penny would put it. Yes, he could grow on me.

Stan admired my home and said it put his to shame. He had neglected his own house. "It's still stuck in the 80s," he said. "Needs decorating from top to bottom, new carpets and curtains. The kitchen isn't very old. It was one thing I did before Sandra died. After that, I didn't incline to do much to the house." He looked out of my kitchen window at my garden. "I've concentrated more on the garden. I find it relaxing being out there, and it occupies my mind. The house was her domain and the garden mine; suppose I have hung on to her influence, but I feel now it's time to change that if I am going to embark on a new relationship."

I asked him, "How does your daughter feel about you dating?"

He held my hand and kissed the back of it. "She is all for it. If it wasn't for Sally, I wouldn't be on the dating site, and I wouldn't have met you."

He then held my chin and kissed me tenderly. I wasn't sure whether to let things progress. Further, I felt that nagging doubt of not wanting to hurt either party. We were both vulnerable people who had lost someone dear to us, and I didn't want to make the mistake of rushing into a physical relationship.

It was obvious he loved Ted and told me he missed having his own two dogs; they died not long after his wife, which must have been a double blow.

We cuddled on the sofa and chatted about our childhoods, who influenced us, our childhood dreams and dreads. He attended an all-boys boarding school; his father was a civil engineer and worked on government projects abroad. He spent the first few years of his life in Africa, and until he reached 5'10", he was bullied.

"I was a gawky kid with pale skin and really skinny, thick hair that stood up on end. I looked like a lavatory brush." He laughed. "I always felt awkward, particularly in physical education lessons. Then I discovered cricket, and I was good at it. I have been sporty ever since. I found other males respect sporty individuals. I suppose that force has driven me to be so competitive in cycling."

I could now understand that this man had a soft underbelly. He helped me wash up, and then, as we said our goodbyes, he gave me a deep kiss on the lips, his tongue exploring my mouth. Yes, he left me wanting more. We agreed to meet again; he would ring and arrange another time.

He phoned the following day and said I had inspired him to tackle his house. He was going to the DIY shop to buy paint and wallpaper, order carpets and probably blinds, start on the sitting room, and then, once that was done, progress to the dining room. He sounded excited and animated. I was really pleased for him as he added he still wanted to see me, but he needed to crack on with his project. I understood and told him not to worry about me; the sooner it's done, the better.

A few days later, he sent photographs of the work he had started, again sounding excited. His daughter was amazed, he said. But it didn't last. He phoned to say his elderly mother, in her 90s, was suffering from dementia, and he needed to sort out some care for her. He would ring me at least twice a day, updating me on what he was doing. I must admit I enjoyed the fact that he could confide in me and ask for my advice.

His older brother, who lived in Africa, started to cause him grieve, worrying about the inheritance being frittered away in care homes, trying to push Stan into caring for his mother. He asked if he could come over to see me. I agreed and told him to bring a couple of pizzas.

A troubled soul stood on my doorstep carrying two pizza boxes. We ate the lukewarm pizzas while he told me what was happening in his life. I had opened a bottle of wine, and we were soon in bed with the two glasses. He was very gentlemanly and white, except for his lower arms and legs, which were very brown. The last time I saw such a white body was hairy back Peter, the shoe and foot fetishist.

I wasn't as confident as I had been in the past and certainly not as sexually driven as I had been with Toy Boy. I was glad Stan took the lead.

I did all the usual things you see in the movies but I didn't have an orgasm. Stan did and almost cried out and shook like a leaf before collapsing on me! No expletives, no shouting for God and no congratulating himself. He didn't even ask me if I had cum or how was it for me? We lay there in each other's arms and stayed silent.

"Next time we will have music on, what do you think?" he spoke softly and then looked sideways at me for an answer.

"Yes, that would be nice."

He didn't stay the night as he was meeting social services for his mother's care.

For several weeks, often on Sundays, he would visit me. He once cycled the 50 miles to my house. I found it hilarious seeing him in Lycra and slapped his arse. He wasn't so amused. There should be a happy ending, but he wasn't as committed as I thought. Excuses included; finding support for mother, which I perfectly understood; decorating the house; tidying the garden after the winter; a pre-planned cycling/training holiday in Majorca, with no mention of a future trip with me (yes, that island again); his intense training for the big competition; looking after Molly; complaining about his daughter's useless ex and how Stan had to support her; the self-serving brother.

On the scale of issues, his were not as bad as some, but I detected a weakness in him. Again, I would never be a priority; was I expecting too much? The sex was nice, nothing special, and the cuddles and music made it better. His cooking was a delight. I never saw his house and when I wrote to say I thought there was too much competition for his attention, it was looking doubtful that we could form a lasting relationship. I wasn't even sure his daughter knew about me. It was best to end our short relationship before we got hurt. Bearing in mind, Stan had been introduced to both my family and friends, oh, how familiar this is; so many men don't seem to think this part of a relationship is essential.

I called him to say I didn't think our relationship was going anywhere and that maybe he needed time to do all the things that stopped him from forming a solid relationship with me.

He responded, not rejecting what I said but saying, "You were the reason I refurbished my house. I wanted you to see it. My daughter was looking forward to meeting you and Ted".

He went quiet for a moment and then said, "I understand that my life is chaotic and leaves very little time for a relationship."

Another pause: "If you are in this area, would you call in for a cuppa? I would love to see you."

I wished him well with his competition and ended the call.

I was saddened by the end of this short relationship as I started to become fond of him, but it wasn't enough. I need a man to want me above all else, not necessarily above his mother or his daughter and granddaughter, but to at least be given some special time. Not just to be there for a shoulder to cry on or a visit for sex occasionally. There was a part of me starting to think that these part-time relationships were all I deserved; life is short, and relationships in your 70s are even shorter.

My two daughters had different opinions regarding Stan. The eldest said she thought he was arrogant and didn't like his eyes. She couldn't see it lasting, so she wasn't surprised. The younger daughter said what a lovely man he was and thought he was right for me and was sorry it hadn't worked out.

When I met my Girls Tribe next, I told them he was a really lovely man, and out of most of my dates, he had the most potential for a future. Unfortunately, he had too many other distractions to allow me to be a priority (I wonder if I sound entitled or spoilt).

"His loss. What is it about men? They are so fixated on their sports, exes and other crap they don't recognise a good thing when they see it. You are a good person, generous and affectionate. You deserve better."

Kitty also comments: "Do you think it's men in your age group, Jay? It may be that new relationships are too difficult for them to comprehend. You have said before that many want a quiet, uncomplicated life. They crave the company of women on their terms without commitment. F*#k them, now what next!"

As she sips her coffee, I agree with everything she said. "Kitty, as the old saying goes, women are from Venus and Men are from Mars' I think we have different needs and expectations. Hard to fathom where I am going wrong, or is it I still feel I'm worth more and won't settle for less, my own arrogance getting the better of me, maybe? Sadly, there seems to be very little choice in my age group, and maybe I have missed the boat, and I am destined to be single."

I sighed; I am not perfect Kitty. I lack patience and may be too strong for a lot of men. I wish sometimes I could be that compliant, housewifey woman, but I cannot. I have too much I want to do; I need to make the most of life; it's too short to spend it with the wrong person; I would rather be alone; I know that now."

CHAPTER 31
THE BLUE DANUBE AND THE PROPOSAL

After finishing the relationship with Stan, I booked a holiday on a river cruise on the Danube over Christmas week to yet again distract myself from the manhunt I had been on for almost five years. Plus, the nagging thoughts of Toy Boy and what he was doing with Laura kept invading my brain. I was three months away from my 72nd birthday and felt I needed to get on with my life now as a single woman. Travel always excites me, and whilst I never hope for a romantic liaison, I always meet some memorable travel companions, many of whom become friends initially. However, once home and after time, the contact fades away naturally. These short friendships always add to the travel experience and have given me a few stories to tell.

Among my fellow travellers on this trip were a group of Americans I befriended; that nation made up 70% of the passengers. A family of mum, dad and three early-twenties children were celebrating Dad's retirement, and he wanted all the family together on this holiday, possibly for the last time.

They seemed fascinated with me travelling alone, being English and from the city where Dad (Eddie) went to university for a year. He couldn't wait to talk to me about Yorkshire which he had visited during his time at University. I was often asked to sit at their table for breakfast when they would quiz me on so many things. I enjoyed their family banter with the two daughters and son, too; it was a pleasure to be around them, and I felt safe.

A father and two sons also befriended me. My first contact was with the youngest son Jak, a 6'5" giant of a man with a shaved head, enormous bushy beard and tattoo-covered arms; some would say he had a "red neck look" about him. I nicknamed him "Big Foot" (I know, not original), which he seemed to enjoy being called. He had one arm in a sling, supporting a broken shoulder; I remarked that only two years previously, I, too, had a fractured shoulder and sympathised with him. We had coffee together and chatted for at least an hour as the boat slowly sailed down the Danube on a misty day. The views were unclear, and we were waiting for our next stop, which was to disembark and visit a small town on our way to Vienna. I would guess Jak was about 35, his brother nearly 40 and his dad in his mid-60s.

He told me how his dad and brother were much smarter than he was; they were doctors. I disagreed. I said people who trained for five years for a career were not necessarily smarter, maybe a bit more dedicated/focused than some. I explained from my own experience that I had met many very smart people in my career who didn't have a qualification to their name, laughing and referring to myself in the process of telling him.

"Oh my, that's so refreshing to hear. It takes a smart person to come up with something like that." I didn't tell him I never felt smart.

I couldn't help but feel sorry for him; there was that hint of him being put down for most of his life by his family members. He also admitted his mother was a stay-at-home "Mom", dedicating her life to looking after the three of them until she passed away from pancreatic cancer. I told him my mother also had the same cancer and he gave me a massive hug with his one arm. He said he wanted to introduce me to the other two family members. I wasn't sure about the prospect of meeting them but nodded all the same.

He was a lovely, warm, gentle giant. His demeanour changed when he talked about how spiritual he was and how his girlfriend, who was an artist, had introduced him to another world of art, theatre and yoga. His parents were never interested in that sort of thing.

As he continued to speak, I felt the boat's engine slow down and could see the jetty of our next stop. This was a particularly beautiful village on the Danube, with its main feature, a blue and white painted Church sitting in the middle. I agreed to join the American family and wished Jak a lovely day.

Bigfoot Jak saw me wandering around the Vienna Christmas Market the next day. He insisted I join his Dad, who had an austere look about him, thinning hair that looked tinted and the shorter brother, who looked up and was more interested in the contents of his phone, his thin, mousy brown hair covering his forehead in spikes.

His brother suddenly announced, "Gluhwein, that's what we should have. It's a tradition here at Christmas," as he pointed to the screen on his phone. At least he researched on his phone to get the most out of the day.

We opted for a traditional mulled wine (gluhwein) in the Bierkeller. While the three of us sat cupping our hot drink, Jak told his dad and brother about me. They were very polite, but they didn't have the same interaction; I felt that they were too dull compared to Bigfoot.

My feet were going numb by the minute, and the oom-pah music was so loud I could hardly hear the men uncomfortably close to me on a bench seat. Once my drink was finished, I made my excuse that I needed to get back to the boat to warm up. They were all very polite and stood up as I left. Manners maketh the man, some say. I valued their respect but couldn't help thinking, do they view me as some kind of elderly English noblewoman that this was expected of them? Felt weird.

A letter was posted under the door while I was getting ready in my cabin for my evening meal onboard.

```
"Dear Jay, myself, George and David, would welcome
your company at our table this evening, signed Jak
(Big Foot)."
```

To say I had mixed feelings was an understatement. My biggest fear was Jak trying to set me up with his dad.

I dressed simply in a plain pale blue floral blouse and navy knee-length skirt. For some reason, I was really struggling with the button on my blouse. My left hand wouldn't stop shaking. "Come on Jay, stop the silly nerves," I said to myself. Although, I had noticed lately how clumsy I had become, tripping up and spilling things, was it my new asthma medication, I wondered?

I arrived at the table on time to find three smiling faces staring at me. Jak jumped to his feet and gave me one of his giant hugs with one arm. George pulled out a chair for me. David sat opposite me, half smiling, and said, "Hi, glad you could make it."

The conversation started a bit slow, with the question of how the rest of my trip was going. I tried not to give too much eye contact because I felt I was being scrutinised. For some reason, my confidence seemed lacking and I wanted to escape from the table, only I knew it would be rude to do so.

Thankfully, Jak started talking about their home in Utah and his wonderful childhood there. George and David became animated about their fishing and hunting game together; Jak explained he was too squeamish to participate in blood sports.

They described how they spent more time on the golf course now watching the game run across the greens and the rough rather than shooting them. I couldn't help noticing the bond between George and David was much stronger, and they seemed to exclude

Jak from their 'do you remember when?' moments. Maybe Jak was a disappointment to his Dad.

From what I was hearing, they were typical Americans who believed in the 'Second Amendment of their Constitution', the right to bear arms. While my father always had a rifle when I was growing up, it was for shooting rabbits and providing food for our large family. Their use of guns was purely for a macho blood sport and possibly for perceived protection. I was starting to feel uncomfortable in their company.

George was particularly patronising with the waiters, and that grated on me. When the waiter delivered the wine list, George opened it. He tried to impress me with his knowledge of European wines, while telling me Californian wines were much better in his opinion, although you paid much more for them. I thought I would throw a spanner in the works and ask what he thought of Australian and New Zealand wines. He just dismissed them as immature vineyards and felt they had a long way to go to be considered fine wines. I commented, "Really? How interesting that you would think that."

I told him I had visited many vineyards, from Mendoza in Argentina and Portugal to the Yarra Valley in Australia, and many in Spain, Germany, and France.

"They all have their special vintages, depending on the climate at that time. Therefore, they all have something to offer to the most discerning of pallets. But we all have our favourites don't we."

I know, deep down, I was bragging about my well-travelled past, but he riled me with his superior attitude, and it didn't end there. The truth was, my Tony had more of an interest in vineyards; he was the one who dragged me around them. However, I did take notice, and this enabled me to comment about what I saw and experienced.

"Oh, I see we have a wine connoisseur at our table. Tell us which of the wines we should be drinking on this list." With a mocking voice, George pushed the leather-bound wine list my way.

I didn't even look at it and responded, pushing the list back across the table. "Actually, the house wines on this cruise are very palatable and I'm sure the chef and wine waiter chose carefully to make sure they complement our wonderful menu," I remembered that at the side of the menu options were recommended wines.

Jak looked across at me and gave a large grin with a slight nod. We both picked up the food menu simultaneously to study it. "Well, that was interesting, thanks, Jay. Let's order. I'm hungry, and tonight, it's fillet steak for me, and I will have a beer with it." I laughed with Jak as he demonstrated with his one arm and a knife pointing upwards in his fist. Cutting his steak would be a challenge.

"I am sure the waiter will cut it for you, Jak; they are extremely helpful." Again, I couldn't help myself having a dig at George's arrogance earlier.

George hardly spoke to me throughout the meal. David was more interested in my travels and told me where he wanted to go on his wish list. I kept my knowledge understated, for I was beginning to hate myself for sounding superior, too. George was clearly not used to women standing up for themselves, misogyny being a part of his nature.

I didn't wait for the desert course. I made excuses that I was very tired and knew we had a long day and night ahead of us, as it was New Year's Eve, and I wanted to enjoy the masked ball and fireworks.

New Year's Eve was fantastic. Our guide took us to a beautiful ballroom in a palace overlooking Vienna, where we were given a brief waltz lesson. As I didn't have a partner, a young man took my hand without a word; he was a perfect stranger, handsome and Austrian. We waltzed to an orchestra playing the 'Blue Danube' (by

Johann Strauss II). He whisked me around the floor at breakneck speed, and suddenly, I became very dizzy, and he had to stop.

Immediately after the waltz, the fireworks began lighting up most of Vienna, with beautiful landmark buildings reflected in various colours. We stood on the huge terrace in awe of the spectacle and listened to the 'Blue Danube' again as the fireworks seemed to crescendo in time to the music. The display finished in time for the clock to strike **midnight**.

In front of me was a young couple; he was of Chinese descent, in an immaculate DJ suit, with a bright red dicky bow tie, hair swept back with a very neat ponytail at the nape of his neck. I watched as he went down on one, with a little black box in one hand and the hand on his knee. Clearly, he was proposing to a beautiful red-headed English Rose. With a massive grin, I could clearly hear him pop the question, to which she quietly accepted with a nod and then screamed the palace down in excitement—jumped on him, striding his hips.

"We are engaged!" she is still screaming and jumping up and down in his arms, kissing his face and neck; he could hardly hold her. He gave her a long, lingering kiss when he saw his chance. Everyone who witnessed it started applauding and those who didn't came over to see what was happening; many men shook his hand, and women came over to hug her. I happened to be taking photos of the festive scene around me when I caught their moment on camera. We exchanged details, and I promised I would forward the photographs to them, which I did. And yes, they did get married a year later.

Oh! How this moment touched my heart. Young love. I struggled to remember an occasion or feeling of elation that someone loved me so much to surprise me and treat me with adoration.

Reminiscing, I was sixteen and had only been kissed once before meeting Tony. He did have his moments, but he was more practical than most, and his idea of a surprise was, he asked me first. It wasn't until recently that I understood that he was insecure about failure and rejection. He hated getting things wrong, and consequently, he was risk averse. Surprises were too risky.

I was the opposite and surprised him a few times. I believed our opposite natures complemented each other, but I now realise I was short-changed regarding emotional connection and romance, which had been my driving force to find "The One" who could fulfil that missing element in my life. It's not a big ask, you might think, but neither did I.

Many people I have met in my life never find love and romance. You would think girls and men who tick most boxes deserve to find the right person, but they don't. Conversely, I have heard of couples in their 70s finding love. However, my cynical self was starting to doubt the kind of love portrayed in movies; perhaps love was an illusion that had passed me by in my later years.

I laugh now but accepted Tony's dour ways over the years. He was very much his father's son.

My engagement was in a café. He asked me over our two cups of coffee, "Shall we get married?" I remember saying, "If you want to," considering I thought I was punching above my weight with him. I was from a single-parent family of six children living in a corporation house, and his father had a good job and owned their house, a car, and a caravan.

Tony also owned a scooter adorned with several mirrors and spotlights. It amuses me now when I remember he responded, "Yes, I wouldn't have asked if I didn't. Shall we go to Leeds on Saturday to look for an engagement ring?"

His mum put on a buffet for family and friends on Christmas Eve to celebrate our engagement. It was the first time I had ever been given a party dedicated to me—of course, Tony, too. I remember how special I felt.

Back to the Danube. When the fireworks ended, we returned to the cruise ship. Bigfoot Jak, George, and David were at the bar, but they clearly hadn't left the ship that evening.

"Did you have a great time? You look very elegant, too!" shouted Jak across the floor.

I asked why they hadn't come to the palace. He said that kind of dressy do wasn't their thing. They were typical Americans, so they didn't take suits on holiday, just shorts, T-shirts, and sneakers. They did see the fireworks, though. He then offered to buy me a drink and told me his dad was very impressed with me.

"Not many women impress my dad, you know." As I suspected, he was trying to set me up with George. I declined the offer of a drink, saying I had already had enough to drink and promised to join Eddie and his family before I returned to my cabin. He politely nodded and said he would see me some other time. The three Utah boys got my body language message; I was not interested in developing a meaningful friendship.

I continued to enjoy the rest of my cruise and the fleeting company of other passengers without feeling committed to anyone. No, Mr Right was waiting for me.

JACQUELINE T. **MAY**

CHAPTER 32
A DATE WITH
MR PARKINSON

When I arrived home, I knew there was something I had to deal with; I had been in denial for at least two years. On a few occasions, Toy Boy had said I was shaking when he was holding me, and I had said it was an adrenaline rush.

My son-in-law had said, "What's up with you, Jay? You are shaking!" when I passed him a glass of lager. My signature was getting really messy and never the same twice. I was struggling to sleep at night with restless legs and cramps down one side. I could go on, but I needed someone to explain what was happening to me and fix it. My doctor referred me to a neurologist.

This was my first date with Mr Parkinson. Yes, I was diagnosed with Parkinson's disease. The neurologist was very matter-of-fact, with no empathy. I was alone and thought, after I left, he could have served that dish a little warmer, with less vinegar. He reassured me I was at the early stage of the disease; medication should control the symptoms, which was a relief. I did suspect my diagnosis before I attended the appointment, as my father had Parkinson's from an earlier age than I, and I knew it was degenerative; therefore, it would not get better, only worse, with no cure.

I sat in the hospital car park for about 30 minutes, trying to remember what the Neurologist said. Many phrases went through my head that I needed to research. He advised me to join the Parkinson's UK organisation for support and helpful information, talk to the specialist nurse if I had any further questions, and he would see me in twelve months.

Chastising myself, I shouldn't have come to this appointment alone. The floodgates opened, and the shock hit me; I thumped my steering wheel (again) out of frustration. "That's it?? Medication and you are on your own to deal with it!" Many expletives came out of my mouth before I switched on the engine to go home. I don't remember driving; I was in such a daze.

If I wasn't sitting at home numb, I was walking miles with Ted, trying to determine what this meant for my future. After a few days of moping, I realised I needed to talk to someone.

I shared my diagnosis with those close to me, which proved to be devastating news for some, mainly Kitty and my daughters. I tried to play down the shock and reassure them that my life would carry on as usual; it wasn't catching, and there was an extremely low chance of it being inherited. Many had noticed the mild shakes before and accepted my explanation that it was my asthma inhalers. I put them right and added, "It's not the best news, but I'm not dead yet! There is still a lot of living to do. I will not be written off or treated like an invalid. The meds should control it, so I will not let it define me, okay?"

Trying to hide the lump in my throat that caused my voice to sound restricted, I looked at Kitty with tears in her eyes. "I know Jay, you will not let this define you. We all know how strong you are. Ask for help instead of trying to be superwoman, please."

Toy Boy (Alan) stood at my kitchen door with a bunch of mixed flowers. "Does this mean I didn't give you an adrenaline rush after all?" His beautiful face and manly body towered over me with empathy in his eyes.

At first, I could hardly smile, but after a second, I was relieved that he had made fun of me and my shaking. Sympathy from others was difficult to bear. "Doesn't stop you having sex, or does it?" He winked, then gave me a huge hug. "I'm still here, as a friend, you know that," as he rocked me gently from side to side.

"Yes, after four years as a fucking friend, you remind me again!" Only I say it to myself, not out loud.

I want to stay a moment longer in his arms. Then, for the first time ever, I cry in front of him, floodgates opening for the first time since my diagnosis, sobbing uncontrollably over my future, gasping for breath, my nose running like a tap.

As he lifts my chin and looks deep into my tear-filled eyes, he says in a soft, deep tone. "Jay, it's okay to cry, you know. You've been strong enough. Just let it all out."

He sits me on the sofa and hugs me for nearly an hour, my head resting on his chest; we hardly speak. He strokes my arm, and I can feel his strong heartbeat in his chest. This is the closest I will ever be to his heart, the nearest to having a loving relationship with him. Although, I know this is just a sympathy hug for a shaking wreck.

I sob some more, then push him away, wiping my eyes with my sleeve. "Now bugger off, you've smudged my mascara."

He laughs. "She's back in the room."

I thanked him for coming over as he moved towards the door. He looked back. "You will be okay, Jay. I know Parkinson's will not slow you down. You've got this."

He was the only one who named the disease; everyone else avoided saying it. I must stop fantasising about him, let him go and get on with my life with Mr Parkinson as best I can.

DEAR MR PARKINSON

When did you sneak into my life?
I don't remember becoming your wife.
I have been trembling over you for some time,
Blaming my moments on drugs and wine.
Yet, as I'm struggling with all my tasks,
You declare yourself mine.
So, I wobble and ask,
"Are we an item from now on?
Will you keep me safe
In the manner I'm accustomed to?"
No, you interrupt my night's sleep
With vivid nightmares and dreams,
Aching legs and cramping feet.
My voice and throat croak,
Telling my doctor, I need help
For life with you is no joke.
No reply Mr P, just the meds?
Put up with the side-effects
Hoping for a cure instead?
However, Mr Parkinson,
I've decided to stay and fight.
Signed, your wobbly wife.

And who would have thought, after all those years of seeking "The One," that it would find me in the shape of a disease in the end? Mr Parkinson will be my companion for the rest of my life now. What hope do I have of finding a man who will 'want' or fall in love with someone with a degenerative disease? I have no idea, but I will stay as positive as I can.

On that cheerful note, reaching 73 years is an achievement in itself and, despite everything I have gone through, to try and meet someone special just for me. I am actually content on my own with Ted, the pup, for now.

I don't have any regrets, and I hope that in some small way, I have made a few men happy, if only briefly, maybe brought a little cheer to their lonely lives, as some have to mine. I might have been their last sexual partner, their last 69, there's a thought.

I have probably scared a few, too, as they have me. The Irish anaesthetist, who loved the same artist as me, enticed me into his bed, only for me to leave him asleep in the middle of the night because I imagined he might have drugged me. He didn't.

At least I don't have to worry about anyone else except Ted and me. I can allow myself to be selfish now more than ever before and take advantage of my loving family and Girl Tribe to keep me on my toes, keeping me young in spirit, if not in body. I will still volunteer for the charity, do poetry recitals, travel, and write whenever possible. I might even have the occasional date.

Regarding finding "The One", never say never. There might be an elderly man wandering around my local supermarket who may be looking for a travel companion with a bit of a wobble, a shaky hand (which might come in useful for a hand job) and a sense of fun. Well, who knows, this old girl might still be dating into her eighties.

Here is a thought: what would I say to my 66-year-old self if I embarked on this online dating journey for the first time?

Well, obviously, life is definitely too short. Get out there as soon as possible and make the most of every day. Don't prevaricate; I know it feels scary, but if you don't embrace Online Dating, this new way of meeting men/women, you have less chance of finding "The One". Many men are just as scared as you are. Besides, I had a lot of fun and some sadness on the way, but that's all a part of being human. I strongly believe good things come out of adversity. It's not always what you expect, but often, there are valuable experiences, self-discovery, adventures, and periods of physical and mental excitement. Do it while you can.

Communication is everything. But don't give too much away about yourself too soon; leave a little mystery. Men love a chase. However, sadly, they often dismiss women who chase.

Don't worry about your age differences; they are only numbers. Slide your age options to the left for a younger suitor on the dating app. And don't be too critical of a little white lie. I know the thought of not being honest is hard, I certainly found it so, but remember, there is no law against it. Most men do it, and we women forgive them for it. So don't be afraid; be kind to yourself and others. Never say never. There are always surprises around the corner, so why close off your options? Enjoy and appreciate the value of short relationships; nothing has to be forever. And at 73, forever isn't that long; I am hoping for quite an exciting ride nonetheless while I can.

Most of all, believe in your worth and trust your gut instinct; if he feels too good to be true, then there is every chance he is. SAY NO!!!!! and move on.

NEXT!!!

Today

On this rainy day my mobile pings with two message notifications.

"Hi Jay, Would you like to meet up for a coffee? I love dogs, too; I am sure Max and Ted would get on. :-).

I will understand if you think this message is too forward. Would love to hear from you.

Roger x

Hiya J,

Happy Monday. How are you doing today? I hope you're okay.

Alan xx :-)

JACQUELINE T. **MAY**

ABOUT THE AUTHOR

I'm the eldest of seven children, the mother of two daughters, and the grandmother of five teenagers. I am self-taught in most things because my education was sadly lacking, and my mild dyslexia was not acknowledged. However, I muddled through life, embracing IT and the Internet, and forged a respectable career until I retired. I have written several short stories and poems.

Printed in Dunstable, United Kingdom